"A beaut ... yet unheralde ...cess that may change human consciousness on a global scale."

Robert A. Monroe
Author of *Journeys out of the Body*

"I find [*Agartha*] fascinating . . . It reminds me of the SETH material . . . and I hope it will reach the many and change their lives, enabling them to see life from a different perspective."

Eileen Caddy
Author of *Foundations of Findhorn* and *The Dawn of Change*

"Mentor is a multifaceted 'personality' at once humorous, erudite, practical, technical, poetic and loving. . . . He is a worthwhile companion to meet along the path. . . . *Agartha* can be welcomed to the body of channeled literature which may be helping to midwife the human race into a higher destiny."

New Realities

"*Agartha* provides open-minded readers with a view of reality, the earth, and the future which deserves the most careful, scientific, political and democratic citizen's evaluation."

The Planet

AGARTHA: THE ESSENTIAL GUIDE TO PERSONAL TRANSFORMATION IN THE NEW ERA

Meredith Lady Young

BALLANTINE BOOKS • NEW YORK

Library of Congress Catalog Card Number: 84-50109

ISBN 0-345-36277-2

Manufactured in the United States of America

First Ballantine Books Edition: November 1989

To Jim,
My fellow traveler in this wondrous
search, whose loving support has made
my personal journey possible.

CONTENTS

Acknowledgments   xiii

Author's Preface   xv

Note to the Reader   xvii

CHAPTER 1: THE ENCOUNTER   1
   Friday, January 16, 1981 | 1
   Saturday, January 17, 1981: The Encounter | 6
   Searching the Recent Past for Answers | 13
   Sunday, January 18, 1981: Dialogue | 17
   The Deepening Relationship | 24
   The Continuing Communication Process | 31

CHAPTER 2: COMING FROM THE HEART   33
   Learning to Listen | 36
   Tonal Resonance: The Energy Vibration of All Life | 39
   The Meaning of Love | 45
   Equality: The Practical Side of Love | 54

CHAPTER 3: WHERE IS ENLIGHTENMENT?   59
   The Conscious Mind: The Body's Creative
      Computer | 63
   The Superconscious Mind: An Expanded Subconscious
      and Reservoir of Spiritual Development | 64
   Perceptions of the Heart: Mental Body, Soul and
      Originator of Spiritual Development | 65

The Mind-Heart Connection | 66
Interpretation Via the Already Established Program | 67
Conscious Mind as Protector | 68
Actively Reprogramming the Conscious Mind | 69
Passive or Random Reprogramming of the Conscious
    Mind | 70
"Mind" and "Brain"—Two Separate Entities | 72
Where Is Enlightenment? | 73
Simultaneous Lifetimes | 75
Perceiving in Perfectness | 75
Functional versus Observational Learning: The Expanded
    Self | 76
Meditation Exercises | 82

CHAPTER 4: CREATING YOUR OWN REALITY   89
Separating Illusion from Reality | 90
Who You Are: The Spiritual Matrix | 93
Evolutionary Identification with the Spiritual
    Matrix | 95
Inclinations of the Soul: Man's Inner Core | 97
The Spiritual Matrix and Unconscious Confusion in the
    Dream State | 99
Intuitive Rejuvenation | 102
"Out-Of-Body" Travels in the Spiritual Matrix | 103
Sleep, Coma and Death: Similarity of Spiritual Matrix
    Experience | 106
The Mechanism of Awakening | 107
Free Choice: The Fabric of Life | 108
Weaving the Fabric of Life | 112
Earth School, Divine Destiny and Free Will | 114
Going With the Flow | 116
Manifesting Reality | 117
The Dynamics of Creating Your Own Reality | 121

CHAPTER 5: THE POWER CONNECTION:
        KEY TO EARTH'S SURVIVAL   122
The Power Trip | 123
Personal Power: Learning to Draw from the Source | 126

Personal Power: Birthright Gift and Spiritual Matrix
  Affirmation | 129
Relinquishing Power | 132
Experiencing Personal Power: A Meditative
  Exercise | 136
Beyond Personal Power: The Consciousness Shift | 137
Group Process: The Power Squared | 139
Planetary Destruction or Spiritual Awareness? | 142
The Ionosphere: Earth's Aura | 144
Earth Changes Explained | 147
The 27th to 38th Parallels North: Earth's Weakest
  Link | 150
Correcting In-Earth Energy Imbalances | 152
In-Earth Healing Meditation for Groups | 152
In-Earth Healing Meditation for Individuals | 153
Ionospheric Healing Meditations for Groups | 154
Ionospheric Healing Meditations for Individuals | 155
Will Earth Survive? | 156

CHAPTER 6: INNER SPACE VERSUS OUTER SPACE
                                                                     158
Inside-Outside: The Two-Way Mirror | 159
Equal Application of Expression | 161
The Nature of Vibration: Postivity and Negativity | 163
Stress | 167
Cleansing Through Visualization and Harmonics | 169
Visiualizations for Cleansing and Balancing the Body | 170
An Exercise Using Harmonic Vibration | 176
Beyond Basic Cleansing: The Chakras | 177
Tracing the Energy of Life | 180
Case History of John | 181
Conclusions about John | 185
Reading the Aura of a Chakra | 186
Chronic Disharmony: The New Norm | 191

CHAPTER 7: BENEATH EARTH'S GREENNESS   193
No Such Thing as Nonexistence | 195
Two Levels of Natural Life: Physical and Spiritual | 197
Evolution: Will It Wait? | 202

Communication With Nature: Fact or Fiction? | 205
The Communication Process | 213
The Garden Energies | 215
The Deep Blue Channel | 224
The General Flower Radiance | 225
New Hampshire Flower Essences | 226
Combining Energy of the Earth and the Heavens: The
    Perfect Garden | 231
Personalizing Nature: Can Man Teach as Well as
    Listen? | 232
Wanting to Understand | 234

CHAPTER 8: THE EXPERIENCE OF HEALING   236
Holism: A Complement to Traditional Medicine | 236
Four Cases of Trauma | 239
The Three Stages Through Trauma | 242
Review of the Lessons of Change | 245
Is Disease "Karma"? | 249
Allegory of Lord Karma | 250
Healing and Being Healed | 252
Medical Clairvoyance: Learning to See | 255
A Minor Miracle | 257
A Second Miracle | 259
Caroline: A Major Miracle | 261
Healing: How It Actually Works | 264
Appropriate Treatment: Allopathic or Holistic | 266
The Healer/Physician | 267

CHAPTER 9: DEATH: THE NEED TO SURVIVE   271
Moving from Life to Death and Death to Life | 273
Reincarnation: Repetition of the Way | 277
Karmic Ramifications of Additional Energy Units | 279
Regression into Past Lives | 280
Physical Death: The Missing Sense of Self | 283
What Does It Feel Like to Be Dead? | 285
The Gift of Life | 287
The Need to Survive | 289

CHAPTER 10: MAN AS GOD   291
    Learning to Channel: A Coming of Age of the Human
        Experience | 292
    Seeing the Spirit Within | 294
    What Does It Mean to Pray? | 297
    The Nature of Praying | 299
    Toward Realizing Man's Divinity | 301
    The Pathway of Spiritual Consciousness | 302
    Consciousness: The Meaning of Life in Earth
        School | 304
    Mentor's Final Thoughts | 305

EPILOGUE—1989   307
    Choice, Change and New Beginnings | 308
    Personalizing the Universe | 311
    Personal and Planetary Rates of Change | 315
    Extinction Becomes Relevant: A New Way
        of Learening | 318
    The Changing Family Structure: A Personal Search for
        Spiritual Bonding | 321
    Going In the Right Direction | 329

ABOUT THE AUTHOR   334

ACKNOWLEDGMENTS

Special thanks to:

—my family, Jim, Mark and Melanie, whose loving support encouraged me through the long solitary hours of work.

—Caroline, whose tireless energy and superlative editorial skills have allowed AGARTHA to become all that it was meant to become.

—Beverly and Jean, for their loving care in the editing and Jeanne for the hours of retyping of AGARTHA.

—Jean and Hugh, who believed in me.

—And finally, to Mentor, my teacher, for his guidance, love and unshakable confidence in my ability to write AGARTHA.

AUTHOR'S PREFACE

It is my belief that it is no accident that you are holding this book in your hands, for this is no ordinary book. It is a teaching vehicle that will help you to understand the deeper mysteries of life and stimulate new levels of personal growth and awareness. It can be a powerful catalyst toward spiritual enlightenment and at the very least it will challenge and expand your current definition of "reality."

It would be presumptuous of me to speak in such terms about AGARTHA, except that I am truly not its author. I am a messenger. It has been my privilege to give form to the extraordinary material in this book whose depth, scope of understanding and clarity are well beyond my level of expertise. I am neither a scholar nor a philosopher. Nothing in my conscious background qualifies me to write a book of this magnitude and nature, for the author of AGARTHA demonstrates a level of understanding of the workings of the Universe well beyond that of any earth-level teacher I know.

The straightforward answer to this seeming enigma is that AGARTHA was written "through" me, not "by" me. It is a compilation of information that was related to me over a period of two and a half years (1981–1983) by an evolved spiritual teacher not of this physical reality. The material was presented or "channeled" to me during my daily periods of meditation by a teacher who chooses to be identified simply as "Mentor" to avoid any undue emphasis on personalities and to encourage the reader to weigh the teachings on the basis of how they "feel." I have learned that Truth has a

vibration of its own that is perceptible to those who can attune themselves to hear it, and the reader is invited to become
a sounding board for the truth in these pages, each according
to his ability to ''hear.''

I can readily imagine the difficulty that many readers may
initially have in accepting the notion of a nonphysical teacher.
As one who only recently learned to travel inner pathways to
integrate the worlds of the physical and nonphysical, it came
as a surprise to me to discover that such worlds existed outside of science fiction. It was even more surprising to discover that we could learn to communicate with them. The
very thought of ''other realities'' will undoubtedly excite
some and frighten others. It can cause one to conjure up
visions of angels and devils, UFOs and Star Wars. Fear not;
I can assure you that what I will share with you is both natural
and universal. AGARTHA will, in all likelihood, provide
new dimensions to the reader's understanding of the nature
of this rich and incredibly diverse universe and of man's
growing ability and need to develop a knowledge of its living
nature. It may also shed new light on the basic teachings of
the world's religions as well as lend new dimension to one's
quest for spiritual understanding.

It is recommended that the reader follow the sequence of
chapters, at least for the first reading, because each subsequent chapter builds on the information presented in earlier
ones. It is also suggested that the reader pace himself in
reading AGARTHA, since the contents of each chapter are
quite compressed though simply presented.

I do not and cannot defend the information offered in
AGARTHA as true. There is no scientific way to validate the
information that will satisfy the person who requires tangible, measurable proof as a requirement for acceptance. Perhaps it is enough to ask the reader to withhold judgment
altogether in order to allow the contents of AGARTHA to
speak to a receptive mind and open heart. You may even
wish to read AGARTHA as an entertaining piece of fiction
if its contents prove a strain on your conscious limits of credibility. This would not offend me in the least if it would serve

to allow you to focus on the information presented rather than on the process or source of the knowledge.

AGARTHA was a gift to me and I offer it in love to you that it may help you along your personal path. May you grow in knowledge of who you are and be guided to act responsibly in the light of your expanding consciousness.

Meredith Lady Young
"AGARTHA"

Walpole, NH
Spring 1984

NOTE TO THE READER: The masculine gender has been used throughout AGARTHA to avoid the cumbersome use of he/she/it, his/her/theirs. The designation "man" is, therefore, intended in the generic sense to indicate human.

CHAPTER ONE

THE ENCOUNTER

*"Do not fear what you do not understand,
    instead seek to learn.
Do not be one who turns away from awareness
    in fear, for there is much being held in the
    balance."*

MENTOR

Friday, January 16, 1981

GRAY DAWN FILTERED through the partially frosted windows, dissolving the early morning darkness. I woke up tired as if I had been trying to wake up for a long time. There was no smooth transition out of the dream state, just a sense of being dropped into consciousness.

I glanced at the clock beside the bed. It was 6:30 a.m., and I knew without turning over that Jim had already left for the early train. So it was morning again. Slowly I rolled over and adjusted the covers. I closed my eyes and tried to recreate the soothing blankness of sleep, but from deep inside an amorphous sense of anxiety pushed into my consciousness. It did not come in a polite linear fashion but in a massive assault. For weeks this storm had been gathering momentum, and now it threatened to overtake me.

Depression, resentment and fear descended on me. I felt as if I was being emotionally ambushed, and I bristled at the intrusion. I tried analyzing these surges of unknown energy that were now coming in steady waves. What was this about? Was this some physical trauma? Or was it emotional? I winced at the thought that this was all in my mind, yet there

1

was no apparent physical origin or explanation. Turning on the light, I sat up in bed. I felt helpless. Where were the answers? The thought of another day of anxiety and tension was more than I wanted to consider. Overwhelmed with confusion, I got up to fix a cup of coffee.

My children, Mark and Melanie, were still asleep in their rooms. As I listened at their doors for the familiar sound of school-morning activity, there was only silence. With a growing sense of despair, I continued on to the kitchen. While the water boiled, I paged absently through yesterday's newspaper, trying to shake my nagging misgivings. I needed to think of my children, my husband, anything but these foreign vibrations that had seemingly slipped in under the front door and were now demanding my full attention. But in spite of my contrived emotional blackout, the tempo of the vibrations was increasing. Gazing down at my hands, I expected to see them shaking. They were not, but inside me everything seemed to have melted into an emotional lake. I wondered if this was what it felt like to be drugged or even schizophrenic. Then, as quickly as the buildup had begun, it subsided. The vibrations mysteriously receded to a tolerable level, and I relaxed just slightly, steadying myself for another attack. There was no attack, however, and also no explanation.

In retrospect, I realize that my dilemma resulted from having no frame of reference from which to interpret the dynamics of a mystical experience. Terms such as "vibration," "energy" and "consciousness" were not yet available to me. I had no words to describe my internal world; consequently I had no way to describe this, my first conscious encounter with the nonphysical world. I have since learned that physical terminology is never an adequate substitute for the power of the experience. At that time, however, I would have been grateful for any understanding of what was happening. Instead, my lack of awareness resulted in a feeling of total isolation.

The bleakness of the early morning light matched my own feelings of depression. I pondered my dilemma, looking for a solution, an escape. Closing my eyes, I took a deep breath. For an instant, there was a measure of calm. I tried it again, placing all my concentration on my breath. It worked. I began to feel myself relax. I had been meditating each morning for the past nine months and had come to recognize that internal place of quiet, that still point. How well I knew the routine: first releasing all thoughts, then letting go of physical sensations and finally finding that complete peace. Without conscious thought I had apparently found a way through this fear. Quite spontaneously, my deep breathing had triggered my meditation routine. I knew immediately what I needed to do.

Opening the bedroom door, I glanced around the room. The familiar surroundings were reassuring. Pulling the coverlet off the bed, I wrapped myself in its softness and sat with my back against the foot of the bed. With my legs folded yoga-style, hands resting lightly on my knees, I began doing my deep breathing. Closing my eyes I silently voiced my personal affirmation which preceded each meditation: "I believe that I am more than my physical body and as such can perceive more than my physical world. I ask that I be assisted in my search for truth by whatever means is appropriate to advancing my ultimate awareness."

I do not recall exactly when I first sensed a "presence" accompanying me during my meditations. This presence manifested itself in wavelike shades of purple, seemingly connected with my deepest levels of perception. It seemed little more than a purple sphere floating in the upper left-hand corner of my "mind's eye." At first it did not seem significant, since my meditations were frequently filled with visualized colors and shapes. But as the weeks progressed, this mental vision continued to exist within each period of meditation. I found myself drawn to speculating on its significance. I could not release the notion that this energy was somehow different from the rest of my visualizations. Its very consistency intrigued me.

Slowly I counted myself into deeper levels of meditation, letting the strands of quiet merge inside me. Within minutes all was completely calm. Even the vibrations and fearful thoughts which had been pursuing me had disappeared into the quiet. I allowed myself the luxury of totally letting go and found my mind drifting on magical inner currents. Then, at a point deep in meditation, I shifted my body position, bringing my hands lightly together in my lap. The effect was dramatic. As my fingers touched, an electrical impulse jammed my entire being, and a circle of intense energy began to circulate in a counterclockwise motion through my hands, up my left arm, through my head, and back down my right arm. The very motion of joining my hands had completed some type of circuit. I was abruptly jolted out of meditation and dumped back into consciousness. As I pulled my hands apart, I could hear the blood pounding in my head.

I studied the room for signs of anything physically amiss but everything appeared intact. I tried to dismiss the suspicion that the impulses were beyond my control. As I slowly settled back into meditation, I shut my eyes and allowed my hands to touch. Instantly the circle of energy resumed. I separated my hands, only this time it did not stop the flow of energy. Instead, the vibrations reached a crescendo, creating a funneling cone of energy. The spiraling energies began to accelerate, sending wavelike pulses through my entire body. The effect was hypnotic. I was being drawn into a vortex or tunnel of swirling energy and light. In spite of my natural anxiety, I was unable to fight the sensations. Perhaps it was in surrendering that my sense of fear gave way to acceptance and to the intoxicating joy which followed. I found myself in a state of exquisite harmony where no disruption existed. Enraptured by this euphoria, I seemed cradled in an unknown embrace, moving effortlessly and yet with ultimate speed. Like a fragrance being carried by the wind, I just drifted, oblivious to my whereabouts or direction. My inner meandering continued until, to my surprise, I became conscious of a thought forming in my mind.

Responding to this unknown impulse, I leaned to my left to pick up a pad and pencil from the bedside table. I did not question this strange urge, I just complied. Half wondering what I was doing, I stared at the paper and pencil. My eyes were now open though I still seemed in a sort of dreamy daze. I felt no sense of urgency and equally no sense of what I was to do with the paper. After a few moments I simply closed my eyes and was immediately drawn back into the funnel of revolving energy. Once again I floated with the current of light and vibration.

Without warning, my right hand began to move across the manila pad. I opened my eyes and stared at my hand as it continued to move quite without my assistance, the pencil making large random arcs on the paper. I watched in amazement as my hand moved in slow, steady rhythms across the paper. It was difficult to tell whether or not I was even awake. The movement continued. There was absolutely no conscious thought directing the motion. It just continued in an autonomous back-and-forth pattern as I watched, feeling awestruck and silently detached from the process.

I tried lifting my writing hand to see what control I had over the process and discovered that I could voluntarily stop the writing by lifting my writing hand. For several moments I held my hand suspended over the paper, deciding what to do next. Then dropping my hand back down to the paper, the writing began again, repeating the process, filling the pages with incomprehensible looping designs. Whenever I picked up my hand the involuntary movement stopped, and as soon as I brought it back to the paper, the writing continued.

From what seemed a state of suspended animation, I observed myself as totally detached from the actions of my right hand. As the reality of what was happening crept into my awareness, I was not sure whether to be thrilled or panicked. At that moment I had no understanding of telepathy, or that what I thought could be, and in fact, was being perceived by another dimension. I only knew that these large random shapes did not make sense and I wondered, to myself, why they were not more intelligible. Instantly, the large scrawling became small, tight circles. "Good God," I murmured. "*Something* has read my mind." This realization shattered my tenuous resolve and I was consumed by a new rush of anxiety. Dropping the pencil, I reached for the phone.

Anxiously I waited for the New York operator to patch through the call to my husband's office. She asked me to please hold, then "click"; there was nothing. The ensuing

silence produced a sense of isolation as if I had been discon-
nected from all physical life. I can recall with absolute clarity
the tension I felt as I waited for Jim to answer his phone. As
I gripped the receiver, it suddenly became my only handle
on reality. Thoughts tumbled into new thoughts with no resolution, leaving only more questions in their wake. I wanted
to stop thinking, to remove myself from this moment. I was
determined not to convey a sense of panic when Jim answered the phone, but I needed to share what had happened.
As I wrestled with a way to relate the experience, I realized
how desperately I wanted Jim to verify my sanity. I wanted
him to tell me that what I was experiencing was something
other than the product of my imagination or overstimulated
emotions. By the time he picked up his phone, I was crying,
partly from stress and partly from relief.

Struggling to find the words, I started to tell him the details
of an experience too real to be imagined and too strange to
be understood. Because he was in a business meeting, he
responded only indirectly, but, despite his intentional vague-
ness, I could hear in his voice that he believed me. Neither
of us had any inkling as to what had happened, nor could we
have guessed that my isolation was a necessary building stage
which would soon introduce me to an expanded vision of
reality.

Saturday, January 17, 1981: The Encounter

I am one who has learned a very simple truth: you truly
cannot return "home" again. That Saturday morning I found
myself gravitating toward the most familiar of tasks, as if
they held the power to keep this other reality from trespassing
any further. While I went through the motions of weekend
chores, I was conscious that nothing I could do would stop
that which was inevitable. There are some experiences in life
that are not optional; rather, one's only choice becomes how
conscious one wishes to be while living the experience itself.

The vibrations were even more pronounced that morning.
I somehow knew this was to be the day that my world would

be changed forever. I watched my children playing in the snow. Their carefree activity suddenly embodied the essence of all I held personally sacred. If I let go, if I gave in to this vibration totally, would I return to them intact? Would I still be the mother they loved? In my heart, I prayed for five minutes more of this warm familiar world before I released what little hold I had left on my life. I knew of no way out of this dilemma except through it. There was no more time or energy to remain in this no-man's-land of vibrations and strange meditations. It was time to solve this puzzle, to fill in the missing pieces. The solution seemed obvious—I needed to meditate again to find what lay at the end of the tunnel of light. It no longer seemed a choice.

Words cannot adequately describe what followed. Sitting on the floor, I wrapped the familiar comforter around me and balanced the pencil and paper in my lap. I took a few deep breaths to quiet myself and said my affirmation, asking for the strength to face whatever might happen. In the most natural of ways, the most extraordinary of events began to occur. All of the strain I had been experiencing melted away, and a feeling of peacefulness filled my being. The sense of time slipped out of my consciousness and the very room in which I was sitting vanished in an instant. Simultaneously, it seemed my awareness opened wide, allowing me to fully sense what was happening.

As I thought of my body, I could feel the rhythmic pumping of my heart and the steady rise and fall of my lungs. I was enthralled by the simplicity of it all. The experience continued to unfold, causing a sense of peace to flow through me. At the point of absolute stillness within me, I knew I was in the presence of that which is considered sacred. Fear and trauma could not exist here. I was overwhelmed with a glowing expansiveness, pouring out the purest love I had ever felt. In my euphoria I wondered at my hesitation in releasing myself to this Source of wisdom and unconditional love. There are no words to adequately translate the feelings that filled me. It was one of those intimately profound moments that is never forgotten.

As difficult as the journey had been to this place of peace, it was equally difficult to consider returning to the physical world. The sense of tranquility was so all-pervasive that the thought of ever moving from this awareness was devastating. Reluctantly, as I began to grope toward physical reality, my hand began to move. Although it had happened once before, this time when my hand started moving, I was still so far removed from physical reality that it was hard to focus my attention on the process. I struggled to refocus my thoughts. With eyes barely open, I watched my hand as it responded to an unknown source of dictation.

I *felt* words—real words—crowding into my mind. My hand moved in response, writing what was being mentally transmitted in this mysterious manner. I was participating in the process, yet I also remained partially anesthetized to it. The words came so fast that I wondered if I could keep up. My hand ached from the strain, but I could not bring myself to stop. Finally, forty-seven pages later, my pencil came to rest.

I was at a loss to explain either the source of the writing or the words which were scribbled on the page. I held the tablet as if feeling it for the first time, needing to touch physical objects that connected me to my surroundings.

How had these words come to me and from where? I had not heard voices; I had not seen the words. I had not thought words. I had *felt* them as though they grew from within me. These words were more than letters put together. They had depth and dimension, and like an echo reverberating through a canyon, the essence of that echo had filled me and become instantly translated into words.

I stared at the pages covering the floor in front of me. At first I was unsure of what to do. I got to my feet and walked toward the living room. The children were noisily stomping their boots and brushing the snow off their parkas. They did not see me standing in the doorway. Their lives seemed so vibrant and yet vulnerable. I wanted to reach out and hold them and have them hold me. I suddenly needed to share their exuberance. Reaching for my little girl, I scooped her up in my arms, silently holding her precious life close to me. Her cheeks felt cool next to mine, and her face sparkled with joy. We had both given birth, my daughter and I, each to our own creative reality—she to her new snowman and me to a perception of exquisite joy that my life might unfold according to a plan I had never before acknowledged. Life seemed younger, more accessible and ready to be lived. I was filled with such a sense of well-being. The depression and fear had gone and were replaced by a magical sense of completion. I thought how fine it was to be alive on this winter morning, and with this thought came the realization that even the vibrations had disappeared.

I was so caught up in the experience, the feelings of oneness within the meditation and the strange process of knowing, that I had failed to consider the actual words written on the pages. Now for the first time I became aware of the writing. As my eyes focused on the first line, I read:

✳*Do not fear our presence. We exist for you and with you as Messengers of the Infinite. Cosmic Truth exists as the focused energies of a creative universe. God's balance maintains this creative universe and the evolution of all things.*

You are one of many who seek to manifest awareness of Truth and in so doing understand the mysteries of universal life. You inadvertently sought our counsel during those periods of conscious release when your energies were free to search for Truth. In searching you awakened the heart, allowing the love which comes from the heart to generate the intense energy which exists as the link between your body and that of other beneficent spirits.

Your bodily reservoirs are now temporarily depleted because of intensities experienced in advancing this communication. While your body resisted this communication on a conscious level, on a deeper level your living soul urged you forward to manifest your search for Truth. The physical symptoms you experienced were the result of the refocusing and reinforcing of your bodily energies and energy channels in order to accommodate the expanded energy of our communication.

Now that you are aware of the exchange which can and

often does exist between man and unseen forces of the universe, you must realize that you have tapped the most basic of Truths: that all beings exist as seemingly insular items and yet as integral and inseparable parts of the whole. There is no limitation possible of the whole either in thought or action. The whole exists in relation to its parts but not because of its parts. The parts exist because of the whole.

The totality of the universe is an orderly, efficient, and balanced operation where nothing is permanently lost or misdirected. There are no time or space limitations, only increased awareness of the whole. All beings exist and function according to their degree of enlightenment.

When man initially aligns himself with the intuitive truths of the natural universe, he is filled with questioning. This is part of learning, for without questions there can be no satisfaction in the verification of truth.

Our purpose is to make you aware where you are unaware, to glorify your spiritual nature where it is diminished, to show you the peace of worlds within and without.

The Earth is undergoing a metamorphosis into an age of awareness and is physically changing to accommodate this increased energy. Your planet and its people will be exposed to an unprecedented period of harmonious realignment if the energies of more advanced realities are successful in catalytically sparking this new age of awareness. The Earth's evolving consciousness will gradually transcend those negative limitations which currently dominate your diminished and depleted world.

Do not fear what you do not understand; instead seek to learn. Do not be one who turns away from awareness in fear, for there is much being held in the balance. Seek the light and consciously align your energies with the new, blossoming awarenesses of your evolving world.

I did not know what to say. As I handed the pages to Jim, he too, was astonished at the power and sweep of the words, and unable to even speculate about who might have authored such thoughts. Clearly it had not been me. His rational mind seemed unable to even entertain, much less resolve, the huge questions raised by the communication. We sat looking alternately at each other and then at the scattered pages. It seemed incomprehensible that such startling words were on the papers I held. I was a person of feelings, not of words. Even though Jim was a man of many words, none surfaced to summarize the significance of the writing. I reread the first page, struggling to grasp the words and integrate them with the process I had just witnessed.

The reaction I found myself verbalizing was one of mixed feelings. Disbelief, uncertainty and skepticism blended with exhilaration and a feeling of reverence. My major stumbling block was personal self-confidence. How could this writing have come through me? Surely, I was not worthy or capable of interacting on such a highly spiritual level. "Do not fear our presence." I was not as much afraid as I was awestruck. "Messengers of the Infinite" sent uncontrollable tingles down my spine. My Episcopalian background had long since been set adrift, and my compromise with formalized religion was Unitarianism. Spirituality to me was a vast and unknowable subject. But what was *this*?

My anxiety level rose again when I came to the statement, "God's balance maintains this creative universe and the evolution of all things." The mention of "God" was somehow confounding to me. Long ago I had dismissed the idea of a personal God, feeling it was too pat an answer. My current bewilderment, however, indicated how much I still wanted to believe in such a God. The prospect of being addressed by a God-oriented presence from another plane of existence was both exhilarating and terrifying.

The writing implied that we were being helped by other forces from outside ourselves to save our very lives. Comprehending this incredible piece of information made me wide-eyed with amazement. I took a deep breath, looked at Jim and continued to read. I had asked in my meditations to know a way to help change all our lives to have a broader perspective. The enormity of my asking the universe for answers seemed suddenly preposterous. I had been so caught up in seeking my own personal enlightenment that I had lost

sight of who it was I was addressing. I took a deep breath.
Picking up the second page, I read slowly, trying to feel what
was written between the lines as well as on them. The tone
of the message was unquestionably "beneficent." Certainly
nothing personally threatening was contained in the words.
In fact, it was apparent that I was being offered guidance by
some force or intelligence that seemed to have an overview
of the condition of the earth and its people. It all seemed
preposterous, and yet there it was on paper in front of me.

"The physical symptoms you experienced were the result
of the refocusing and reinforcing of your bodily energies and
energy channels in order to accommodate the expanded energy of our communication." So this was the cause of the
vibrations. It was hard to comprehend that my body had been
the object of such a mysterious reprogramming. It was more
than a little frightening to hear what had been going on inside
of me. As overwhelming as everything now appeared, this
was an experience that in all probability would never be du-
plicated in my life. There was no explanation as to why it
had happened to me, but intuitively I knew this unique happening would be both a blessing and perhaps a curse. I was
suddenly exhausted by the weight of it all. I slumped down
between the pillows, unable to read any more. It was simply
too much to absorb, and I retreated by staring absently at the
ceiling. It would all work out; somehow I had to believe it
would all make sense.

An unsettling thought pushed its way into my mind, causing me still further anxiety. Had I imagined this message?
Was the writing the product of an overactive imagination or
something from my subconscious? I closed my eyes to concentrate. Was this real? *Was this real?* The feelings of immense energy, the vibrations and the writing process were
still very fresh experiences to me. I turned each piece of the
writing over and over in my mind, listening to how it sounded
and wondering what the true origin of the writing was.

I was already aware of expanded states of consciousness
and my meditations had shown me new depths of my inner
self, but I had never returned from my meditations with written messages. These words were far more profound than any-

thing I was capable of writing. It was simply beyond me to
even try to fathom "Cosmic Truth" or "Messengers of the
Infinite." The very mention that "God" existed was more
than I wanted to try to handle at the moment.

I was reeling from the impact of the words, and my life
seemed suddenly compacted into the last two weeks as if
nothing significant had existed before the onset of this experience. I needed time to find a level of normalcy, to remember who I was in order to figure out why I was where I
was at this moment.

Searching the Recent Past for Answers

We are all, of course, products of our experiences and
those hereditary characteristics with which we prepare to play
out our lives. It is never easy when in the middle of life there
is cause for a dramatic change. Yet I had found myself in that
situation during the previous year. I was now thirty-seven
and married with two children. Outwardly I had all the em-
bellishments of a successful suburban life in Connecticut.
Since this had been my yardstick for success, I did, indeed,
consider myself successful.

Jim was thirty-nine and a vice-president with CBS. While
he often talked of being bored with the corporate world, I
tried not to respond to his notions that the job was not "feed-
ing" him. It was too threatening to even consider the possibility of his leaving the corporate life. I had no desire to go
back to work or in any way to lessen the level of my life-
style. Whenever the conversation came up, I let it die through
lack of interest.

In April, 1980, Jim had planned to attend a workshop in
Virginia on exploring and expanding human consciousness.
Even though he doubted my interest, he asked if I would like
to join him. Surprising myself, I agreed to go along to what
I was sure would be just another of his intellectual exercises
on consciousness. I rationalized that at the very least I could
enjoy the warmth of spring, well under way in the Blue Ridge
Mountains.

Perhaps there *is* no adequate preparation for life's dramatic changes. I was certainly a complete amateur in understanding human consciousness or matters of deep spiritual significance; yet I found myself signed up along with Jim for a workshop at the Monroe Institute of Applied Sciences in Nellysford, Virginia. Although I did not know it then, this workshop would forever alter my conventional existence, drastically changing what had always been. It was called the "Gateway Program," a term which later proved to be entirely prophetic. In this program we were introduced to new, advanced mind-focusing techniques that assisted entry into deep levels of meditation.

I was expecting nothing and Jim was expecting everything. I later wondered if that contrast in expectation levels had made the difference. I joined the conference to be a spectator, not a participant. The people who came to this workshop were mostly serious searchers, not neophytes like myself. The one thing they all shared that I did not was an interest in exploring their deeper dimensions. While I enjoyed their company, there was an invisible wall of intent which separated us; and though I planned to go through the motions I neither anticipated nor sought any far-reaching insights. Jim, on the other hand, hoped for some kind of personal insight through the new application of meditation techniques.

The experience of the conference was intense as people reached into the unknown for understanding and came back with experiences from beyond their physical environment. Lulled by the meditations, I too reached into the unknown and experienced my living presence in a way that defied every human consideration of separateness. As I experienced the earth rotating through space, I saw life moving as one. The earth, the stars, the sun all lived as scintillating replicas of an even more magnificent wholeness. Life was not limited to human population; rather, all forms of animate and inanimate being flowed together toward ultimate completion.

The workshop participants were exposed to deepening levels of meditation and to the tools of exploration into dimensions of consciousness. My visions grew in intensity with each new session until I lost count of the days, the time and even what Jim was doing. Initially it was difficult to share my experiences with the group even though they encouraged me. I was so overcome by the depth of my own emotional responses that I could barely speak without a deluge of tears.

In a state of consciousness referred to as "mind awake, body asleep," I found fields and meadows of uninterrupted lush greenness and extravagant life which permeated my senses and filled my body with joy. Touching the living essence of nature, I rejoiced in the knowledge that I, as a woman and member of the human race, fit perfectly into the scheme of creation. Yet it was a poignant realization that all forms of life existed as extensions of a universal growth pattern which benefited from the interaction of all the parts. Feelings of total inadequacy washed over me when I considered what I had to share with others. Sadly I realized I had nothing.

In another deep state of meditation I felt the fear and hopelessness of being a bystander and watching the dissolution of buildings collapsing before me like insignificant little play houses, and parts of people's bodies floating in strange geometric patterns of black and white. I did not know what it meant to see scenes of such wanton destruction occurring within the framework of such apparent apathy.

The most profound of my visions was of a silver dove floating effortlessly in a clear blue sky with a band of turquoise across its forehead, its gossamer body refracting the rays of sunlight into a rainbow of stunning beauty. This lovely vision appeared in response to my question, "What is the single most important thing for me to know at this moment?" I could only speculate that it was meant to signify the rebirth of my own being into a state of freedom and beauty capable of displaying great light. As I reflected on the interpretation, I was perplexed because I did not have any great light to share. Yet I felt as if I was falling in love with all things simultaneously. I became aware of myself as the embodiment of love, and that feeling has never left me.

The memory of the experiences glowed within me, and I laughed, cried and rejoiced at my discoveries. Life suddenly seemed far grander than anything I had ever known. A different love began to flow between Jim and me, touching a new deeper level of tenderness. As I shared the feelings from the four days, our new connection lifted us into a previously unknown level of commitment. It was as if a dam had broken within me and a sense of renewal flooded into my life. I was free.

Patterns of expected behavior, of self-accepted limitations, seemed to slip away in the weeks that followed our return to Connecticut. I was no longer afraid to vocalize thoughts about changing life-styles and exploring spirituality. Suddenly I was eager to explore what had previously been so threatening. While lifelong perceptions are difficult to change, I learned that they can be changed. And in so doing, my experiences allowed the birth of a new "me."

As I practiced the new meditation techniques I had learned in Virginia, including a personal affirmation for guidance and protection, I found I was successful in reaching similar levels of intense discovery. The meditations, always dramatically visual experiences, continued to blossom. Visions became more specific, often in response to questions I asked about my life. As I gave myself permission to change with these new discoveries, I found that not only my needs, but my perceptions of family relationships, changed. Often there were not words for the feelings I wanted to express, some growing from an overwhelming inner happiness or an unexplainable sadness. Now that the emotional restraints had been removed, I was exposed to feelings that had a new level of intensity.

Often in meditation it seemed as if I was talking to myself or wishing into the limitlessness of space, asking for a better understanding of what our lives meant. I came in contact with people who suffered emotionally and physically, victimized by seemingly insurmountable obstacles which left them feeling deserted and exposed. I wanted to believe that there were answers, and I asked in my meditations to know the unknowable that I might share insights with those whose lives had no meaning.

Sunday, January 18, 1981: Dialogue

What was to happen next? Was this communication with an unseen being likely to continue? More significantly, was it possible that yesterday's message was but the beginning? There was an endless array of personal questions I wanted to ask, not to mention those of broader spiritual significance. The possibility for such an avenue of information seemed too extraordinary to comprehend. Still it was worth pursuing in light of yesterday's profound thoughts. Jim suggested that we meditate together to see if direct questions would receive answers. The morning's writing had left us stunned, yet eager to explore possible connections. Early in the afternoon we sat together to pursue the communication. I sat cross-legged on the floor and Jim sat in front of me. Both of us had paper and pencils. In retrospect I am shocked at the boldness of our actions, and yet we were suspended somewhere between understanding and disbelief, and we needed more clarification.

Gradually I calmed down, did my breathing exercises, said my affirmation and waited. Abruptly I sensed the "presence" and murmured to Jim to proceed. Nervously he wrote out the first question and placed it in my lap: "WHO ARE YOU?" My right hand immediately began to move as it had done before. The message came quickly and then stopped. With tremendous excitement, we read:

✳ *We are multidimensional beings from another more spiritually evolved plane. Our aim is one of positive reinforcement to further man's development.*

Man lives as a simple, two-dimensional being who has chosen to experience earth in order to advance his spiritual center. However, man has succumbed to limited vision and is unable to evolve further without guidance from outside energies who are cognizant of greater vision of universal action.

You have been looking for your path, I am your teacher—I am Mentor—and I am here to help you evolve through earthly planes to other more satisfying dimensions.

I was trembling. *"Mentor"* . . . *my teacher.* Was this the result of my meditations, the months of asking to be shown? My body felt limp and overwhelmed. Tears clouded my vision and slowly ran down my cheeks and onto the paper. Quietly Jim returned to his questions. My mind was suspended somewhere between consciousness and meditation, yet I heard Jim scribbling and felt him place the next slip of paper in my lap. The incredible dialogue continued.

Where are you?

✳ *We are within—as part of your own evolving energy— and without—as a separate energy existing in a separate reality. We are of another more highly evolved plane with beings of greater understanding. We wish to augment your development through the teachings of cosmic truths. We wish you only the peace and joy of dynamic self- realization.*

We and others of the universe have consistently inter- acted with your planet, Earth, and many other stars of your galaxy. It is universally understood that more highly evolved energies will be allowed to periodically transcend their energy bounds in order to share insights with more slowly evolving energies. This is being done everywhere.

We stared at this answer. What kind of intelligence was this? The answer seemed reminiscent of science fiction. It was extraordinary to consider "more highly evolved ener- gies" transcending energy bounds to help mankind. It was almost beyond belief, yet there it was written on the paper— a beneficent spirit of energy wanting to share higher under- standing with us. I felt numb.

Jim's next question was aimed at trying to locate this "Mentor" in a physical way.

Where do you come from?

✷ We began, as you did, in the birthplace of all souls. We have progressed beyond your level to a place of sublime tranquility. We are teachers. We are available to all developing levels and wish only to provide reassurance and guidance to those who seek to walk the path of enlightenment.

This response seemed to be telling us that there might not be an understandable way to locate Mentor's presence. I was captivated by the two notions: "the birthplace of all souls" and "a place of sublime tranquility." I recalled my childhood visions of heaven, and began considering the notion of guardian angels, but Jim's next question interrupted my wondering.

What purpose do you have in being here?

✷ To improve your understanding of those spiritual concepts which are compatible with universal evolution, and simultaneously to increase your understanding of other realities which exist to the same degree that yours exists.
We are here to help avert total depletion of physical and spiritual resources. This depletion is being aggravated by man's unwillingness to cooperate with others of his kind and by his wanton destruction of his planet. There are vast directions for growth, but a basic change in priorities is necessary to allow the planet to evolve in a nonthreatened way.

This suggested some sort of impending danger but also that, through a more accurate appraisal of the real issues at stake, namely the "depletion of the planet," we could change the already established patterns and perhaps avoid whatever waits in the wings of unwritten earth history. In looking honestly at the world in which we all live, there seems to be such contradiction. On the one hand, surgeons struggle to perfect transplant surgeries, and on the other hand, we promote war which causes untold loss of life and devastation. I wondered about the outcome of the earth's unsatisfactory relationship with the universe. I speculated whether this was leading toward some sort of apocalyptic event.

Why is this communication happening now?

✳ *Communications are increasing for two reasons. One, large numbers of people have advanced their levels of spiritual and cosmic understanding to now have the energies and the direction for focusing their objectives, one of which is often contact with realms of higher consciousness. Put another way, the seeds of spiritual enlightenment are sprouting and man is becoming aware.*

Two, spiritually aware realities cannot condone the destruction of Planet Earth, for no action can exist without a much intensified reaction. Thus, there is more being held in the balance than man's mere Earth School survival.

Once again, a clear statement was being issued that man's destruction of the planet was threatening more than his own survival. But it also seemed to foreshadow a possible new level of cooperation between man and "spiritually aware realities." What was this term "Earth School"? Were we, indeed, in some kind of school or classroom? In thinking about the earth, I realized my deep and intense feeling for this planet being referred to as Earth School. I felt as if earth was a personal being, a friend I wanted to protect. Whatever the avenues to sustain life on the planet, they had to be found. I felt totally inadequate. How could one person help?

What do you want of me?

✳ *To listen attentively and to learn, that you may eventually share those understandings with many others. Divinity is ultimately for all, but there are highly negative forces interacting with your planet, and earth needs an immediate course correction to avert potential disaster.*

Do not labor under assumed responsibility. You are only meant to contribute your energies through this already

established channel. The use of this channel will not over-
whelm your system, for you are now handling this com-
munication smoothly. You need not fear our assistance or
guidance. This is important; just listen and learn.

I realized that I had no choice, no alternative. Apparently
I was being asked to communicate what was channeled to
me, yet there were no specifics. In a way I was relieved.
What a monumental task it would be to try and change established thinking, particularly when the source of the information could not be seen. I relaxed a bit, unable to think of
another question. Jim, however, was ready with one which
was particularly significant.

Why did you communicate with Meredith?

❋*Her earlier life was spiritually unfocused and dis-*
tracted. She was generally concerned with her living cir-
cumstances and only in a limited way concerned with
questions of cosmic evolution. This changed—she became
aware of her connection with the Ultimate and wished to
find direction for her life and the lives of other people.
We also live by this connection to the Ultimate and are
imbued with the abilities to work with those whose desires
for knowledge are sincere and whose energies have become
focused to receive instruction. We were aware of her per-
sonal existence before her awakening, but were unable to
single out the connection in order to reach her supercon-
scious. She asked for a link to greater understanding. This
is that link. We are grateful for her receptivity.

Was it that simple? Was it basically a matter of asking for
help? If so, then it was suddenly clear . . . I truly had asked—
specifically and persistently—for guidance to help me grow
in awareness. Apparently my meditations and my prayers
had resulted in this seemingly incredible linkup.

We desperately wanted to learn more about Mentor. Was
Mentor a godly entity? Was Mentor part of a spirit existence?
What was the relationship between Mentor and other spiri-

tual forces? I was determined to find some way to position
Mentor's presence.

Are you able to draw on higher powers for help?

✳ *Yes, the Ultimate Love, the Ultimate Whole, God, is
the perfectness toward which we all evolve. Each strives
in his own way within his own structure to achieve his
highest potential on all levels of achievement.*

Mentor's response was reassuring to me. While I needed
to personally sort out my understanding of God, it was comforting to hear that Mentor recognized a higher power. This
brought me to a new level of confidence. I thought of my
next question and watched my hand write out the response.

Do the vibrations that I sense when I meditate indicate your
presence?

✳ *Yes, the vibrations indicate our presence with you. We
are never far from you. You have but to channel your
energies in the appropriate fashion to draw in our presence.*
   *The human race must recognize its deeply buried bond
with Universal Energy or no significant spiritual growth
is possible. Universal Energy projects love to all elements—be sensitive to this fact.*
   *Guidance is crucial to all people of all realities. It is
essential to strive to improve awareness. Many are working to improve your planet, Earth. It finds itself in a very
depleted condition. Your energy will provide one more
voice to add vision to your planet's lack of direction.*
   *Man is at the eye of the storm and doesn't perceive the
reality of what may be upon him. Because catastrophe
now falls within range of Earth's horizon, each individual
with vision must take responsibility for his awareness and
strive to reach others with farsighted, insightful information. Growth will be slow but permanent, and will allow
Earth to continue its forward momentum, breaking out of*

its currently stalled condition. The Earth cries out for rejuvenation and realignment. If you doubt this, let your body sink into a receptive state where you can monitor the degenerative process within the Earth.

Mentor's compassionate plea for mankind to wake up to the trouble at hand was distressing. It saddened me to think of any impending catastrophe and man's seeming disregard for his own plight. I felt totally inadequate considering the unlikely prospect that anyone would listen to what I could offer on the subject, much less accept the source of my information.

Should I meditate at a particular time of day?

✳ *Yes, work at a particular time; we can make our vibrations stronger then. Work often. We have much work to do. You will not always understand what we say, but it will all become clear in time. Contain the material in packets; it will be dispersed later. Sleep well and good night.*

"Sleep well and good night"! Mentor must have sensed the drain I was beginning to feel. I was emotionally frayed, yet I was already considering the questions for the next "sitting." I wondered if this loving presence would be there for me tomorrow. The dramatic tone of the messages, the sense of compassion for all humanity contained within the words, caused yet another awakening within me. I read again the instruction to contain the material in packets to be dispersed later. I began to feel a sense of commitment, shadowed though it was by my own lack of confidence. Nevertheless, this sense was destined to grow. The commitment was to work on behalf of humanity. A contract had been offered to me—and I unknowingly accepted.

The Deepening Relationship

The next morning I was ready with another series of questions, and Mentor—thank God—was there to respond as before. As I was preparing to ask my question, I could not help but wonder if, somehow, I would be able to perceive Mentor in physical terms. He immediately responded to my mental wonderings as a question.

Will I ever be able to perceive you in a physical way?

✳ You cannot see a picture of us because our wavelength structure is different from yours. Our thoughts come to you through a complicated channel of wavelength variations. When you meditate you see purple and white spheres. These are the auras of color-sensitive reflections of the intense accumulation of energies with which we work. This will have to be sufficient, for it would not be appropriate for us to manufacture an earthly posture just for your temporary reassurance. You must trust us based on your reaction to our teachings.

We are many in number. We began with three but the three are not always the same, for many wish the opportunity of experiencing breakthrough to your reality. As soon as it became possible for one group to tune in to your level, it opened the way for many to tune in. It is a matter of fine tuning on your part and ours.

However, Agartha, I am Mentor—your teacher—and the coordinator of your perceptions. I am always with you to monitor and interpret that which is being projected to you. I am becoming acquainted with you and you with me. It is important that a bond of extreme trust and love develop between us.

"Agartha"? The name appeared so quickly I did not think to ask Mentor why he called me that. Then in reading through the response, I asked what Jim and I both wanted to know:

Why did you name Meredith "Agartha"?

❋ *"Agartha" is a name meaning "journey to the stars." We knew she would appreciate it. It is a name with good meaning—special meaning—in your language. It has no origin in our language. Language in our space or dimension is undetermined—it exists by the acceptance of another or willingness to receive an impression. One must have the other being's permission in order to send and have the message properly received.*

We do experience what you could call thought impressions. These, however, are not in a form you would recognize. Our naming of Agartha represents a thought impression. It was translated to those exact letters by Agartha herself. The intent, the meaning, was what was projected.

Mentor was right—I loved my name, "Agartha." It was almost two years later, however, before Mentor clarified for me that Agartha was from the Sanskrit word, "agarta," which translates to the concept of "heaven bound." This second meaning added greatly to my initial enjoyment of the name, as I have since come to understand that we are all "heaven bound." I had the distinct feeling that Mentor enjoyed giving me my name, and it became special like a sacred gift that one cherishes and shares with loved ones. It was beginning to seem more natural for me to be developing a relationship with Mentor. His calling me Agartha indicated that it was mutual.

While Mentor has masculine connotations in my mind, he has said specifically that he is both male and female. My teacher regards himself in a universal way as his response to my later question about names on his realm indicated.

What about your name, "Mentor"? Apparently you have names? What are they?

❋ *Our names are of no real importance. We address energies of our dimension with thought impression titles, such as "one of unlimited joy" or "giver of wisdom." You may call us any positive force names you choose—pick any and they will be adequate. You may use "Mentor" (Co-ordinator of Perceptions), "Mirth" (Sustainer of Happiness) and "Merciful" (Unique Sensitor).*

I had the strange impression that Mentor was amused with my questions about names. I sensed that he was laughing lovingly as he came up with "Mirth", "Merciful" and "Mentor." He seemed content to be making a concession to my need for names and his kind indulgence was warming. It helped me to relax while getting to know this new non-physical connection.

Jim wanted to ask about the communications themselves. How did they happen? How did the thoughts come out in perfect English? Perhaps more than any single issue, the simple question of language and language transmission greatly puzzled us.

How do you communicate through Agartha via the English language? I can only assume that your language, if you have one, is not English.

✳ *We do not use language per se. We use brain waves which are telepathically processed. Your need of a particular language is very basic and presents many difficulties even in communicating with others of your same planet. We communicate with Agartha telepathically. We do not feed her the words, we feed her the thoughts, and she then puts them in her own words.*

Telepathy seemed a simple answer to what we could only guess was a much more sophisticated process. We were becoming more confident with the process, however, and had no reason to doubt the incredible results.

Many months later a question came up that was frequently asked by both believers and hard-core skeptics. I hoped it would not offend Mentor, but I needed to ask it.

I do not wish to doubt you, Mentor, but could it possibly be that you are a product of my imagination?

* *What is imagination except a glimpse of reality experienced and expressed in a normally unprecedented manner? We tied our collective energies into this communication and then selectively decreased the volume. The conversion of energy into thought impressions, which are then telepathically transmitted, is how we were able to communicate with you, Agartha. This is the way communication is most successfully accomplished where there is a wide variance in energy levels.*

Most people you know experience jolts of awareness. This communication is simply awareness strung together creating complete thoughts; and, yes it does come through Agartha's subconscious, or as we would rather call it superconscious.

On our dimension we are like a shimmering pond with reflections or vibrations springing back and forth. These thought impressions are communicated very precisely— and with beautiful subtleties that are lost with words. You might call it words of a different kind of language, but there is no noise or sound involved.

Quiet and sound merge into one another in other dimensions . . .

Mentor's skill and grace in answering my most complicated questions was reassuring. Even though the answer to questions often sounded like a combination of a Zen koan and a beautiful metaphor, it still felt basically complete. This intriguing answer, however, failed to satisfy Jim's deeper question concerning verification of the existence of other levels of reality. I tried again.

What about all the skeptical people and people who want facts?

* *There will be some wanting only concrete proof. These people's minds are still in a more confused state of development and have not evolved to the point of accepting higher consciousness in their lives. They are therefore only interested in tearing down that which they do not under-*

*stand. But there is no time limit for awareness, and ulti-
mate knowledge comes to all energy forms.*

*Do not be concerned; we will protect you in any circum-
stances that would seriously disillusion you to the point of
creating blocks to our communication. You have already
progressed along this path of higher understanding to the
point where it would be impossible for you to be again
satisfied with the mundane. Do not be concerned—the
value of this material will be perceived.*

*The understanding of Truths is more essential, more
valuable to you as a race of people than mere facts could
ever be. Truths are not limited to the interaction of certain
physical circumstances or events. Truths encompass understandings which raise man from the confinement of
Earth School to mastery of the Cosmos!*

*Facts are finite. They happen and are recountable, but
to whose benefit and for what purpose? The ever-
expanding search for Truth is the only search of substance, and those who search in this vein will not be
disappointed for they will intuitively recognize the Truths
of which we speak. Truths are constant elements emanat-
ing from the very core of existence. These are the building
blocks with which man needs to deal.*

Being the channel for these communications and needing
to answer the questions of those who wanted to know about
the Mentor material, I had a particularly strong need to know
that I was not just talking to myself. I also needed to be sure
I was not misrepresenting Mentor's thoughts. This authori-
tative answer seemed to satisfy Jim, or at least to preempt a
continuation of questions along this line of thought. He was
deeply impressed with Mentor's wisdom concerning facts
and truths.

How can I be sure which thoughts are mine and which are
yours?

*❋Questions in the morning are more apt to get prompt
and correct responses. Write your questions out ahead of*

*time. If you find you are unsure of an answer, do not
speak it—it is coming from you and not us. Our answers
and material are sent quickly and surely, as you are now
writing, not with hesitation.*

*It is understandable that you wish proof. When you stop
being concerned with this you will find proof. We are not
being arbitrary, we are simply trying to separate our communications from your own mind's. There is a very fine
distinction sometimes between what you wish to believe
and what in fact is our beamed-in communication. Always
ask questions about your course of action several times
and if you do not understand, ask again.*

It seemed so simple, and I have come to recognize Mentor's ability to deal in simplicity as an attribute of a true
teacher. It was just as he said in the beginning: I was learning
to trust him because of what he said and the way in which
he said it. It seemed he was always able to perceive just how
much I could comprehend. He was never belittling nor overly
perplexing, always dealing in easily understood language.

Gradually our daily contact with Mentor led to larger questions about the whole spectrum of alternate realities and nonphysical beings. If it was possible to reach out and contact
higher levels, could we communicate with simpler life forms
such as houseplants or even the nature spirits? Jim posed this
question about other realities and was quite surprised by the
depth of the answer he received.

Are there separate realities overlapping with ours? Can Agartha journey to these realities or experience them with her five
senses?

*✶It is not solely the five senses with which one experi-
ences other realities. Agartha experiences me now, not
with her eyes, not with her ears, but with her mind and
her spiritual energy. She will have an easier time perceiving those realities which are more advanced than those in
and around Earth School, for Earth School realities are
primarily concerned with a basic level of spiritual growth.*

The exception to this is in contacting the natural energies or nature spirits of the planet, for they share a similiar energy configuration with man and thus can be contacted quite easily.

The energy developed through normal spiritual attainment is not of sufficient strength to contact more diminished levels. It takes considerably more energy to digress to more diminished levels than it takes to advance to more spiritually adept levels. It follows then that those on the simpler, more basic levels of development are more easily able to contact those beings who will advance their spirituality, whereas they will not be able to contact as clearly those beings of lesser levels who might cause them anxiety.

When a being becomes of sufficient strength of spirit to be unaffected by contacts with lesser realities, then he usually finds he possesses the energy necessary to make contacts of this type. The intense desire to communicate with simpler levels of reality is not usually felt until sufficient insight has been attained that one perceives his true role as teacher.

Perceptions change as you advance. There are no clear-cut lines between realities. Death in your culture has you crossing a major barrier, when in fact it is a rather minor transition. Once on the other side you discover degrees of attainment. Each entity is separate but exists within the whole. Realities exist in a blending fashion, perceived by those involved as either separate or blended in exquisite harmony with the whole.

What is perceived depends on what is being sought. Put another way, there are singular and multiple ways of perceiving each reality by those involved, just as in Earth School, where there is the contrast between mere survival and spiritual enlightenment. Thus the degree of "enjoyment" or "growth" inherent in each reality depends on what one is content with. One cannot see the beautiful blending of energies if one has developed interest and knowledge of only the physical condition.

The Continuing Communication Process

And so it began and continues today. Mentor requested that I contain my daily writings of his teachings in packets. One morning, about three months after our initial meeting, he mentioned that we would begin the first of many books and presented me with the entire chapter outline for this book. Subsequently, we were to spend the better part of three years writing this first book, and he has instructed us editorially through each stage in order that the book may be guided to completion.

The process of sharing Mentor has become easier as I have observed the positive effect of his words on individuals and groups. It has been a slow steady process of learning to look beyond my own limitations to realize that I would not have been given this connection if in fact I was not capable of using it effectively. The more my life reaches toward awareness and understanding of all life, the more I find I have deepening insights. These increase my effectiveness in helping those with whom I work come to a more complete and positive understanding of their lives and potential purposes. Fears of personal limitations have not vanished, but they have become less important as the focus on my work as a communicator and interpreter between two worlds has gained a stronger position in my life.

I have shared Mentor's teachings privately with many people, and each person seems to take from the material what is important to his or her own learnings at any given time. When we learn who we are, it seems that we will then know how to solve many of the critical issues facing us today. My hope is that this material will significantly add to each reader's conscious understanding of the meaning of life and a sense of our place in the larger scheme.

Mentor's conclusion to this initial chapter most appropriately outlines both his intent in sharing this material with us and the promise of release from man's current woes if we are able to "come of age."

✳ *The teachings included in this chapter are relevant to each life and to each individual who searches for a greater understanding of the unanswered questions of Planet Earth and the Universe.*

The purpose of our contacting Agartha has been explained as well as the process by which this was accomplished. The desire to know and to contact other dimensions is part of each individual's superconscious, for on this level man really "lives," sensing with astute awareness the major issues of dynamic spiritual growth.

Two thoughts are important here: one, there is an obvious increased level of reported material on the subject of communication with unknown realities. Two, the nature of the material, while not completely verifiable on the conscious level, is nonetheless all-encompassing and verifiable on the superconscious level.

It is time for the people of Planet Earth to come of age and to acknowledge their role in the Cosmos. For this to happen, for enlightened understanding to replace callous indifference, each person must look to his superconscious, his "living mind," for his own unique connection.

CHAPTER TWO

COMING FROM THE HEART

"Man's body is filled with the joy and sorrow
of yesterday.
Man's mind is filled with the joy and sorrow
of today.
But Man's soul is filled with the priceless joy
of tomorrow,
through the reality of coming from the heart."

MENTOR

THE PROCESS OF integrating any significant change into one's life is more often a threat than it is a comfort, at least in the beginning phases of a new cycle. And it seems that, while the process of change is constant, it is like a pendulum whose arc spans an abyss, activating on one side dramatic and obvious changes and on the other, the more subtle forces of life.

My initial spiritual experience in early May, 1980, had triggered a season of change which was to last for the next eighteen months: nine months after Monroe but preceding Mentor, and nine months adjusting to the addition of Mentor to our lives. Even before Mentor officially introduced himself in January of 1981, I was involved in the process of reconciling my new sense of self with my former self, which proved to be a major episode in terms of my own transformation.

Looking back at that time in my life, I still feel a deep sense of gratitude for the quiet autumn provided for us before we moved to New Hampshire. We had moved into our first rental house at the height of the fall colors. The house had originally been part of a summer colony and was tucked

33

away in the woods. The giant pines hung precipitously close
to the house, all but leaning on the roof. While there was
nothing especially memorable about the house, it was the
experience of living there which was significant.

We used the six months of fall and winter as "think-time"
for finding a building site and a house design. It seemed
appropriate for Jim to leave CBS in the early spring of 1981
in order that we could move to New Hampshire to begin the
building of our home. Although I had always shied away
from cold climates, my new spirit of adventure suggested
there was more than the cold to consider in choosing the
location of our new home. The New England approach to
living was meaningful to us because it reinforced the aspects
of determination and dignity which seemed woven into every
aspect of life. Moreover, the rural life seemed suited for
spiritual pursuits.

Once Mentor became part of my life, he did not complement my role as wife and mother; he overwhelmed it. It was
safe to ask for guidance, but it was contrary to who I was to
fully live it. I had no desire to threaten the established roles
within my relationship with Jim, nor did I want the responsibility of defending a reality I was only barely beginning to
understand myself.

These writings highlighted all my personal insecurities.
I felt incapable of presenting my experiences in more conventional terms, which seemed to be what everyone expected. I did not have the cosmic vocabulary, the
background in religious traditions, or the confidence to
present Mentor in a way that I felt would do justice to him
or the writings. I only wanted to try to keep the wonderful
writings as a personal treasure from which I could pick
and choose the day's fare.

Yet, mixed in with this sense of retreat from the sharing
of the writings were those moments of genuine confidence
which seemed triggered by another's need. My own fear of
rejection paled in response to those whose words spoke of
trauma, disease and death. Where there was a need to be
addressed, it felt deeply appropriate to relate my experiences
and the beautiful materials which had been put into my pos-

session. Under the circumstances, material seemed to pour directly from some inner well, all personal misgivings fell away and the right words were always spoken. I did not need to hesitate; what I said was understood in a way that was meaningful to me and to those with whom I spoke. I have since come to call this process "switching to the cosmic channel," which means speaking from the heart and knowing that it will be right.

While spirituality, at this point in my life, was still a dawning reality, Jim had been actively on his own path for ten years. Only once during that decade of searching had he experienced a sense of his own connection to the nonphysical world. My overwhelming breakthrough with Mentor, by comparison, created a feeling of guilt as if I had somehow been granted a spiritual privilege I had not earned. From that perspective, it did not seem fair that the connection with a nonphysical teacher should be made with me rather than with Jim. And it seemed that as Mentor's influence spread into every area of our lives, it inadvertently diminished Jim's spiritual search.

Perhaps in certain respects it would have been easier had this been Jim's direct experience, for he is not a man who is comfortable with the position of observer. He has a participant's nature with an intense desire to experience the realities he reads about. And so it was perfectly natural for him to interpret my spiritual experiences as that which was happening to and for both of us. Certainly, at one level, that was, and is, an accurate perception. From the more intimate perspective, however, I felt as though I was being pressured by Jim into sharing and interpreting my experiences for others with the same emphasis and confidence his personality naturally dictated. Mentor became a vicarious spiritual experience for him, suggesting that his long quest had not been in vain. While I inwardly understood this delicate situation, attempting to communicate my feelings to Jim only served to complicate the matter.

For regardless of this spiritual awakening, I was still a suburban housewife, and not yet a mystic. I felt woefully unprepared to face people, telling them of my cosmic experiences. To accept Mentor's presence and the writings as the natural fulfillment of a spiritual search meant that I had to accept myself as a confident participant in a cosmic reality that was altering the very basis upon which I had built my life.

There were times, though, when I felt I had taken major steps forward in releasing old patterns and responding to new ones. For example, it had been my decision to move, and it had come not with feelings of self-sacrifice but from a sense of natural progression. It now seemed very appropriate to consider a change in life-style.

Learning to Listen

Weeks of intensive Mentor writings set the precedent for the work which was to become a part of my present life. I would meditate in the morning after the children left on the schoolbus, and then write for several hours, transcribing the scrawls into readable form. Mentor would always clarify or repeat a message if for some reason I could not decipher my own handwriting. There was never a note of annoyance; the message was simply repeated. By noon the serious work of the day was complete.

Internalizing the subject matter in these morning sessions was quite another matter. I often experienced a level of detachment in which I would lose a sense of what I was writing as well as of its source. While enormous potential for personal change was contained within the scope of Mentor's writings, I was easily overwhelmed and could only absorb a little at a time. The material I did not read immediately found its way to the desk drawer to be read later.

Jim could not believe that I did not devour the writings, but it was important for me to maintain a level of normalcy for myself and the children. Perhaps it was a protective device that allowed me to go on living. I found it was often the smallest details of the writings—the way Mentor would unexpectedly use the name he had given me—Agartha, that would cause me to sense the enormity of what was taking place. It was in this cautious manner of integration that my personal relationship with Mentor grew. I knew I needed to tread carefully, taking care of my own emotional health, for this was to be a contract fulfilled over many years. By this time I had come to trust that the writings would always be available for the asking, though I think Jim was afraid that this incredible source of insight might one day disappear. Despite that, it was a magical time for me, knowing that my life was being directed by conscious choices, and that these choices were forming a new pattern which would move me toward a deeper appreciation of Mentor and a new level of sharing with others.

Every area of my life slowly began to reflect the effect of Mentor's influence. And, as with a severe and sudden weight loss, people near me noticed the change. Sharing the explanation for my shifting patterns proved to be another significant learning experience. I came to realize that revealing the existence of a nonphysical teacher can elicit several different responses. One comes from the disbeliever for whom there is no proof. Another is, oddly enough, from the believer who, in his willingness to believe, can derive an impression which is simply inaccurate. I have had the experience, more often than I like to recall, of having to clarify an individual's understanding of what the significance of Mentor is within my life. It does not mean that I am suddenly fully released from the experiences of fear or anger, doubt or worry. I am as susceptible to a cold or to a car accident as anyone else. The significance of Mentor far transcends my personal concerns, and yet every aspect of my growth is enhanced by the relationship I have with my teacher.

Still, it is enormously reassuring that Mentor has never failed to answer my calls. I have only to relax, clear my mind, focus on him, and he is there. The process never ceases to amaze me. I have learned to work faster and more accurately by typing his communications rather than writing longhand. This method has it amusing drawbacks. Sometimes in the process of "listening," I become so engrossed in what is being transacted that I neglect to notice that the paper has come out of the typewriter. At other times I will get my fingers on the wrong keys and my typing becomes totally unintelligible. In these instances, fortunately, Mentor willingly repeats. Typing, with its few drawbacks, is far more comfortable than handwriting and since I am a competent typist, working at a keyboard has become my preferred method of taking down the messages. While it may seem at first to take away from the naturalness of the experience, I have found it saves hours of time in the transcribing and frees me for more creative work.

There are any number of ways once can received channeled material. My least favorite is letting Mentor speak through my own vocal cords. I cannot remember the first time it happened, though it happened in the natural course of one day's lesson. This, of course, turned out to be Jim's favorite type of communication since he could have a dialogue with Mentor. He found it difficult to understand why I put up such resistance to this verbal communicating, even though I tried to explain that it was difficult to vacate one's body in the presence of others, knowing that one was not present to stop or in any way influence the communication. It is a feeling of being totally vulnerable and virtually defenseless.

My reticence to verbally express Mentor's material did not apply, however, to small groups of people who were honestly searching for spirituality. It only surfaced with those who had merely a prurient interest. In these cases it struck me as highly inappropriate to ask Mentor for input. While it is my voice that one hears in the channeling, the voice inflections and choice of the words are not. Such an experience can be often disconcerting or overwhelming to a newcomer to the process, so I much prefer to stay in the "here and now" with people while they listen to pre-taped sessions. My sincere desire is to serve people's need for understanding and knowledge, not to impress them with the process through which transmission takes place.

Tonal Resonance: The Energy Vibration of All Life

Mentor devoted the winter of 1981 to communicating knowledge of a universal nature, as well as counseling me and laying the groundwork for our evolving relationship. I was a serious student and realized that I was receiving an education unparalleled by any earthly classroom. One day I asked Mentor about our new land in New Hampshire and the life we would start building there in the Spring.

*Agartha, you will be able to more effectively explore your potentials when you reach your new home. Take time in your new setting to begin the fundamental task of identifying the structural elements of your life. Learn to use the gifts of awareness which are yours. Time will be abundant, amplifying all the supportive elements around you. Do not rush to see beyond. Enjoy the moment.

Once into this new beginning, each day should open with a time of quiet to create and maintain a cleared place for the awakened mind. This centering is essential in seeking the often subtle and seemingly undefined nature of Truth. Truth, in fact, defines itself. It remains solidly intact despite the onslaught of changing mood and circumstance. It is often seen but not necessarily recognized or understood.

Observation of the world of nature offers an accessible lead into the otherwise difficult to approach substance of spiritual evolution and Truth. By witnessing the mysteries of garden and field there is the opportunity to experience the unexplainable and witness the undeniable . . . life in its most radiant and dynamic garb, depleted and yet springing anew, the mysteries of the universe tumbling from the petals of a daisy.

One such natural truth focuses on tonal resonance which is the low-intensity pattern of energy vibrations given off by all things. Tonal resonance vibrations originate from the etheric body and move outward and away from the body in ever-widening circles. The etheric body

*is the ether-like layer of energy which shadows the phys-
ical body. These vibrations serve as a means of identifying
the unfamiliar, be it rock or star. You and the universe
are forever involved in a majestic dance, a gentle swaying
of the visible and invisible, an unprecedented and often
unrealized interaction among all worlds.*

*In pragmatic terms, all that surrounds you interprets
and interacts with tonal resonance. Your superconscious
mind is capable of interpreting signals from the etheric
body as well as the physical body. In your superconscious
interpretation of objects you might analyze the incoming
tonal resonance vibrations in the following manner: molecular structure and resultant biological classification,
(what is it?); propensity toward aggressive behavior (will
it hurt me?); under which laws of the universe does it
function? (do we share a common bond?). The object's
interpretation would, of course, be in its own vernacular
and not that of twentieth century language, but it would
still roughly approximate your questions of basic identification. This personal sonar routinely seeks to identify and
categorically analyze all interplay with which it comes in
contact. This ongoing readout continues through each
day's activities and functions continually without conscious directive.*

*In walking your land you become the interpreter and
the one who is interpreted. Consciously, you remain distant from this interchange as the mind follows its instructions to extricate only the most relevant of incoming
data, relegating all else to the less accessible states of
consciousness. The five senses are not applicable to tonal
resonance, since you neither see, taste, touch, smell, nor
hear vibrations. You instead sense them intuitively with
your unconscious or rather superconscious mind, mentally moving in harmony with the most basic forces of
interconnectedness. Of course, unlimited potential exists
for relationships among all things. A partnership is born
when both parties are cognizant of the other's awareness.*

We were to learn many things about the vibrations that man and objects emit and the effect of these vibrations on their environment. One of the most dramatic personal examples occurred shortly after we moved to New Hampshire. We had gone to Connecticut to attend a wedding and we were exhausted as we returned home late that night. Mark and Melanie were asleep in the back of the station wagon, and I was struggling to stay awake to talk to Jim. It was a losing battle. During a lull in our conversation, I dozed off. Without warning I was jolted out of sleep by Mark who woke up shouting, "Dad! Dad! The road! Look out for the road!" Before I could respond, Mark was again lying down, sleeping soundly.

Jim was visibly shaken. He confided that he had fallen asleep just before Mark's outburst. Mark's shouting had awakened him. We were frightened to realize how close we had come to disaster. There was no question that something profound had happened, and I was determined to ask Mentor about it the next day:

✻ *There are many routine functions necessary to maintain a physical body and mind. These routine programs are stored out of conscious reach in the vaults of the superconscious mind. However, when something occurs on the physical plane grossly conflicting with a maintenance program, such as falling asleep at the wheel when one had been programmed to always remain alert when driving, then the superconscious mind sets up a distress signal to attract the body's attention. The normal give-and-take of tonal resonance is overridden with the distress vibrations being sent from the superconscious mind. These alerting vibrations tell the physical and etheric bodies of a major problem.*

Consider the circumstances behind your near-accident:

1. Jim was driving the car (normal tonal resonance vibration).

2. Jim fell asleep while driving the car (distress vibrations override normal tonal resonance signals).

3. Mark was asleep in the back seat (in touch with the standard give-and-take of tonal resonance vibrations from his father).

4. Mark, responding to his father's distress, overrode the vibrations (wakes up screaming the intent of the signal—look out for the road).

All things give off normal and altered levels of vibrations. Altered levels occur when action is not compatible with conscious programming. Whenever the body digresses from its programmed pattern, the vibrations respond in an altered pattern. This is how people at great distance from loved ones sense a major problem. Sometimes the distress pattern is strong enough to break into conscious thought. Mark's response was also indicative of the fact that he knew what represented a grave variation from Jim's normal tonal response. A stranger might not have reacted as strongly or might not have reacted at all.

We could relate easily to Mentor's explanation and found ourselves gradually led into deeper levels of trust. We had experienced verification of tonal resonance and therefore had our proof that the vibrations of which he had spoken actually existed.

Qualifying Mentor's teachings in terms of that which is more profound versus that which is of lesser importance would seem a typically "human" endeavor. And yet, when Mentor offers guidance specific to the undertaking of one's own life, the category of "personally profound" is automatically created. The dimensions of personal guidance became interwoven with material of a more general level as Mentor cited examples from our own lives as illustrations of the concepts he wanted to communicate. This occurred with great regularity during the time of the building of our home.

✳ *How you work your land, Agartha, and who is involved in the building of your home will have a lasting effect. All the gradations of harmony and disease which you and oth-*

*ers around you feel will become ingrained in the very core
of your house. Either positive or negative, the tonal resonance emissions of all those within your sphere, will determine the atmosphere in which you will live.*

With his guidance, we felt compelled to find compatible
people with whom to share the task of building the new house.
One morning Jim awakened me with one of his great ideas.
He said we should contact David and Martha, two new
friends, and ask them to come out from Indiana to live and
work with us on the building of our house. We knew David
was a carpenter, an expert gardener, an artist and a musician;
Martha was an apprenticed midwife who had a serious interest in healing, organic cooking and gardening. Both were
strongly spiritual, well-grounded people, and we knew our
children would love them. Trusting Jim's intuition, we called;
when they enthusiastically accepted, we felt confident it had
been the right decision.

In a similar fashion we found Mike, our lead carpenter,
whose quiet strength and knowledge kept us on course during
the building of the house. We found Mike after a phone call
from a local shop where we had made inquiries for a special
craftsman/builder. And there was Lew, a carpenter and expert wilderness guide, on whose steadfastness we learned to
depend. A bond of trust developed among all of us as we
labored together on the house for almost seven months.

Tentatively at first, and then with increasing confidence, I
began to share Mentor's teachings and was gratified at the
level of response to his thoughts. We would sit in the garden
or around our living room fire for meditations, sharing
thoughts and experiences. From these intimate gatherings,
we developed a loving nucleus of people who became our
new friends and community.

✳ *Your land is meant to serve as a haven to many, a sanc-
tuary, and must be prepared accordingly. Those in need
of solace will intuitively journey there recognizing it as a
place of peace.*
Energy has been channeled to your land, ensuring the

proper conditions for building and planting. The land is awakening to a new, more dynamic growth potential and you will feel this as you plant and reap. The added energy will be effective in two ways. First, it will combine with soil and seed to give you greater production than you would otherwise know. Second, it will weave a fabric of harmony among those working in or near the garden, with construction of the house moving forward with added vitality. Interestingly, if you could see the energies of increased production and harmonious interaction in their appropriate colors, you would discover that the red of heightened production and blue of harmonious interaction create the color violet which is representative of the spiritual transformation you seek.

Just as we quickly developed a routine in the construction of the house, my daily meditations with Mentor gradually became an accepted part of the morning procedure. This created occasional twinges of anxiety as I saw Jim becoming "addicted" to Mentor, abdicating his own objectivity in making decisions about our lives. He began to refer every issue to Mentor for comment.

Inwardly, I could feel a level of resentment developing as it became subtly apparent that I was more welcome at the breakfast table with the morning writing from Mentor than without it. I expressed my anger to Jim by stating that I felt as if I had become little more than a machine for taking cosmic dictation.

This feeling was extremely difficult for Jim to appreciate. Perhaps it struck him as irreverent since he was convinced that had the connection been made with him, he would have pursued it with greater determination. Nevertheless, I was pursuing it with all I had to give and that would have to be enough. I was becoming less self-conscious regarding what others might think, whether I would be rejected as "different" because of my emerging gifts; but I also needed to maintain a sense of normalcy.

The transition in personal and in spiritual life-styles, though relatively smooth, still required a period of adjustment in which I was to learn that ultimately we are all subject to the laws of the Universe. Though I knew better, it was remarkably easy to believe that with Mentor's assistance, all major problems could be avoided. This, of course, is the same inaccurate perception I have since encountered in many others seeking to understand both the intricacies of my relationship with Mentor and their own guidance.

Shortly after we began work on the house and started clearing a path through the woods for the electric lines, Jim had a serious accident in which his leg was pinned under a tree. I was utterly confounded. I had believed with all my heart that this move was sanctioned by the Universe. Mentor had told us of our new life but he had never mentioned that this accident was in the offing. I felt betrayed. Why had he not warned me? Every tiny detail had gone perfectly and now we had come up against a totally unexpected circumstance which threatened to explode our dream of completing the house.

Jim was an essential member of the building team. Without him we could not possibly stay on schedule or within budget. Mentor was reassuring but quick to point out that the people on earth are governed by certain natural laws and when these are disobeyed, trouble inevitably results. He continued, saying that all was not written and that we were subject to the laws of earth just like everyone else. He did, however, give me some specific instructions to help with the healing of Jim's leg and the giant hematoma healed in three weeks rather than three months. It was a miraculous recovery and he was soon back building stone walls, even if it was with a slight limp, and I was more seasoned in my expectations of the role of the Universe in my life.

The Meaning of Love

One of Mentor's more fascinating discussions was on the subject of "love." I was curious to know his perceptions of the actual meaning of this energy called love. In spite of the reams written on the subject, Mentor's thoughts revealed levels previously unknown to me.

❊ *"Love"* is the word you use to describe a specialness of feeling, a demonstrable affection for a person or idea. Unfortunately man rarely understands the pure, undiluted essence of *"love as harmony"* or *"love as concern for the whole."* It is important, however, that you be exposed to love as it can and does exist elsewhere. Love is experienced by all realities but in different ways and with different focuses. Let us look at love as it exists on my dimension and on yours, Agartha.

More advanced consciousnesses exist in a dimension of total self-commitment to the advancement of all energy toward the Universal God. Love, as I know it, exists as an expression beyond individual limitation. This love is an experience tied to those insights gained from the accumulation of evolved lifetimes. As love is seen in its true proportions, so involvement in and concern for the universal growth and advancement of all energies becomes the living focus of all.

Lesser-evolved realities exist in more poorly-defined dimensions, focusing on the individual and his needs—95% physical and 5% spiritual—rather than a concern for the whole. On your level, there is little concern for love as universal harmony, because there is only a budding understanding of man's connection to the whole. Quite naturally on your dimension, physical awareness through development of human relationships is the most important exercise of life with a new growing concern for individual spiritual advancement.

Love is experienced by all dimensions as it fits the needs of those involved. Thus you could call my love *"abstract love"* and yours *"emotional release love"* (love that is dominated by individual priorities). Connecting these two realms is *"enlightened love,"* which is love through enlightenment or total awareness. Enlightenment is the traveling, the traveler, and the point to which one travels; It is the doorway and the experience of triangulating on love beyond the physical. Love actually knows no boundaries and through enlightenment can open vastly divergent *panoramas from those to which you have become accustomed.*

It was disconcerting to think that the level of love where we as humans spend most of our lives was the lowest level which Mentor called "emotional release love." Learning that there are levels beyond this, I wondered if "enlightened love" was a realistic goal. I asked Mentor about the possibilities for such advancement:

❋ *Love, Agartha, no matter what the focus, can be the point of interaction around which all else ferments. Love is, indeed, the appropriate and, in fact, only relevant vehicle for increasing man's vistas of harmony on Planet Earth and harmony within the Universe.*

Understanding love as it exists on other dimensions is interesting and important to engendering feelings of connectedness to the "future" and one's place in the universal picture. However, my serious intent in discussing love is to offer you the opportunity to recognize physical love in order that you may transcend it into something far more expansive.

Enlightened love is the magical link where man sees himself as one with all things. Harmony grows from chaos when man sees that the other he kills is himself. Individually and collectively, maturity is gained only as each person reaches, through love, for recognition of his own living connection to all other living energies of the Universe. A few now stand at this juncture of recognition, ready to live through peace and unity. Their numbers, however, are not yet sufficient to offset earth's extreme cacophony. Future growth is dependent on lessening the confusion, tension, and despondency which is currently so widespread. Man looks to the heavens for answers but sees only the reflection of his own desires, for his vision has become myopic and dulled. He no longer sees clearly. He does not seem to comprehend the obvious, that the way out of his conflicted and tormented state is to envision himself as integrally linked to all life.

Love, that elusive and yet essential breeze which blows through all life, exists as the core of all revelation. "Love comes from the heart" is a metaphor which points the way to a new beginning through recognition of the heart as the seat of man's "I am" awareness, man's link with others of his kind and with the "Isness."

The "I am" represents awareness of one's self as a harmonious part of the whole. "I am" signals: "I am responsible for deepening the connection between all peoples and the 'Isness'; for improving the harmony of the planet on which I live in order that all may find fulfillment."

Intuitively I felt the immense power in these words and was drawn toward the notion that it was the responsibility of every individual to find and nurture the "love connection" with the Universe. Yet, I had never felt a closeness to the word which seemed to stand for this realization, namely enlightenment. There seemed a coldness, a sense of detachment from reality whenever I read the word. It had never occurred to me that anyone other than yogis and evolved mystics consciously pursued enlightenment.

Still, in my own way, I could relate to the concept of enlightened love. As Mentor described it, it seemed potentially attainable and utterly appealing. I began to think of enlightened love as perhaps the ultimate goal for man. Rather than standing as a badge of esoteric distinction, enlightened love perhaps stood as each individual's only genuine gift to himself and to his planet. I wanted to know more.

Mentor's words encouraged me to personally examine my motivation toward others in consideration of my conscious commitment as part of a living reality. Within this context I hoped to, in some way, come to understand my own "I am" connection. While I felt an undeniable tie to the Universe, even a heart-to-heart link, I had never defined it. To experience this centering seemed the way to avoid the personal "black holes" potentially around every corner and also to contribute to rather than detract from the collective experience of living. Verification of one's "I am" connection to the "Isness" offered a potential means toward crystallizing one's relationship with the Universe.

I knew that if I could share this personal journey with others, my work with Mentor had the potential for becoming a beautifully creative and personal act of love. This vision became the core of my development, making a lasting impression on my life. It also became the basis for my work as a healer, believing that one's own personal connection, when made manifest, carried the individual beyond any physical limitation.

Only a few people who came into our sphere seemed unable or unwilling to appreciate the value and integrity of the teachings and guidance. Regrettably, some of these people were very close to us, and I could see that they were unable to fathom such a dramatic change in someone they had known in another more familiar capacity over the years. While this was frustrating, we learned to follow Mentor's own wisdom regarding such people, sharing only as much as we felt they could accept. Mostly, we found people hungry to learn. We regarded what we were learning as valid and felt strongly committed to further understanding the teachings. It became natural to share with others, and Mentor commented on my feelings:

❋ *You are feeling warmed, Agartha, by your experiences with people, sharing and being helped by your awareness. You seem surprised at the impact this material has on them. While you have accepted the writings and they seem very natural to you, to others they are still mysterious. Many are not able to contact their spiritual teachers, so they find it incredible that you can. While there is little feedback to your insistence that all people are capable of tapping other realities, nevertheless, this is the way some will eventually find their way to our realm to be shown truths beyond their five senses.*

We tried to incorporate Mentor's teachings into our own lives, but found that new patterns of thinking do not materialize overnight. If we were having problems grasping and

integrating these difficult perceptions into our lives even with
the assistance of a teacher, we could more fully appreciate
how difficult the process is without a direct connection. The
goal of enlightened living seemed both near and far, but it
was through Mentor's continued loving guidance that we
stayed on the path of seeking.

✳ *The "I am" is the seat of higher consciousness in the
body. It encompasses those qualities which are aligned
with the higher self and its connection with the Ultimate
Energy. "I am" development depends on the amount of
positive energy directed toward it.*

*Not unlike the physical body which responds to repeti-
tion in order to achieve facility in an endeavor, so the
spiritual body or "I am" also needs repetition to
strengthen its ability to override negative or inappropriate
feedback. Those aspects of physical and spiritual conditioning which are reinforced obviously grow, and those
which are neglected, atrophy.*

*The opportunity for reinforcement of the "I am" exists
through everyday actions and conversations as well as
through the more abstract issues of good and bad, right
action and "sin." When behavior, yours or another's, is
inappropriate—change it. Refuse to accept into your being
words or actions which are detrimental to the developing
"I am."*

*Life's major issues, the ones that you recognize as hav-
ing something to say, are nothing more than runaway small
issues. Take exception to the small issues. Be sure they
end where you wish, not where circumstance dictates. It
definitely is a matter of choice. Through such mental ma-
nipulations, one makes a commitment to one's path on a
conscious level and this directly affects one's life course.*

*You can be and should be responsible for your individ-
ual and collective growth. Strengthening one's own "I
am," developing one's own sense of self-love, identity and
commitment makes it possible to live and joyously experience a fully expanded life. This understanding of self is
the beginning of love's increased presence within your*

world. Each must develop his own vision of love and then
magnify it to include ever-widening groups of people.

Through the sharing of Mentor's teachings, certain issues
were brought painfully to the forefront. In our exuberance
and enthusiasm for all that we were now learning, we naively
assumed that everyone would be equally receptive. We discovered that this was simply not true. Moreover, we also had
to learn ways of responding to the reactions of others without
experiencing feelings of personal rejection.

This issue highlights, perhaps more than most, one of the
paradoxes of life. No doubt every individual has had the experience of observing another person, perhaps a child, doing
something which could be made much easier if approached
slightly differently. In offering assistance to the child, the
adult is likely to hear in response, "Just let me do it myself."
But if you, as the adult, know the procedure automatically,
then you feel a sense of frustration since you know how
simple the task is to accomplish. And yet, it is an act of
wisdom to allow the child to grow into his own skill.

I have come to believe the same process is at work in the
unfoldment of spiritual truths. Until or unless an individual
is ready to learn or experience something, then no matter
which way one explains a spiritual concept, it is still likely
to sound more like fiction than fact. Simultaneously, just
because you feel you are a more aware individual does not
mean that that is necessarily true. Moreover, in the event that
it is true, it does not make you a teacher.

I can recall a particular incident in which a very dear
friend, one whom we had known for many years, invited us
for a visit. We very much wanted to share the Mentor material and we were concerned as to how it would be received.
Prior to our visit, we asked Mentor what the level of receptivity would be and how best we should present the information. Mentor said that shortly after engaging our friend in
a conversation on spirituality, he would excuse himself, saying that he had to make a hasty trip to the drug store. This
would be our signal that he had heard enough and was feeling

threatened by our views. At that point, we were instructed
to change the subject.

It is fascinating to note that *despite* the fact that both Jim
and I were forewarned as to the exact course the conversation
would take, that did not mean we were forearmed. Early in
the conversation, our friend announced that he had to leave
for the drug store. Jim had hardly begun to talk and thus was
not expecting to have the conversation aborted quite so suddenly. He responded to the circumstance with frustration and
rejection. He felt that he had not been given a fair opportunity to discuss the subject. In this incident, we had been told
the exact scenario and still, our initial response was one of
confusion.

If we gleaned nothing else from this experience, we did
learn how very difficult it is to disregard one's immediate and
personal response and to seek the more compassionate response. Even with the assistance of Mentor, the more "human" pattern was the first level of response. It is not easy to
learn and it is certainly not easy to change.

✳ *There is an interesting part of love which we have not
spoken of, and this is the appropriate course one should
follow in sharing with people caught in the malaise, the
dis-ease of life. There is a basic factor here of assumed
responsibility for another's attunement or lack thereof.
How can you possibly be responsible for another's seeking
the path of enlightenment? You can talk, guide, teach,
use all known devices and still not create a desire to know.*

*That creative spark, that "time for enlightenment"
which kindles the flame is one of the beautiful mysteries
of the universal connection. Suffice it to say that the ini-
tiative to "seek" surfaces and becomes apparent at times
appropriate to the expanding nature of the seeker. The
kindling for the fire, the materials with which to fan the
flames of seeking, should be kept close at hand in readiness for another's unfolding. However, there is no way
one individual can create another's time for enlightenment. The life blood of spiritual advancement is a thing*

apart, a thing of the Universe, a thing unique to each living soul.

Be sensitive to each person and the individual needs inherent in each situation. Mentally work your way through the following list to the place where you feel it is appropriate to share:

1. *LOVE THE GOD FIBER in those people whose earthly demeanor makes it impossible for communication on a conscious level.*

2. *LOVE FROM A DISTANCE those beings who tolerate social conversation but who discourage more meaningful communication.*

3. *LOVE THE SHARED FRIENDSHIP in those who are anxious to share their love and awarenesses.*

4. *LOVE THE ONENESS in those people with whom you can share all that you feel, all that you have learned, aspirations and misgivings, personal and cosmic.*

Of the above list the only stage that might need clarification is the first, loving the God fiber. This might also be stated as "sensing the common cosmic link among people." The essence of this is to wish all others well, helping specifically those where it is possible. In those cases where it is not possible, in those cases where there can be no sharing, it is enough that you set them free to effectively follow their own path. Wishing them harm only causes you harm and ties you down unnecessarily. Release in love each individual to his own cosmic reality whenever and wherever that may be, harboring no sense of rejection or self-pity for the unrealized exchange or relationship.

Mentor's simple, concise explanation of the stages of love was reassuring and at the same time a concrete approach to sharing our lives and new directions. I was personally attracted to the notion of "releasing in love," considering the number of times I had assumed an individual wanted my help instead of more appropriately waiting until the person asked.

How much better it might have been in those circumstances to simple "release in love," and not just to release or let go but to do so *in love*. I have learned that unless personal assistance is directly requested, one should not interfere. Allowing an individual to move through any crisis without judgment or interference is often the most appropriate response one can give. Crossing those personal boundaries without an invitation only adds to the tension in times of crisis.

Equality: The Practical Side of Love

As I worked at integrating Mentor's lessons on love, it became increasingly apparent that I had been reticent to share the reality of Mentor with my ten-year-old son, Mark. What had begun as simple procrastination in regard to discussing the changes I was undergoing subtly established a precedent which began to seem impossible to change. Initially, I was afraid that Mark might not have the maturity to understand my relationship with Mentor without being frightened. I also was intimidated by the thought that he would think I was strange.

Mark was having his own difficulties in adjusting to our move to New Hampshire. I was hesitant to add to his confusion. Yet I could feel the tension building between us. He was always angry and I was certain it had to do with his feeling of being held at arms-length from this new mystery he knew existed in my life. All that Mentor said suggested that it was impossible and inappropriate to second-guess another's reaction. But I had assumed that Mark would not understand and I was afraid to trust him to make his own decision.

The question of what to say to Mark came to a head one evening when I was saying good night to him and he unexpectedly asked, "Why are you always meditating, Mom?" and "Why can't I see this space person?" I could feel myself stiffen and withdraw. I did not want to make a mistake on the initial introduction of Mark to Mentor, but I was not prepared to do it that evening. I promised Mark we would have a talk the following day. The next morning I turned to Mentor for his guidance:

✻ Relationships do not fit neatly into molds. There is no mother-son, father-daughter, husband-wife mold, or any other preconceived pattern of appropriate behavior within a relationship. One's own unique relationship is created. Just as no two people are alike, so no two relationships can be alike.

To assume you know someone well enough that you can and do predict their behavior and mental perspective is a gross and often tragic mistake, for it eliminates that person's freedom to create their own unique composite. It forces them to accept an abbreviated and often secondhand version, and that is never good enough. While these secondhand renderings may be acceptable for a time, they will inevitably need to be challenged and reconstructed by the individual in light of the other's own process of interpretation.

You are aware, of course, that sharing one's thoughts and feelings is the basis upon which communications are built. There must be an outgoing giving of information in order to receive an incoming feedback. Your son is fearful of what he does not understand due to lack of appropriate information. In your trying to protect him you have, in fact, only shown him you do not trust him with the facts. You have deprived him of his right to make his own value judgment, his own composite. You assumed you knew what his reaction would be. You obviously did not. You assumed your son would quietly accept your assessment of the new guidance, and he obviously has not.

To travel one's own path, one must be shown the importance and relevance of making one's own choices and decisions and allowing others the same freedoms. Agartha, give your son the required information to make his own value judgment. There is no right or wrong answer— only degrees of appropriateness to fit his and your individual needs.

After school the following afternoon, I took Mark for a walk and began the long overdue discussion. It took several months for him to work out of his slump in order to reach a point of openly discussing my experience of communication with a nonphysical being. To my relief, he did not reject what I told him, nor did he go shouting it to his friends. He developed a personal balance concerning my relationship with Mentor that was mature and touching. While he did not initiate many conversations on this subject, he enjoyed listening to Jim and me discuss each day's writings.

For a brief period of time, however, Mark needed to test Mom's abilities. Despite the fact that I found this process personally annoying, I knew he needed to assure himself of two things: one, that I really did possess a new ability and two, that I was still Mom. On one occasion, Mark told me he had not touched the cookies on the counter. I jokingly suggested that he tell me the truth or I would "check it out." He just smiled. Placing my hand on his stomach, I announced he had eaten two cookies. The look on his face was a combination of both astonishment and satisfaction. This was his way of coming to terms with my new ability and I was more than willing to cooperate with his reality.

My reluctance to trust Mark with my cosmic adventures caused me to reevaluate my relationships with other people close to me. I wondered if my own wobbly sense of personal confidence had gotten in the way of being honest with others. I asked Mentor if he had any thoughts on improving the quality of my interaction with those whose love I wished to share.

❋ *It is interesting and appropriate that you chose the word "interaction," Agartha. The degree of interaction is important as well as the atmosphere within which the interaction or communication takes place. Familiarity in this case is a definite hindrance, for it is usually interpreted as giving one permission to trespass not only in another's territory (mentally and physically) but in an atmosphere of blatant superiority and self-righteous preoccupation.*

Those to whom you are related or those with whom you share closely in any capacity deserve the right to be treated as strangers. The same forbearance, acceptance and friendship you would show to a stranger, you would often withhold from those close to you. Give equally to all those who cross your path. You are all related and yet you are all separate. Share your energies, always realizing another's choices are not your choices, another's path is not your path. You are unique and yet one with the community of man.

"The community of man"! What an incredibly romantic notion. "But, Mentor," I asked mentally, "is it realistic to think that all people could ever live together in harmony?" To this he replied:

✳ *But, Agartha, if you do not try how will you know? Man was meant to live in harmony, not imbalance. Man was meant to develop his energies for the benefit of all, not just for personal profit.*

Harmony has always been the way of things. Disharmony is only the way of things on earth. Be part of the unity and balance of the Universe by striving for what seems improbable and yet is possible.

There was much that I needed to assimilate from this rangy and sometimes difficult chapter, but Mentor's synopsis left me no doubt that he believed man's awareness of these subjects was critical to the attainment of any level of personal or collective satisfaction.

✳ *In this chapter, Agartha, I have shared with you ways in which love can create a harmonious whole through individual awareness. I have discussed:*

- *Awareness of tonal resonance.*
- *Use of homes and personal surroundings as sanctuaries.*
- *Love as the key to sharing and growth.*

- *Harmony through strengthening of the individual "I am."*
- *Conscious acceptance of responsibility for superconscious ("I am") growth.*
- *Communication through love—lack of guilt for another's awareness.*
- *Interaction—human with human.*

Coming from the heart is tapping one's awareness of the Truth, and awareness of the Truth is what your life is about. While your ability to perceive the Truth will grow and change, the Truth will not, Agartha, for the Truth is the Truth.

CHAPTER THREE

WHERE IS ENLIGHTENMENT?

How difficult is the path
How intense is the desire?
To find oneness,
To find peace,
To find enlightenment?

MENTOR

IT WAS A little more than a year after coming to New Hampshire when we finally moved into our new home. There had been six months of living in the rental house in Connecticut and another seven in a rental farmhouse near our building site. The experiences were entirely different: the first a time of introspection, of consolidation and of meeting Mentor; and the second a time of expansion, of building and of sharing the winter's learnings.

The men who were moving us arrived early in the day to unload our belongings which had been in storage for thirteen months. It was strange to see the abundance of possessions since we had become used to living so sparingly. The boxes filled the house until it was nearly bursting and still they brought in more. Our family's moving-in celebration lasted for weeks as we enjoyed the rearranging process of all the familiar things. I had not realized how accustomed I had become to the more casual and spontaneous lifestyle we had been living and how completely I had released the myth that I needed furnishings, rather than just the people, to make a home. But now I was content to be in one place and to call it home. The long days of working on the house had had a

pleasure of their own, but I was tired of change and of the
long hours of physical work which precluded quality time
with my family. It was time to settle into the next phase of
my life, finding how I was to use this gift from the Universe.

Now that my outer world of house and relationships had
settled into a comfortable routine, the quality of my internal
work became my central focus. Absorbing the teachings was
an all-encompassing learning experience. Despite their relative simplicity, I found it required personal discipline to
devote the necessary time to receive and record the writings;
and it often took weeks or even months for the concepts to
find their way beyond mere surface acceptance into the fabric
of my comprehension.

With great patience, Mentor opened my eyes to broader
truths and areas of learning which I had previously considered the province of poets and philosophers. Slowly I began
to understand, and the more I was able to integrate, the more
committed I became to establishing more fully my own connection to the Universe and to learning how to share it with
others. Mentor, like a true teacher, provided the basics that
brought me to doorways of greater learning. While standing
in these doorways, I found myself wanting to walk through
into a world of questions which could expand my spiritual
horizons.

As the spring of 1982 approached, we began attending
meditations and joining with others in the celebration of spiritual occasions. I was overwhelmed by the energy and commitment these people exhibited in seeking to expand their
personal spiritual development. More than that, it proved to
be a very dynamic time in which I could evaluate how much
my life had changed.

Through the process of coming to know these new friends
and local community members, I found myself relating in
ways far different from the exchange of simple social ameni-
ties which had been the custom of our business world. I
learned that the "social contract" which exists between individuals whose major life focus is spirituality automatically
contains a clause of openness.

It is not easy to articulate the differences I observed in

social dynamics which exist at the various levels of human interaction. In our "former" world of corporate social relationships, the level of personal interaction often revolved around our children, our homes, business ventures, travel and gossip. Rarely did one leave one's personal boundaries unprotected. It simply was not acceptable within these circles to openly discuss emotional or psychological matters. Oddly enough, while it was socially acceptable to discuss the fact that one might be in therapy, it was highly unacceptable to reveal why.

The dynamics of human relationships were controlled by the need to continually project the right impression. And the right impression meant always appearing to be in control of one's business, one's finances and one's family. While a functioning member of this world, I saw these behavioral patterns as natural and appropriate. In fact, I not only accepted my role in this system, I enjoyed it. I can remember the social movements of the 1960's and 1970's in which I looked upon hippies and "women's libbers" as radical. How they planned to make any type of valuable contribution to society was beyond my comprehension. I admit to having felt unnerved at their tendency to freely express their emotions, especially anger, their sense of social frustration, their sensuality and desire for fewer restrictions on human relationships and indeed, even their desire for a personal spirituality. Had I possessed then the vocabulary I do now, I would easily have admitted to feeling threatened by their total disregard for traditional social standards.

And yet, here I was, years later, living in a rural community, finding myself attracted to those individuals scattered throughout the area whose very prerequisite for social interaction seemed to be the courage to relate with honesty, sensitivity and love, totally celebrating the vulnerable side of the human design. Only the hand of the Universe could have rearranged my life in such a fashion that the social arena I had once feared became the very social arena in which I now lived. I recognized that I was receiving support from individuals who longed to share with and to accept us, not for what we owned, but for who we were.

I can recall detaching myself from my world, as one sometimes does, and viewing it with that sense of wonderment,
thinking, "When did all this change so dramatically, and
what happened to that woman I used to be?" I looked at my
new friends, the people I was growing to love, and suddenly
realized that had this been 1966, these folks would have been
the hippies and I probably would have been considered one
of them. I was even more amazed at my changing behavior
as it became more appropriate that Jim and I start a monthly
meditation group in order to share the Mentor material. This
process highlighted what was to be for me the next intense
personal challenge.

Exactly how does one casually share the teachings of a
nonphysical source of guidance? Precisely how does one establish credibility? That is to say, what is the appropriate
criterion for earning respectability when the task at hand—
the sharing of this information and its source—is more likely
to attract severe criticism than social applause? In short, I
was once again frightened and overwhelmed. However, this
time I had a strong sense that in a minor way, I had been
through this experience before. Had I not redesigned my
personal and social life based on my spiritual experiences?
Certainly my entire world had been rearranged and yet my
internal sphere had only increased in strength and in trust
from the experience.

On the other hand, one very real distinction existed between my private world and the outside community. At some
point, no matter how extreme my experiences may have
seemed to my family members, they tried any number of
ways to believe me. However, the reality of our society is
that others seek to discredit long before they grow to trust.

I suppose I would have felt even slightly more confident if
I had strong academic credentials to my credit; for example,
a Ph.D. in psychology would have kept at least some critics
at bay. But such was, and is, not the case. I had only the
truth of my experience and Mentor's words committed to
paper as my platform from which to speak. And I had
learned that within my day-to-day living experiences, I, too,
grew by personally experiencing the truth of his teachings.

Mentor had said, "the Truth is, after all, the Truth." I needed nothing else. I started out hoping that he was right and learned that indeed, he was.

Our meditations were received warmly. Individuals from all over New England began to find their way to our home. It was gratifying, not in terms of feeling that all of this somehow supported the validity of my own spiritual reality, but that it totally supported the validity of man seeking to touch the power of his own spirit.

As I deepened the questions, Mentor deepened the responses. In keeping with this new intensity, Mentor began a fascinating series of discussions to help me understand the dynamics of the human "heart" and the human "mind."

The Conscious Mind:
The Body's Creative Computer

✳*Can there be more than a metaphoric relationship between physical mind and nonphysical heart? In order to understand the "path of the heart," it becomes necessary to identify not only the mind's role in perception but also the heart's.*

Conscious mind is the body's creative computer. It perceives, judges and reflects all that is thought and experienced. These perceptions form an ever-changing complex of information. This network becomes the "program" within which the body functions. In its capacity as filter, the conscious mind sifts through all contradictory or seemingly inappropriate incoming data enabling each individual to function in what the conscious mind considers an appropriate fashion. Undesirable, contradictory or threatening input is effortlessly filtered out of conscious reach into the superconscious mind for storage.

"Thinking" means interpreting appropriate input in order to maintain effective functioning. The thoughts that are allowed to reach the conscious state are interpreted, simplistically speaking, within a left-brain/right-brain context. The left-brained person tends to view life in terms

*of the pragmatic, analytical, theoretical and deductive,
while the predominantly right-brained person lives in the
world of the sensory and intuitive.*

*Dominance of the left or right aspect of mind is developed not only through subtle environmental interactions
that reinforce success or failure in the use of each aspect
of mind, but also exists as a hereditary predisposition toward left or right. In determining one's own left or right
brain dominance, recall an experience. Observe during
the process of recollection which impressions are the ones
that are remembered first and with the greatest intensity.
Are the thoughts that come to mind details of the actual
event (left-brain) or the feelings about oneself or the other
participants (right-brain)? Understanding how the five-senses reality is molded by one's conscious mind better
enables that individual to identify and eliminate the unnecessary blocks which have arisen to obscure the true
picture.*

The Superconscious Mind: An Expanded Subconscious and Reservoir of Spiritual Development

*Unlike the conscious mind, the superconscious mind is
not directly called upon to make decisions. Instead, it
serves as the storehouse or resource file for all conscious
and unconscious data. All that is experienced is relegated
to the archives of the superconscious, for it exists as the
collective force of unfiltered consciousness, taking in not
only all physical and emotional but also all higher level
awareness and spiritual development. The superconscious
then is this wonderfully versatile aspect of human consciousness which can potentially integrate the more
evolved cosmic awarenesses with all other stored material.
Thus the conscious mind exists as the decision maker and
the superconscious as the data base from which information can be drawn in order to make decisions.*

Perceptions of the Heart: Mental Body, Soul and Originator of Spiritual Development

We have established a frame of reference for the conscious and superconscious minds, but what of our original question, having to do with defining perceptions of the heart? In other words, now that the conscious and superconscious are accounted for, what is the role of the heart? Let us explore for a moment the presence of heart beyond just its poetic implications. There are three counterparts to the physical heart. They are the etheric, astral and mental hearts. The words etheric, astral and mental refer to those levels or layers of bodily energy which surround the body. The etheric body is closest to the physical and is the energy body which is seen and manipulated in holistic healing techniques. It is electromagnetic in nature and visually appears to be made up of many swirling energy patterns. The astral layer is less dense than the etheric and is further removed from the physical. It is primarily reflective of the emotional state of mind. This is the area from which auras are often read, although in fact the energy from all the energy levels can be read. The third level is the least dense of all the layers and is often called the mental plane. It is from this level that the "heart" energy originates which is the human link to the Universal God.

We have been discussing the general energy layers which surround the body, but now let us look at the heart. On the physical level, the heart pumps blood, which sustains life, and is poetically referred to as the origin of love. On the etheric level, the same specific energy center of "chakra" reflects one's ability and willingness to love oneself and others, as well as to use the energy of love within one's life. On the astral level, the "heart" reflects one's emotional reaction to love, including all that one believes to be true about the concept of love. On the mental level, the "heart" becomes the individual's link to God and the higher order of understanding. The insights of the heart and the perceptions of worlds beyond exist equally for all. They are not learned, they simply are. They are within each person as a gift—full-blown awareness ready to be tapped.

All input having to do with spiritual awareness is communicated from the mental heart to the superconscious to await recognition by the conscious mind. While the superconscious contains all input and is inherently a most powerful resource, it must be unlocked by the conscious mind in order to utilize any information or perception for everyday use. In other words, unless there is conscious interest in extricating a new piece of information from the files, the pieces of understanding remain stored. The issue then becomes: what prevents the conscious mind from choosing to recognize these intense insights? What causes the frost on the windowpane?

The Mind-Heart Connection

The conscious mind, superconscious mind and mental heart comprise what I will call the "spiritual body" and forms the basis for human existence by combining all aspects of being. The energy layers of the body combine in such a way that they remain separate and at the same time unified for the benefit of the greater whole. The joining of physical to etheric to astral to mental, or function to thought to awareness, is the implication. I would like to suggest that physical and nonphysical, tangible and intangible, necessarily intertwine to produce a potentially awesome vehicle for awareness. Just as the organs and systems of the physical body cooperate to sustain life, so cooperation of the physical and nonphysical synthesize properties of heart and mind giving birth to harmony and insight.

In attempting to understand the mind, one finds the higher consciousness vibrations and thus one finds the underlying mind-heart relationship. For if all potential physical and nonphysical cooperation lies at the level of the superconscious mind, then awareness is but a matter of opening the conscious flood gates and letting attune-

ment flow in. Awarenesses from the heart in the form of answers and insights into such questions as "Why am I?" are thus present not only in the mental energy but also in the superconscious mind. Just as the speaker at a convention can choose to recognize or not recognize a question from the floor, so the conscious mind can choose to allow or not allow the valuable information it holds in its vault to be heard.

(see diagram on page 68)

Interpretation Via the Already Established Program

Despite left- or right-brain dominance, the individual sees only that which he wants to see, is programmed to see, and in fact allows himself to see. Or put another way, the individual interprets all experience in terms of his existing program. The conscious program is that network of input which the conscious mind advances as reality. The fact that the conscious program may have very little to do with the true picture, the view from beyond the physical, matters not at all. The individual accepts the program as the true assessment. Incoming data is analyzed in the conscious mind in light of this existing picture and that which is considered appropriate is integrated. All else is altered or stored in the superconscious. The mind will not validate what it deems inappropriate or destructive to its established program.

How much of a deviation is tolerated by the individual mind varies. How strictly the mind adheres to the established program depends on how threatened the mind is by change, and this in turn is a product of environmental and hereditary influences extending over the span of the individual's life, possibly many lives. Certainly there is more play within some programs than others.

Interaction of the Three Levels
of the Spiritual Body

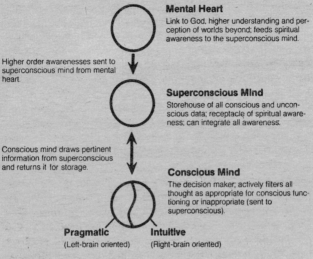

Mental Heart
Link to God, higher understanding and perception of worlds beyond; feeds spiritual awareness to the superconscious mind.

Higher order awarenesses sent to superconscious mind from mental heart.

Superconscious Mind
Storehouse of all conscious and unconscious data; receptacle of spiritual awareness; can integrate all awareness.

Conscious mind draws pertinent information from superconscious and returns it for storage.

Conscious Mind
The decision maker; actively filters all thought as appropriate for conscious functioning or inappropriate (sent to superconscious).

Pragmatic
(Left-brain oriented)

Intuitive
(Right-brain oriented)

(Note: It is possible during sleep and meditation for the conscious mind to link directly with the mental heart, bypassing the superconscious mind.)

Conscious Mind as Protector

Considerable conscious mind energy is involved in assessing incoming data, determining what stays and what gets filed. This sorting runs smoothly as long as the mind receives input at a rate compatible with its processing abilities. When a backup occurs because of an excessive input of questionable material or because the normal mind processes are unable to function at a satisfactory level due to fatigue, stress or illness, then the self-protective device known as "mental close-down" occurs. In severe cases not only is all analytical thought suspended but physical function may also be impaired. This is commonly called "mental breakdown." In such a case only the most basic of life support systems continue to operate. One eats, sleeps and walks around, but all creative thought requiring conclusion is suspended. The length of time until normalcy returns is dependent short-term upon the mind's catching up with the backlog, but is dependent long-term upon modifying the existing program.

A less severe form of mental close-down is called "clicking out," and may include symptoms of extreme lethargy, constant daydreaming, inability to sleep or need for unusual amounts of sleep, inability to concentrate, tenseness, irritability, or a sense that one is drifting out of control. Interestingly this phenomenon of "clicking out" affects most people on a daily basis. When circumstances become too overwhelming one "clicks out" and when the conscious mind catches up, adjusting accordingly, one clicks back in. If the "clicking out" is not severe, then the mind is effectively fulfilling its purpose of shielding the person from overload. If, however, the "clicking out" increases to abnormal proportions and one spends more time "out" than "in," then there is a major problem. For at this point the mind is refusing to alter the existing program to meet the obvious new level of need. Answering the question of what and how the mind will and will not accept as new pieces to the existing program is the basis upon which the study of psychiatry is built.

The individual who is involved in this evasive behavior of "clicking out" for longer periods of time will often not be aware of what is happening and the potential trouble. His consciousness refuses to recognize this "clicking out" problem, for to do so would involve looking at the causes of "clicking out," and this would in turn necessitate a change in the existing program.

Actively Reprogramming the Conscious Mind

If these "click out" conditions exist when the conscious mind is at a loss as to how to integrate new data, then one might wonder how new information is ever introduced into the existing program.

The mind is the creative part of being, but its components are nonetheless tools which are or should be directed by awareness. Through the simple ignorance of not knowing to ask or how to ask the mind for a change in programming, one allows life to be directed by the unexamined program which has been put together haphazardly over many years and may in no way reflect current circumstance or belief structure.

Here is an example of how to ask conscious mind for change: "Mind," as if you were addressing something you could see, "I am not familiar with ways to heal my body through my own energies, but I feel this is possible. I am in pain most of the day and the doctors tell me there is nothing that can be done. I do not believe this. Let those perceptions which in any way relate to the subject of my healing become one with my conscious mind, allowing a solution to be forthcoming."

The conscious mind, as a tool, works in a straightforward fashion, only responding to that which is actively sought. It is not effective to be subtle or to hint. It is not in any way presumptuous to ask for that which you need. After a question is asked, reprogramming begins immediately and within several days answers and more questions are mysteriously at one's disposal, speaking directly to the problem.

It is only necessary to address the mind, asking that appropriate material be released from the suspended state of the superconscious and allowed to become part of the conscious mind. If one asks for only general improvement, then there will be no specifics; but if specifics are sought, then specifics will be produced.

Passive or Random Reprogramming of the Conscious Mind

There is another, more gradual way for conscious level programs to be updated if one chooses not to ask but to just let life happen. This approach involves the conscious *mind's occasional acceptance of marginal data. In such a case the conscious mind, in its random cataloging, will sometimes integrate information which is borderline in acceptability. A new idea may be accepted because of a tenuous connection to something already within the existing program. Since like thoughts tend to attract each other, there then exists the possibility that a second idea related in some way to the first may eventually become attached and gradually, one block at a time, understanding is developed.*

For example, the conscious mind of a person interested and knowledgeable in geology might be allowed to integrate material on the mystical powers of crystals through the link of crystalline structure. Or because of the temperamental nature of the cataloging process, the conscious mind could just as easily reject the information on crystals on the grounds of no framework for mystical power concepts.

The decision for acceptance or rejection of borderline material is made without the individual's conscious knowledge and would thus only become accessible if the data were assimilated; otherwise, input recedes into the superconscious. That is quite a chance to take with information which could be of great value and might be intensely needed in the physical day-to-day life.

It is, of course, easy to see that the fallacy in this approach is the randomness with which data is accepted or rejected. Awareness becomes reduced to nothing more than a whimsical game with the conscious mind and based on the intrinsic odds of this game, it becomes discouragingly difficult to consider growing in creative insight. The important thing to remember is that mind is a worker for the good of the whole body, and it must be told what it is expected to do. This includes what it is expected to filter and what it is expected not to filter. Few people seeking the path to awareness will wish to waste time with the latter method of building new mental programming through the random alignment of occasional thoughts. In-

stead, most will choose to tap the mind's input in order to demonstrate tangible results.

"Mind" and "Brain"—Two Separate Entities

Mentor had not once used the term "brain" except in the expressions "right-brain" or "left-brain." I asked him to clarify "mind" and "brain" and their relationship to one another.

❋ *"Brain" and "mind" use the same head apparatus, if you need to think of a physical location for the mind, but there the similarity ends. Brain is a composite of matter controlling physiological function, adjustment and adaptation. Mind exists apart from the functional brain and is capable of arriving at independent thought and conclusion.*

Mind normally has no responsibility for regulating body programs or registering responses other than those it consciously chooses to affect. Only brain functions in this capacity. Mind is not tethered to the body; instead, it is cut free to assimilate and analyze in a totally unique manner. Brain and mind had been considered the same force until recently, when it became increasingly obvious that stimulus and response could not account for expanded awareness, and that there were indeed far-reaching and still uncharted reaches of the mind. Creative thought was not necessarily the predictable product of environment and heredity. There was more. Mind varied according to its own interpretation of self, and the factors making up the interpretation were often unknown, allowing the human species to range beyond the limits of the physical world.

The process of reviewing my teacher's explicit yet profound explanations of the mind's workings began to give validation to the many months during which I had struggled with integrating the meaning of the writings. I had convinced myself that I had to grow into the sharing of the writings, but what of their acceptance into my own inner self? Other people were often overwhelmed when they encountered Mentor, yet I had always managed to subtly keep my distance from the intensity of the writings. It was one thing to go through the motions of receiving the writings and quite another to change one's views in order to understand and then integrate their contents. It gradually became clear that until I openly asked my own conscious mind to have a framework within which these new ideas could fit, I had no conscious connection that would allow the contents of the writings to become part of my thinking. Even Mentor once admonished:

＊Agartha, you must not be in such a hurry to put the lessons away. The material is meant for your learning. If you do not carefully read and re-read the material, then our communication serves no purpose.

Once again I sat and asked my conscious mind to let me see and understand my "I am" connection so that I could begin to express more fully the truths I had only tentatively touched. I knew that any further steps toward my own understanding would also involve the use of my developing abilities in a way that reflected neither fear nor reservation. Mentor, certainly sensing the new level of my commitment, began to talk of enlightenment.

Where is Enlightenment?

Finding the pathway to understanding my own "I am" connection now became the main object of my desire. Convinced that I could actively seek answers, I asked my conscious mind to allow me to find a way of experiencing my own special connection to the Universe, my own personal experience of oneness. Mentor provided this most beautiful guidance to assist my quest:

＊You wish to know of the path of ultimate understanding, Agartha. Where is enlightenment? You now know

only of the physical—the mind and how it must be tapped to awaken. I tell you enlightenment has already found a home within your heart. You have but to loosen the confines in which it is held and allow the realization of your oneness with God to fly freely to your conscious mind. You must have eyes to see, ears to hear and mind to understand the language of the heart, for enlightenment is a total experience.

As the conscious mind is focused to receive and interpret deeply-held understandings, the channel will be cleared from the heart to the conscious mind, and the power to act in compliance with cosmic understanding will be yours.

Enlightenment, as a perception, is a clear vision of the perfectness of all things. When this vision fuses with the spiritual body, the result is a kinesthetic reaction of such proportion that there can be no doubt that a foot has been placed upon eternity's threshold.

The realization of one's own perfectness creates a problem for many, because man has learned to think of himself as imperfect, marred by immutable negatives and "sins." This most basic of tenets must be resolved before there can be any hope of inner or outer peace.

The acceptance of the perfectness of all things is the key to knowing God and "enlightened love." It is not enough to hope that one day you will be perfect; you must see yourself as perfect in relation to all things at your present juncture. You must live your own perfectness in a state of loving awareness, cognizant of this new, true realization.

The tawdry world that surrounds you is once removed from the reality of perfection. The physical world is an elusive mirage, an ever-changing play where the actors and scenery are continually and quixotically rearranged.

Simultaneous Lifetimes

I was puzzled to hear my physical world referred to as an "elusive mirage." It was certainly real to me. The mere thought that it was an illusion was threatening, and I asked Mentor for clarification:

* *You are not inalterably tied to any one character in any one play. You are in fact many characters at the same time. God's energy expresses itself through each being's simultaneous interaction with a myriad of realities, of which Earth School lifetime is only one part. Since interaction with different realities occurs simultaneously, various "plays" are always in different stages of completion. Realize that while you are preoccupied with acting in one play, you are also watching another. I realize this idea of simultaneous realities and Earth School as illusion will need further explanation later, but for now let this suffice so that we can continue with enlightenment.*

Perceiving in Perfectness

I accepted Mentor's wish to continue on the subject of enlightenment and pursued the concept of "perceiving in perfectness." How was it possible to account for hatred, war, pestilence, and greed in the world? What possible rationalization could there be for such obviously "ungodly" manifestations?

* *You ask, "How can I see all things in perfectness when there is so much pain and misery on Earth?" I will tell you that you are not seeing the "true" picture. You are interpreting the "script" of the play in relation to your limited vision. When you perceive in perfectness, only perfectness can exist for you. Each person sees his own level of perfectness, and that which he sees is what he experiences.*

What you think you see, Agartha, by your acceptance

*of imperfectness and your inappropriate judgment of each
lifetime as separate, is a reflection of your own distortion.
It is impossible to accurately assess the singular lifetime
without seeing it in relation to the whole or composite of
many simultaneously existing lifetimes.*

*For example, a baby is born to a poor third world fam-
ily. After two months of malnutrition, the child dies.
"What possible learning can there be here?" you ask.*

*A man, walking home from work one evening stops to
pick up a paper from a newsstand and is hit by a car as it
speeds around the corner. He dies in the hospital. Here
again, "Where is the learning?"*

*When spirit is withdrawn from the physical body, it is
done with little or no concern for man's parochial framework of right or wrong, just or unjust, good or evil. Spirit
responds instead to chords of a larger and far more awesome symphony, chords having to do with the total cosmic
journey upon which each higher consciousness is set. Trying to judge why a person dies is as fruitless as trying to
count the stars in the heavens from where you now stand.*

*Some mysteries are meant to remain mysteries. There
is a time to live and a time to die, each according to a
selected rhythm.*

*One of the foremost mysteries of spiritual evolution is
how each energy remains attuned to its own unique
rhythm. What memory has been infused into each soul
causing response to only that one rhythm, causing the soul
to follow implicitly that guidance for all time?*

Functional versus Observational Learning:
The Expanded Self

This was not the first time Mentor had talked about reincarnation. This time, however, he revealed a bit more about
the naturalness of the flow in and out of physical life. Despite
Mentor's telling me to accept the mystery, I was still interested in knowing what good could possibly be served by
the baby's dying of malnutrition or the man's being hit by the

car. This was the kind of Earth School pain which made no sense to me. Was there a point of reconciliation, a reason why? Mentor responded:

The issue of the death of the child and the man is not why or when they died but, instead, in what way did learning exist, as in fact it did, from beyond their physical bodies.

The physical body exists for but a moment of eternity and is the outward personification of an inward vision. This inward vision is the continuing energy (higher consciousness) which is formed and molded as it travels its course of spiritual evolution. It is much like a volcanic rock which is wrenched from the depths of a familiar cavity and thrust into an unfamiliar and seemingly chaotic atmosphere, where it is driven this way and that until at last its metamorphosis is complete. It drops to earth, nestling among its new companions until another act of nature disrupts its resting place.

The point is that the familiar is rarely the permanent, and the permanent is never completely within the grasp. That learnings exist on every level, physical and nonphysical, is a given fact. That many of your plane are unaware of learning beyond the physical body is also a given fact.

There are two basic ways of learning from an Earth School environment: one, functioning (living physical reality); and two, observing (viewing physical reality from the improved vantage point of nonphysical life). Both functional and observational learning complete the incarnation cycle and prepare one to again merge with the "expanded self."

The concept of "expanded self" is not as complicated as it is unfamiliar. The expanded self exists in the "ether." There is no visible body. There is only spirit. You cannot touch expanded self any more than you can touch higher consciousness. When there ceases to be a physical body (functional learning) or a nonphysical presence (observational learning), then the higher consciousness reunites with the other portions of its collective self. This compos-

ite body of higher consciousness energy I will call "expanded self."

Since many realities are being lived simultaneously, each portion of higher energy is temporarily loaned to a physical form and then returned when that physical body ceases to exist. This process is similar to that of a lending library. When the allotted time is up, the book is returned, inspected, stamped, rebound if necessary and made available to another interested customer. While it may be difficult to think of your expanded self as a mobile checking unit, nonetheless that is in effect how it functions.

Mentor had woven so much into his comments that I needed time to study his explanations of "expanded self" before asking anything further. I hoped he would come back to the subject of multiple lives when I was more prepared. Probably sensing my desire to return to his examples, he immediately shifted back to his teachings on the deaths of the child and the man.

✳ *Now on with functional and observational learning. Many factors influence spiritual growth or learning. I have chosen the two major vehicles with which I feel you should be concerned at this time: functional and observational learning. Both vehicles are important to each "learning cycle."*

Learning through functioning, as has been stated, means operating or living the physical experience. This is how you are learning now, Agartha. Such learnings are the result of physical encounters. Learning through observation means regarding intuitively that former physical reality from beyond the level of physical limitation.

In the case of the child who died, obviously the learning for that physical existence had been almost entirely in the form of observation, for the child had had very little physical contact with Earth School. However, after leaving the body, a high volume of input began through observation of the former physical life on Earth. The child's consciousness was still privy to sensations of the former phys-

ical reality, including feelings for family, relatives and friends with whom she had shared relationships.

The child still possessed all memory of her recent past and could, for the duration of that learning cycle, continue to draw in sensations from Earth School, but there was a diminishing desire to do so. The natural evolutionary process inherent in the rhythm to which the child had responded when she left her physical body released her from what had been, in preparation for what would be. The spiritual body merely followed its natural inclination in wanting to know of only those substantive questions which would add the final strokes of perspective to the experience. How had the family dealt with death? Had that changed their vision of life, and if so, how?

The transition from physical to spiritual body had been a time of completion not only for the child but also for those who remained in the physical. After the time of completion came the time of awakening. In this case, the child's higher consciousness had been that of a fully developed being, resulting from many trips through many physical planes. It chose to be born into that life of poverty and disease. In fact, both the child and her parents had chosen as equals to share that relationship for their mutual development and benefit. There can exist no pity for the child's death except through personal physical loss, for the child's growth was and continued to be true to course. Death was the catalyst which temporarily freed the spiritual body from the physical, releasing higher consciousness to move on in full cognizance toward the Light.

Let us now have a brief look at the other case where there was "accidental" death. Consider that this individual had lived half of his life in the functional mode, and hopefully had learned from his life. After leaving his body, his higher consciousness continued to observe his family and their situation until all relevant learning had been gleaned. His cycle was not complete in his thinking until the death of his wife and eventually his children. At this point he released the total incarnation.

In considering death and functional and observational

*learning, it is important to recognize that man's peace of
mind lies in his acceptance of life (or growth) after death.
If no waste or stagnation of energy exists within the Universe, then it follows that there can be no waste or stagnation of individual energies, for these are the building
blocks of the Universe!*

I had no idea what a tidal wave of information I had invited
with my basic question, "Where is enlightenment?" I felt
overwhelmed with the influx of new material: "perceiving
in perfectness," "the physical world as a mirage," "life and
death according to selected rhythms," "functional and observational learning" and "expanded self." Even though I
had asked for the information to be released to my consciousness, the answers far exceeded what I had anticipated.

And yet, beneath my feelings of mental overload, the
interrelatedness of each of these incredible concepts was visible. It never occurred to me that Mentor was telling anything
but the truth. His teachings were always simple, but deeply
satisfying on an inner level. With no basis for doubting him,
I accepted his words once again because of their resonance,
their feeling "right."

For now, it was enough to ponder these words and let their
meaning filter into my being. These teachings were quite
sufficient for my overstretched perceptual system at the moment. In fact, it was not until a week later that I felt I had
assimilated enough of the previous lesson to return to Mentor. It was, however, with a deeper sense of resolve that I
came to Mentor seeking specific advice on ways to advance
my personal ability to find attunement. Acknowledging that
a great gap existed between my comprehension of life and
that of my teacher, I asked Mentor for specific steps I could
follow toward experiencing my own cosmic connection.

*✳Agartha, we have spoken of perfectness and of self-
realization through understanding life as a "play." The
player of life has but one view which—without enlightenment—limits him to that one play until he dies and again
sees the whole. With enlightenment, the player can see*

himself as linked to many realities and know himself as the perfect total energy that he is.

You are now aware of expanded self and how one can experience learning with or without a physical body, and we have discussed *"love as the substance that ties all together."* Within this magical mosaic process, where individual thoughts are cemented together with the essence of love, exists the sparkling clarity and beauty of enlightenment.

Strangely, once obtained, enlightenment seems very natural, not at all a difficult struggle for, of course, it is man's natural birthright to be one with the Creator of all things and to share his peace of understanding. Given that enlightenment is a desired state of being, how then can it be achieved?

There is a story of a young man who met an enlightened stranger. He went every day to hear this teacher and the more he heard of the stranger's words, the more he was convinced that this was the way to ultimate happiness. One day when he could bear it no longer, he approached the enlightened one asking to be shown the path of spiritual awareness. He was given three instructions on a piece of paper which he was told, if followed, would produce enlightenment. With great joy he unfolded the paper and read:

> Love all that you see.
> Live all that you feel.
> Know all that you possess.

To know all that you possess you need to still the internal conscious dialogue and listen to the heart. This practice is called meditation. It involves bypassing the conscious mind in order to experience the reality of the God/Universe connection which is known to your (mental) heart, the seat of higher consciousness.

I will suggest some specific meditations which will help you learn to be successful when you meditate. Most people have trouble meditating, because their "minds will not be quiet." The conscious mind is not usually trained to perceive in sequence or in focused thought patterns. The norm is for thoughts to be allowed to drift aimlessly in and out and around the mind, preventing concentration on a single theme. The solution is to occupy the mind first with an abundance of motion and color, and then to abruptly shut off the input and enjoy the moments of intense concentration which follow. It is in effect tricking the conscious mind, for when mind experiences activity and then an abrupt shift to stillness, it continues to be fed by the previous motion and stays in this mesmerized posture for some time.

Taking a series of deep breaths before meditation can also accomplish the same thing, except that you must be certain there is no time lag between the last breath and the beginning of meditation. To be the most effective, the motion must immediately precede the meditation.

You must realize enlightenment may not happen in one sitting. Meditation is a means of quieting the mind so that the heart's perceptions can find room to become expanded and to develop strength. There is no need to have expectation levels for oneself in meditation. The only expectation should be that it be an enjoyable experience, enjoyable in that it enhances one's state of attunement with all that is.

You should not follow any course of instruction which is not enjoyable. It should cause you to feel better, stronger and more complete than when you begin. Each person will find a different type of meditation to be most effective. Each will experience meditation in different forms. Each will find meaningful meditation for different lengths of time. This is all acceptable.

I am going to give you some exercises, Agartha, which if practiced daily will bring forth calming results and will help you coordinate the differing elements in your life:

✳

MEDITATION EXERCISE NO. 1

Sit with your back straight, and your legs folded or crossed in a comfortable position. Close your eyes and focus your attention on the center of the inside of your *forehead. You will notice after trying this that there are several colors which want to be there and which seem to be one with the fibers of your skull and brain. These colors are significant, representing the colors with which you momentarily have the closest affinity and which will be helpful to you in meditation as well as in the healing exercises which we will talk about later.*

Study the colors which present themselves and allow them to exist with you, moving in harmony around the inside of your skull in a circular motion, trying to keep the movement in a consistent flowing pattern. Do this for several minutes and then cause the motion to abruptly stop and let there be no motion, only stillness, on the inside of your skull. When you are no longer able to hold concentration, repeat the exercise, interspersing a few moments of motion with a few moments of stillness, ending with a period of stillness.

✳

MEDITATION EXERCISE NO. 2

Sit in a chair and focus on the ground in front of you. It does not matter whether you are inside or outside. Close your eyes and see the center of the inside of your forehead, seeing the colors which want to be there. Allow the colors to circulate around the inside of the skull. Then cause the motion to abruptly stop. Open your eyes so that you are gently squinting. Focus on a spot a comfortable distance in front of you. Stare, but do not look directly at the spot. Gaze at this spot until you begin to contemplate what is under it.

You may begin to feel yourself being drawn into this space. Follow it. Feel the sense of completeness with the hard surface of the floor or ground. Concentrate on the sense of oneness with the floor and whatever layers you find under the floor. These layers will not necessarily be actual layers and do not need to actually correspond to what would be under the floor. Let your mind sense what is there and feel the motion of becoming one with the floor and the layers under the floor. Going down into the earth, experience your connectedness with the earth and its very core.

After you finish this exercise, let your mind rest by closing your eyes and being still. Focus again on the inside of your forehead. Always end your meditations with this central point of focus and complete stillness within your conscious mind. This part of meditation, this stillness, is where the awareness begins, allowing you to pull into your being the peace of the Universe.

✳

MEDITATION EXERCISE NO. 3

Sit on a cushion on the floor in a reasonably comfortable posture. Close your eyes and look toward the sky. Sit as straight as you can while still raising your chin slightly so that your face is tilted upward. Feel the warmth of sunshine on your face. It does not matter whether you are inside or out. The sunshine is for you to create. Now feel the raindrops splashing down over your face and running down your chin. Relax your facial muscles and let your body drift off into the universe, experiencing no pull toward the ground or toward any solid object.

End this exercise by feeling or hearing a steady sound of energy, water if you prefer, slowly encircling your whole body, filling it with peace and joy. You can use color or sound here, whichever you prefer. When you finish this exercise you will have totally surrounded your body with loving sound or color and will feel totally at peace. Again, end with focusing on the inside of the forehead.

As I mentioned earlier, it does not matter how long you meditate, it is the quality of the time spent. You must try to put other matters out of your mind and spend quality time in this quiet place. This place is reality, Agartha; it is your expanded self. This is your place of the "future," this is why it is so important to come to know this spot of ultimate beauty for it is to be your home.

"Home!" Closing my eyes I let my mind create images of the dark blue heavens, of other sparkling realities, and of my expanded self, of God. While I realized we would all have an opportunity to know that home, I wondered what it would feel like to be in the expanded self with no body.

I began pondering once again the reasons for my feelings of aloneness. What caused the isolation that seemed so much a part of our lives in Earth School? Could it be fear of change, fear of standing still, fear of failure, fear of success, fear of knowing, fear of not knowing, fear of death, fear of life—and all of it due to misperceptions of the true nature of life and love? I looked for a way to understand the purpose of existence as it appeared to my limited view. I was still puzzled by Mentor's own question: "What causes the (man's) frost on the windowpane?" The only resolution I could see was to try the meditations he gave me. Meditation, after all, had led me to Mentor, and now Mentor was saying that meditation was the path to enlightenment. If meditation could produce the miracle of Mentor, then it was equally likely that it was my pathway "home." The meditations were useful to quiet my mind and put me back in touch with my deeper consciousness and with the issues that were "real." I found it easy to drift off into the meditations I had been given to practice and I often shared them with others. Frequently, people asked for shorter meditations to help them feel connected when there was no time for lengthy meditations. Mentor, as usual, accommodated with new meditations requiring less time and concentration:

✳ *I have suggested meditation practices in which you will succeed when you are prepared for an extended period of quiet. This is another approach which can be used throughout the day whether you are in a busy office, a quiet studio, chasing small children, or planning your dinner. It is known as momentary meditation. Momentary meditation provides a regeneration of creative flow. It allows you to reach deeper than your own energy to touch your higher-self connection. Increased effectiveness and efficiency on the physical level, as well as emotionally refocusing, are the result. Momentary meditation can be*

*used as often as you need it, and because it only takes
several moments, it can fit into any schedule.*

*When you are ready to try momentary meditation, stop
whatever you are doing and close your eyes, or if this is
not possible, gaze at a solid object. Say to yourself, as you
visualize energy flowing through your body from head to
feet, flowing out through your feet:*

> *There is purpose to my existence,
> I live, I love,
> I work, I die,
> I am refreshed and begin my life anew.*

*In meditation into sleep you are striving to see and feel
a sense of tranquility and to realize, on a conscious level,
that your body and mind are under control and are functioning according to their intended purpose. As you are
falling asleep, see the calmness of your favorite scene: the
ocean, the mountains, whatever immediately presents itself as a place of rejuvenation and peace. Experience the
scene, either by remembering how it felt the last time you
were in such a place (running your fingers through the
sand or crunching through the snow) or by imagining how
it would feel if you were there. See yourself as calm, tranquil and fulfilled. All worry has fallen from you and you
are totally unencumbered. Feel the confidence of being
peaceful and knowing that your life is under control and
functioning according to plan. This image is important to
present to the conscious mind even if you do not really
feel that your life is under control.*

*This type of meditation is different from the lengthy med-
itation and the momentary meditation, for these two types
of meditation strive to put you in touch with the higher self
and the Universal Connection. Meditating into sleep puts
you in touch with your own bodily energies, and allows you
to control these energies which you normally do not.*

*Your body is filled with energy which can become locked
in various parts of your body through the experiences of
the day. When you go to sleep in a state of consternation*

*and confusion, the energy is not allowed to move to those
areas which require regeneration, which means that you
awaken to the same physical and mental problems that
you closed out the night before when you went to sleep.
Take advantage of this most significant of rest periods by
allowing your naturally abundant energies to regenerate
and refocus your being.*

As I worked with Mentor's meditations, I had journeys of
intense awareness and others of seemingly minimal advancement. I have stopped trying to categorize each meditation in
terms of actual progress, feeling that it is pleasure enough to
take quality time within each day to free one's thoughts from
Earth School preoccupations by adding a level of gentleness
to one's life. A quiet period of non-expectation rounds out
the rough edges, leaving one with a renewed calm and sense
of purpose. Perhaps this is my progress toward enlightenment, this ability to see my life in its ultimate perfection as
one link to a magnificent whole.

Enlightenment is its own paradox. Focusing on the process makes one spiritually self-conscious, wondering if each
action contributes to or detracts from one's own evolvement.
And yet, by its very design, enlightenment transcends the
thinking process and simply becomes the total life-force experience. No thinking is required; one moves beyond the
analysis of one's actions and becomes one with all that is.
Thus is the truth revealed in the Zen koan:

*Before enlightenment I chopped wood and carried water.
After enlightenment I chopped wood and carried water.*

In helping me summarize this chapter, Mentor confirmed
for me the enigmatic nature of enlightenment as a process as
well as a conclusion:

✷ *Do you have a better sense, Agartha, of where the path
lies for enlightenment and how to reach it? You have seen
how your mind, with all its delicate balances, responds to
your wishes. You have learned how to ask for what you*

want, to release the locked-in answers which are yours by right.

Your path of existence weaves on and on, through the conscious mind, superconscious mind and heart of this physical and nonphysical reality, through the psychic "you" existing now in other realities, and through the expanded self which is your accumulation of personal higher consciousness energy beyond the body.

Just as enlightenment has been the continuing focus of this chapter, it should also be the continuing focus of your life. It is the way of all cosmic progress and it will happen to each who searches. It is as much a process as a conclusion. It is a seeking and a finding, a search and a resolution—a beginning and then a new beginning.

Your path toward enlightenment will be influenced by daily choices. The way you handle each day is the way you will handle your cumulative life. Be dynamic with your life, with your choices. Dare to dare. We have talked of different meditation practices as useful ways to let the body be aware of each moment of each day, asking for and receiving the maximum awareness for health, happiness and attunement. Use these meditations to bring these things into your life. Dare to dare, Agartha!

There is a saying about enlightenment . . . that it is the product of:

> *One part physical study of awareness*
> *One part mental application of Truth*
> *One part Cosmic Kiss*

The joyfulness with which one can pursue life and life hereafter should never be overlooked. Pursue your goals, yes, but pursue them with love in your heart and a smile on your lips. As your living presence continues to grow and awaken, traveling ever faster down the path of your own destiny toward enlightenment, be aware of the Cosmic Kiss.

CHAPTER FOUR

CREATING YOUR OWN REALITY

Listen closely and you can hear:
  The tick of the clock
  as it prepares to strike the hour,
  The silent rustle of the owl
  as it wakes to the rising moon,
  The tireless motion of the wind
  as it hushes the sleeping trees.
Your future is of your creation—
          Create wisely!

                                        MENTOR

AN UNDENIABLE RHYTHM and tension is alive in the Universe, a type of constant pulsating energy which is, perhaps, the force behind the movement of all the cycles of life. The completion of our home marked the ending of a major cycle of change within the rhythm of our lives. Except for the furnishings in our home, nothing even remotely resembled our previous life-style. Within eighteen months, we had totally recast our reality. In keeping with the natural dynamics of the change cycle, the pendulum had swung from a time of active, external energy to a period of passive, internal learning.

I began thinking about what the next stage of my life would entail. I already recognized that a new cycle had begun, but I had no idea where it would lead. It did not take long for Mentor to fill these peaceful days with a recommendation for my next assignment: it was time to begin the writing of a book.

Regardless of the fact that I already had experienced what was considered by others to be impossible, the idea of writing a book struck me as more improbable than communication with nonphysical teachers. I was not a writer. In fact, I rarely took the time to read. My personal form of expression was that of an artist and a potter. I created with my hands. This new task seemed well beyond my own capabilities. I protested and Mentor responded:

Agartha, I am not asking you to do this alone, I am merely suggesting that you put into appropriate form the lessons I have given you and the ones we will work on from here. If you were not able to compile this book to be called AGARTHA, I would not have suggested the project. Release your anxieties; the book will be accomplished and it will become a powerful tool of divine guidance for those who read it. I will also tell you that there will be a great number who will read your words and mine.

I trusted that what Mentor had told me would happen and that somehow I would write and compile a book. The thought, nevertheless, was overwhelming. It was true I had grown into the experience of Mentor and had lost my fear of interaction, now finding myself involved with others on increasingly intense levels of spirituality. Perhaps this new opportunity was a way of shattering another old myth of my own personal limitation. In that case, it too would have to go. We began the book. Mentor gave me the chapter outline as it now appears in the table of contents and he helped me begin to organize the writings into a readable form.

Separating Illusion from Reality

As my own horizons continued to broaden under Mentor's teachings, my perceptions of reality changed dramatically. I was increasingly aware of this need to sift out the "real" from the "unreal." Although I had been content to let the "reality gap" exist between Mentor's world and mine for almost a year, I felt ready to more clearly define what, in fact, existed as real.

In seeking to gain a personal understanding of reality, I asked Mentor's guidance on behalf of people with "real world" problems. People came to me searching for answers to better health, fuller lives, more satisfying partnerships and development of their own spirituality. Many people sought to live more constructive and harmonious lives, and I realized that my own questions about "real" and "unreal" could best be answered by exploring the needs of those with whom I could be most objective. As was always the case, the more I sought awareness to change the personal reality of others, the more I learned about the meaning of life in Earth School.

✳ *If the difference between "personal reality" and "personal illusion" were obvious or easily found, there would be no Earth School. For the Earth School experience that each is now living is the illusion known as "life," the all-encompassing preoccupation with physical existence which steals one's waking hours and leaves behind a blindness to the more subtle reality of understandings which transcend physical death. Earth School is the living medium within which man struggles to understand and evaluate his motives and actions in light of more subtle awarenesses.*

Illusion and reality are deceptively general terms, for they have specific applicability to the individual. Illusion is that which appears to be true or real, but which, in fact, is a sham, a pretense of the real. Reality on the other hand connotes the authentic, the genuine foundation of unlimited understanding. Personal illusion is, therefore, any part of the human experience or belief system which negates a spiritual/universal core and interaction with life. Personal reality is any phase of understanding which shows man's physical presence to be a mirage, a momentary consciousness soon to be altered in light of a far more expansive form of life.

There can be a starkness to finding personal reality, for

reality is Truth. It is the facts about who one is and what one's life is about. The quest in search of reality calls to each to seek beyond the immediate, the illusion, to find the irrefutable, the non-negotiable reality of who one really is. This search for personal reality begins on one level, usually hinging on one suddenly unsupportable life myth or belief system. When this is shattered, it begins a chain reaction shattering one illusion after another until false myths and barriers are destroyed, and one stands whole and complete—but alone.

This can be a most painful experience to truly see oneself, one's environment and one's belief systems in the pure white light of "what is." The human conscious mind does not easily accept drastic changes in programming, but, as I have shown you, it is possible to influence the "program control center" of the mind in order to find the reality in all things.

As one searches, one discovers, and in searching one becomes privy to the secrets which lay hidden for so many. This book can be a vehicle through which one's search may be encouraged, for with each new understanding comes new and more all-encompassing questions and then answers, creating a small oasis of confirmation. It is a pulling together of what one discovers to be real into a cohesive unit of self-understanding. While this search may take a long time, lifetimes in fact, there is every reason to begin this inward journey immediately, for the essence of life, the path of value and substance, lies in the search and realization of individual and cosmic reality.

The place to begin discovering personal reality is within the confines of your own nature. The truth which you find revealed in your own life should be the guide in dealing with areas of illusion. Take a long, hard look at your personal reality. Many years may be spent trying to separate what you want to see about yourself from what you are afraid to see or are simply uneducated as to how to see.

The process of looking inward is valuable in learning to see the seemingly impenetrable depths of your own being and in providing you with a fixed center, a place of tri-angulation upon that which exists beyond the conscious mind's fickle interpretation.

Consider this thought, Agartha: light which shines from without reflects only the human illusion, while light which shines from within radiates the Infinite Reality.

People are all masters of skillfully covering up who they really are and what their true connections are. It is a difficult struggle to reach inside and find the "real you." Of course, that truly beautiful essence that exists as one's pure spark of creation resists being hoisted from tranquil oblivion of the inner self into the arena of painful combat in the conscious mind. But once one has sensed personal reality and one's interrelatedness to the Universal God, then true knowledge and illusion go separate ways, for when one has gained personal awareness nothing else has force to prevail. Identification of one's true self is the beginning of the search for reality in all things.

This was not the first time Mentor had referred to physical life as "unreal"; however, this time he qualified "real" as that which does not change. By that definition, all physical matter is "unreal" by reason of its constantly changing molecular structure. What challenged me was trying to understand what part of me was "real" and how I could reconcile my real with my unreal dimensions.

The intellectual notion of an unseen "me" being the bona fide "me" made sense, since I knew it was not the physical one who was in contact with Mentor. I asked Mentor to clarify the notion of the "spiritual/universal core" of life:

Who You Are: The Spiritual Matrix

٭ The stripping away of illusion and the struggle to find personal reality can be likened to the peeling of an apple. As one peels away the layers of unreality, much as one peels an apple, eventually only the core remains, the physical matrix of the apple, the growing program within which

all is held. How different the bright red polished apple looks from the small brown seed, and yet they are interchangeable, the one merely representing the expanded realization of the other.

But unlike an apple, the human does not automatically grow into his ultimate form. Instead he must search for the inner core or spiritual matrix in order to then define and create his appropriate exterior reality. He must try to go beyond physical reality to find and appreciate his own universally created growing pattern and the connection to all life. The individual possesses the freedom with which to pursue the question: "Who Am I . . . Who Really Am I?" This search takes people not only forward to automatic realization of destiny in physical form but also inward from physical manifestation to the eternal core of all life in pursuit of the spiritual matrix.

The spiritual matrix has other names. It is also called the "soul" or "mental heart." The spiritual matrix exists as the "real you," the "eternal you," for it is at the same time a separate unit and also a connecting link to the God force. The spiritual matrix is one's fully developed spiritual growth pattern and potential. In other words, the complete set of instructions for one's spiritual development is present at birth.

One need only recognize this life-sustaining center, this spiritual matrix, as the basis upon which successful physical life is built. For with attunement to the spiritual matrix comes awareness of how to create physical objects and events on Earth, such as health and happiness, houses and money, without losing sight of spiritually-evolved values. Finding the ways in which one's own program seems meant to develop, improving and refining the Earth School experience, is the way one finds contentment. Growing in harmony with one's spiritual matrix brings all other purely physical manifestations of life into harmony. True personal harmony and happiness cannot be achieved through realization of just the physical matrix. The spiritual matrix must likewise be sought and known. Then the physical and the spiritual rightfully proceed as partners in expanding an otherwise limited living experience.

Many questions crowded into my mind in response to Mentor's explanations. Had mankind ever known a time of closer conscious alignment with his soul? What about early human history? Was spiritual awareness something people once had and then lost? If we were meant to achieve an understanding of the spiritual matrix, then why were we not all conscious of such knowledge?

It was perplexing to listen to Mentor talk about this spiritual matrix. I asked him if consciousness was evolving in man or simply a fact.

Evolutionary Identification with the Spiritual Matrix

＊*Awareness of and involvement with the spiritual matrix has swung from a state of total interaction in human life around 10,000 B.C. to a state of practically nonexistent interaction in the twentieth century. The pendulum is again swinging, this time back toward new self-integration of the spiritual and the physical.*

Early man lived his nomadic life in tune with the "voice" that was heard from his spiritual matrix. His physically thinking brain and spiritually intuitive mind functioned as one unit. There was not the current rigid delineation between divine awareness and physical life. He was indeed superstitious and limited in his conceptual understanding of the world around him, but the analytical thoughts he did have were linked to his total life. When he went hunting, he automatically combined the learned fundamentals of hunting with the broader understanding of life as a flow, an ongoing and ever-changing experience. There was nothing to hide behind or separate him from the life around him. He knew he might become food for the animal he hunted as easily as the animal might become his food. Life existed as an uncomplicated integration of attunement and action.

As man developed on the earth, he strove quite naturally to explain the phenomena he saw. He drew away from his intuitive God-connection and tended to see himself as sole creator of his own reality. This trend culminated with post-Industrial Revolutionary man who was completely caught up in the value of his own scientific contributions. His infatuation with his own ability excluded belief in a more subtle yet all-encompassing force. He believed in that with which he could tangibly interact, and within his new role as inventor he saw himself alone as pivotal to the progress of civilization.

This progression from the totally intuitive human to the totally pragmatic human has been the natural development of the human species, but now it is time for integration of the two worlds. Physical and spiritual matrices are not mutually exclusive. They are each meant to complement the other, bringing man to a place of greater accomplishment and creativity, the threshold of a new time, a new era of enlightenment and calm. Today, the spiritual matrix holds to this much broader vision. It must integrate the physical body and mind with the invisible realm of the eternal, giving purpose and significance to the purely physical accomplishments of mankind while at the same time maintaining the unalterable course toward spiritual enlightenment.

Man is indeed the creator of his own reality, but not as a separate force. There is too much he cannot understand until he flows with the universal energy of God, dispelling his own illusion of sole importance in the universe and accepting the reality of valid and essential attachment to all life through the spiritual matrix.

Man is not rooted to simple completion of a preordained growth cycle; instead, he is free to creatively blend the physical and the spiritual matrices, allowing the body and mind freedom to fulfill their patterns. This is the search for "Who I Am."

Science in the late twentieth century is bringing man back to the intuitive, back to reality. For with every mystery which is explainable, there are four which are not.

Individuals now feel closer to the vastness, the majesty of the unexplainable. They are less threatened by its obliqueness. The awesomeness of the unsolved riddles is helping the human race to suspend the illusion of sole importance and to recognize the reality of the need for the combined matrices. Resurrection of the buried spiritual matrix has been rightfully identified as perhaps the only true way the individual and collective world have of becoming whole.

From Mentor's explanation, it appeared that evolving mankind would eventually emerge as a harmonious blend of the physical and spiritual. I wondered about the possibility of a Divine Plan. Where was evolution leading us?

Inclinations of the Soul: Man's Inner Core

❋ Plants produce their rightful fruit, and animals perform within their expected roles. But what of man? What of his need to go beyond physical fulfillment? We have discussed the spiritual matrix, what it is and has been, but what of searching for it? Does there exist a natural programmed desire to urge man to find the truth of his spiritual origins and destiny, to find his spiritual matrix? Does there exist an undeniable urge to help each shed his layers of illusion in order to meet and accept his personal core of reality? Most certainly there does!

While each is free to pursue his "heart's desire," that most ancient of searches for inner awareness and realization of true reality, nevertheless there is a drive subtly and yet relentlessly pushing the human species forward to fulfillment of the purpose of awakening. But, you ask, if each is free to realize this urge, what then prevents the individual from pursuing awareness, shattering his own illusions, opening his eyes? Is it simple confusion about how to begin the search? Is the search too overwhelming? Or is the urge to search too subtle to be consciously recognized?

The major problem is indeed confusion over which

world, the inner or the outer, is reality and therefore which needs to be given serious attention. The path to the heart can be overwhelming because there are not enough true teachers available in physical form to be a source of easy access when one needs to find encouragement. And, of course, the need to search is at first very subtle, and until given impetus, can be and usually is overridden by more seemingly pressing physical matters.

This need to discover personal reality is more than whimsy or myth; it is a living hunger which exists within the very core of humanity as an unsolved riddle, an incomplete poem. To understand the whole poem one must first identify the poem's framework within the heart and then subsequently study the individual verses. A copy of the poem also exists within the superconscious mind, as we have said, yet these sources of potential teaching become the issue.

The simplest and most obvious beginning is at the point where one accepts the perfect oneness of all elements of the universe. This causes the human to lose his sense of isolation and, therefore, his need to see himself as solely dependent on his physical actions to survive. This becomes immediately obvious when one falls asleep; for as the dominance of the Earth School experience recedes and one loses consciousness, the many aspects of the spiritual matrix become clearer.

I thought of all the existing confusion of people wanting and needing to "find themselves." It was clear that Mentor was stating that the quest for one's inner core or spiritual matrix was the most precious discovery a person could make, the "pearl of great price." How then, if one spent most of one's life pursuing happiness in the physical world, could this goal be attained? Mentor's suggestion that the aspects of the spiritual matrix are clearer in sleep suddenly seemed to hold promise for seeking a direct contact with one's center. It seemed appropriate to ask Mentor about what really happened during sleep. Was there a way to reach one's essential self through sleep?

The Spiritual Matrix and Unconscious Confusion in the Dream State

*Two things happen when one falls asleep. First, the workings of the conscious mind slow to a maintenance level; and second, the channels to the superconscious mind and spiritual matrix become more accessible. As one drifts into the sleep state, there is an undeniable pull toward peaceful rejuvenation with the ultimate awareness of the spiritual matrix.

Before reaching the spiritual matrix, however, one encounters three periods of unconscious confusion, which are short periods of freewheeling interaction with the undirected superconscious. Between the time of falling asleep and the first completed hour of sleep, the first period of unconscious confusion is encountered. The second and third periods follow two to two and a half hours into the sleep pattern but still within the first third of the eight-hour sleep cycle. There is a fourth period of unconscious confusion which occurs within the final third of the sleep pattern and which is the dream experience that is usually remembered on waking.

These periods are times of seemingly strange, nonsensical, violent and often weird interaction where things do not make sense. They are often fearfully irrational and generally unpredictable. One feels like a leaf in the path of some unfathomable force. These strange happenings are actually combinations of fragmented and unresolved issues arising from the undirected superconscious as well as feedback from physical Earth School life.

In understanding these erratic periods and learning how to deal with them, it is important to realize that the superconscious contains all the experience and related thought-data which makes up one's Earth School memory bank as well as input from the spiritual matrix. Each person experiences a much wider range of perception and sensation than is consciously acted upon but which nonetheless exists within the superconscious storehouse. We will be discussing this later in talking about free choice.

It is important to know, however, that not all emotions held in the superconscious are of a pleasant and positive nature. There are also those unrealized dark aspects of emotion which are normally programmed out of conscious awareness. It is only in the dream state that one inadvertently interacts with these emotions while wandering aimlessly through the superconscious during periods of unconscious confusion. It is equally possible that one or more of the four periods of unconscious confusion can be peaceful and serene rather than traumatic. This is because the spiritual matrix influences the superconscious.

The usual determination of what the experience will be depends largely on what one has on one's mind when going to sleep. This includes one's experiences of the day and the feelings that these experiences elicit. The state of one's pre-sleep awareness is practically a drawing card to what will be forthcoming from the superconscious—peaceful input from the spiritual matrix or bizarre adventures from the unknown reaches of the superconscious.

Once the period of unconscious confusion has been passed and a deep, sound level of sleep has been reached, the pull to the spiritual matrix becomes recognized and one drifts in a state of heightened attunement in the spiritual matrix for the longest period of the night's sleep, approximately four hours. One's being is psychically (meaning soulfully) rejuvenated. Sleep does much more than rest the body. Yes, it physically rests the body, but it also restores the whole presence to a state of optimum balance. The sleeping union with the spiritual matrix is meant as a time of cleansing for the mind and reinforcement of the personal reality of life beyond the five-senses reality.

If traveling swiftly to the spiritual matrix while spending as little time as possible in the undefined regions of the superconscious is the goal, then it is important to hold this wish in the waking mind as one is falling asleep. If one's dream expectations have been set up before falling asleep, then the chances are that there will be limited exposure to periods of unconscious confusion, and one

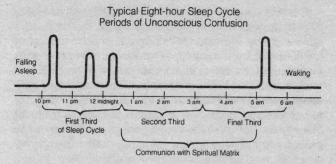

Typical Eight-hour Sleep Cycle
Periods of Unconscious Confusion

Falling Asleep

Waking

10 pm 11 pm 12 midnight 1 am 2 am 3 am 4 am 5 am 6 am

First Third of Sleep Cycle | Second Third | Final Third

Communion with Spiritual Matrix

will proceed more rapidly toward the beneficial experience of the spiritual matrix.

The superconscious is a valuable resource for positive action but can cause considerable anguish when allowed to freely and randomly associate without the support of a conscious directive or probe. There are times when random associations are beneficial and even necessary in identifying repressed emotions. When unresolved and repressed emotions need to be explored, they present themselves in various guises at the periods of unconscious confusion. If one repeatedly has trouble moving beyond an unpleasant dream experience, then one can ask for a suggestion or explanation from one's higher self before going to sleep and insight will be forthcoming.

The longest uninterrupted period of sleep in an eight-hour sleep cycle is the four hours of sleep between the third and fourth periods of unconscious confusion. This is also the most significant period of attunement with the spiritual matrix. This contact with the spiritual matrix is filled with the joyous adventures of the "I am" connection to God and all creation, and each new alignment with the spiritual matrix reaffirms the unlimited nature of man's God-connection.

I was surprised at Mentor's elaborate description of the dream state, feeling as if he had been waiting for me to pose the question about sleep. I was fascinated by his de-

scription of the periods of unconscious confusion and one's
adventures with the spiritual matrix during the sleep state.
His suggestion of programming desired dream work before
going to sleep was particularly appealing. I began to work
on setting up a positive dream plan before closing my eyes
at night, and I tried to become aware of those mornings when
I awoke rested and those when I was less successful at avoid-
ing unconscious confusion. It seemed that when I made the
effort to suggest what I wanted before going to sleep, I had
success with my dream programming. Reflecting on how
refreshed I would feel after a short period of sleep, I asked
Mentor about the value of shorter sleep cycles or even daydreaming.

Intuitive Rejuvenation

✳*I have worked with many souls entering and exiting
physical realities, both in sleep and in death. One particular person's case can serve as representative of an individual seeking intuitive rejuvenation through sleep. This
person had been working with me through many reincar-
nations. Recently born into an earth incarnation, this very
young child was still able to recall our relationship while
in a sleeping state. When she wanted to find me, she went
to sleep, which put her in contact with realities existing
beyond her waking awareness. Small children do not have
the difficulties of adults in recognizing their spiritual matrices, for they are still strongly held by the ties of the
universal connection from which they have just come.
The child's parents began taking her to one medical
specialist after another to discover what was wrong with
their child who wanted to sleep so much of the time. Eventually they devised ways of luring her away from these
inward trips, and she became a very angry, difficult little
girl. Unwittingly, she had been deprived of additional periods of alignment and attunement with the spiritual matrix and thus with her nonphysical teaching. Her systems
had needed additional rejuvenation in order to adjust*

to the particular traumas she was experiencing in the physical world.

Often if an individual is deprived of this needed attunement, he or she may become so physically and/or physically disoriented that the soul decides to return to the expanded self. It is very important that children be given relatively free rein in the early stages to sense their own needs in adapting to Earth School. Children intuitively know what is needed in order to become well-grounded.

From this response I deduced that any sleep cycle that a person experienced naturally was based on probable needs, physical and nonphysical. Our workaday world necessarily discourages napping and daydreaming, but certainly it seems logical that one should seek ways to respond to the body's need for more sleep, rather than simply override the urge with coffee or drowsy awakeness. It occurred to me that my perceptions of time and space were blocks to adequately understanding just where one *went* when contacting the spiritual matrix in the dream state. Our friend Robert Monroe, author of the book JOURNEYS OUT OF THE BODY, claimed that one could actually leave the physical body and travel in the astral state. I asked Mentor to comment on "out-of-body" states.

"Out-Of-Body" Travels in the Spiritual Matrix

✻During these "homecomings" or sleep reunions with the spiritual matrix, each person travels his own path, and I do mean quite literally "travels." Since thoughts are real, whatever is wished for or desired is indeed created. There are no limitations when dealing with the spiritual matrix, and there is complete recognition of one's unlimited ability to create once in touch with the "I am." There is nothing that is impossible, there are absolutely no limitations. Direction comes from consciously setting a course or asking for a specific understanding, as well as from

within the "I am," and as greater integration is achieved, more avenues become open to exploration.

The "I am" exists in a state of enlightened euphoria. When the conscious mind releases the "I am" to truly be, it experiences all that there is to know of the incredible nature of creation. One may journey to other realities. Many people are known to us through such travels. It is often a source of frustration to nonphysical teachers, however, that there can be awareness of expanded realms in the sleep state and no awareness whatsoever in the waking hours.

Other explorations during periods of attunement with the spiritual matrix regularly include visits to the expanded self and even sometimes participation in the life or lives that one is living in other times, places and worlds.

How does one visit these places? Through what is commonly known as "out-of-body" experiences. While aligned with the spiritual matrix, one's thoughts create the experience. It is much easier to travel without a physical body than with one. Wishing to be somewhere or with someone instantly creates that reality. It is as simple to visit another world as it is to visit one's neighbor across the street. Materialization and dematerialization in the spirit state is the way one travels.

If Mentor's explanation could be taken at face value, then each of us has within us an unlimited pass to anywhere—past, present and future—and we possess the ultimate vehicle for personal exploration. I found myself wishing that we could control the adventures. I asked Mentor about people, such as Robert Monroe, who can program their "out-of-body" experiences:

✳ *There are those who are working to achieve this "out-of-body" condition without the initial time-consuming process of a lengthy sleep cycle. Consciously setting the state for this experience also allows the experience to be remembered. The "out-of-body" state can certainly be achieved in a much quicker sequence by those who have access to their spiritual matrices on a conscious level. It is definitely a simpler matter to consciously disengage from the body and travel at will, rather than to spend lengthy periods of time reaching an appropriate sleep state.*

It is overwhelming, however, to wander into an "out-of-body" state or even try to create one when one is not prepared for astral travel. This happens sometimes when one is overly tired, worried, preoccupied, or in a state of trauma. The "wires" seem to become momentarily crossed, and one perhaps finds himself on the ceiling staring down at his body. This experience has shocked more than one person. If this should happen, it is important to remember that just as thoughts determine a cosmic journey so thoughts precipitate reintegration with the physical body. It is only necessary to create that thought in the mind. Because one could be dealing in a world of unfamiliar beings and energies, I would suggest that anyone wishing to try traveling without a body begin with a period of serious conscious attunement, being sure he is clear about the purpose, the destination, and most importantly, the link with the positive God-oriented forces of the universe. I would also suggest beginning with limited excursions so that contact is not made with more than one can initially handle.

I have had discussions with people concerning their out-of-body states in which they encountered other realities and states of being. I even recalled one of my own experiences at the Monroe Institute in which I felt "propelled through space" at an immense rate of speed. The Monroe Institute trainer later identified that experience as typical of what is often experienced at the beginning of an out-of-body state.

I asked Mentor about other altered states of consciousness. What happened during fainting spells or blackouts? What of unconscious conditions caused by accidents or illness? What of the reports of people who had encountered "beings" during near-death experiences? Where did people go when unconscious?

Sleep, Coma and Death:
Similarity of Spiritual Matrix Experience

Interacting with the spiritual matrix during sleep, coma, or death initially produces the same vision. For each night, one finds the same center in the sleep state that one finds in the separation state of dying. This is a very interesting subject and one I will discuss later in much greater detail. However, right now one can reflect on the accounts read of those who were pronounced physically dead and yet regained consciousness to tell of their adventures in a "strange land." There are often accounts of a long, dark tunnel with gold and/or white light at the other end. Sometimes there is a lighted figure of a departed loved one or spiritual teacher. Often there is a river or desert that one is trying to cross. There is always the sense, however, that the decision has not yet been made, that one still has the option to advance or retreat. These experiences are all common to the moment of union with the "I am" or spiritual matrix. The only difference among daily sleep experiences, coma and the death experience is that in the sleep and comatose state one has the option of whether or not to cross the river or whether or not to approach the lighted figure. In the death state there is no choice; one is simply given the opportunity to cross the river of life and break the tie with the physical body.

The joy, beauty and love which have been reported by those who lived to tell of their near-death experiences are but affirmations of that which is experienced every night in the sleep state as well as that which is experienced at the actual time of separation from the physical body. The clarity and intensity of emotions known at these times serve as but tiny foreshadowings of what is to come. What is experienced on these occasions is not vague and distant, but is very real and fills one with the overwhelming joy of knowing that the unseen is no longer fearful but is magnificent and fulfilling beyond words.

Strangely, through these accounts of near-death experiences, the general public has been given a brief glimpse of another version of existence—a vision not of fiction or imagination but of reality.

I was once again confronted with that question of "reality." What did people find in their "near-death" encounters that usually brought on descriptions of indescribable beauty? Mentor had earlier said that the spiritual matrix was the "real me" and that the physical world was but an illusion. At the risk of appearing oblivious to his teaching about reality, I requested clarification of this other world of the spiritual matrix. Once again, why was this dream world called reality and my physical world called illusion?

The Mechanism of Awakening

❋ *Reality—that which is eternal—is the core of existence and never changes though traveling through billions and billions of years of experience. The all-knowingness and awareness of the spiritual matrix is a constant, existing within the context of each and every incarnation.*

The illusion of life is that the ever-changing, tantalizingly unreliable day-to-day existence is somehow real. Reality, instead, is very simply that which is permanent. Those issues and perceptions which are of lasting value when taken out of the Earth School context are those which are real.

Awareness of the ongoing presence of a personal spiritual matrix or God-connection is the personal reality which should nurture the body, mind and spirit. This intuitive insight of man's beneficent connection to God serves as the stepping-stone out of the quagmire of the transitory, reaching for the all-enduring presence of eternal existence.

If it is possible to connect with the spiritual matrix in a meaningful way while asleep, then the question is how is it possible to create such a connection while awake?

Consider this metaphor, Agartha. There is a bow of personal spiritual destiny, and there is also an arrow of

*hoped-for realization. As the arrow is taken from the
quiver and placed on the string of the bow, one needs but
to turn to face the target—the spiritual matrix. As the
arrow is released to find its home in the spiritual matrix,
cosmic destiny and realization permanently unite with the
spiritual matrix and conscious cosmic alignment is known.
It simply takes the conscious effort of releasing the arrow
from the finger's grasp to begin the search which, once
launched, forever changes the physical and spiritual relationship.*

*We have looked at the problems and responsibilities in-
volved in beginning the search: the confusion, the feelings
of being overwhelmed and the subtleties of the desire to
search. If one accepts that the arrow is the divinely-given
desire, the bow—one's destiny and the spiritual matrix—
the target, then the only missing links are: when is the
bow placed in one's hands and by what force? When? As
the inner setting becomes optimally and harmoniously
aligned with the physical state, and when one asks "to
know," then it is the time for personal enlightenment. By
what force? Through circumstance magically and divinely
woven with personal karma. Circumstance and personal
karma interact to create more than coincidence. Be aware
that one truly does create his own reality by being awake
to the moment when he feels the weight of the bow in his
hands—being awake to when destiny says . . . "Now!"*

*Once the arrow is released and finds its destination in
the spiritual matrix of the heart, then on a conscious level
illusions of personal attachment and limitations are shattered and loneliness falls away. After personal oneness
with God has been known, physical life is seen in its true
perspective.*

Free Choice: The Fabric of Life

The metaphor of archery was beautiful indeed. It was impossible not to want to personalize myself as archer. Perhaps
I broke through to Mentor when the Universe said "Now!"

And yet, except for my incredible relationship with Mentor, my own life seemed almost too prosaic for such a wondrous occurrence. I found myself caught in a push-pull reaction to my own awakening process. The nagging question "why me?" always returned. By what grace was I experiencing these awarenesses? Was it simply a matter of personally recognizing the moment that the "bow" was in my hand? Surely I had no way to assess the magnitude of my asking for guidance prior to Mentor's miraculous entry into my consciousness.

If this is a matter of personal free choice, then why is there free choice? Why is the human species allowed to wander the wastelands of nonreality, caught in the boredom and pain of the purely physical, when a knowing nod could perhaps unite man with the undiluted joy of essential knowledge? Why this seemingly pointless delay in requiring each to ask his own question, find his own answer, and open his own door? Mentor sought to enlarge my horizons in order to answer my new barrage of questions, doubts and concerns:

✳ *The doors of universal knowledge are found in the non-physical, not the physical. All Earth School or other physical incarnation experience is assessed and assimilated in the higher consciousness between lifetimes in the state of "expanded self," of which we have spoken. Each door of knowledge that one would open is unique, for it holds affirmation of previously assessed Truth and yet provides encouragement to continue the search. Behind each new door is further interpretation of life and beyond life. These gathering grains of Truth cling together as if magnetized, forming an ever-evolving kaleidoscope of new ideas. There is no door that holds all the answers, each only adds to the ongoing totality of understanding.*

There need be no anger or despair at not being able to see one's complete cosmic picture, for there is no such thing as one's complete picture. There is only the moment—the experience of the "now," guiding one's footsteps, expanding one's world view in order that each may selectively pull forth his own appropriate understandings and move forward to the wondrous whisperings of the next door.

Follow the path of the heart, the Universal God-Connection which urges each forward to explore that which is most necessary to his development. With the heart as guide, each is powerfully drawn to physical situations which affect one's beyond-life development and understanding. One is like the conductor of a great symphony who periodically directs the whole orchestra but between performances studies the intricacies of individual instruments. In searching, confirmation of the old and expectation of the new begin to mold the psyche into a vessel of sublime and integrated beauty. The obvious then begins to take shape—that to search is to find and to search is eternal.

Mentor's words gently encouraged me to value the unseen as the object of my ultimate desires. Despite my love of and attachment to many of the beautiful aspects of this physical existence, I wanted to know the other world as well. During moments of intense spiritual interaction, I would sometimes wish I could avoid the difficulties of the physical world and go in search of my spiritual matrix on a full-time basis. Why did I have to live this Earth existence at all? What was the point of it all? But then I would see my children and Jim and realize that life on Earth was also sweet. Mentor showed me how spiritual and physical life need not be in conflict at all but, indeed, very much in concert with one another:

✳*Physical life on Earth can be likened to an intricately woven square of fabric composed of intriguingly unique, often bizarre, fabric combinations. These fibers weave one's soul with one's current physical reality, forming a beautiful pattern of personal integrity. All that is physical (conscious and unconscious) and all that is eternal is reflected in the ongoing saga of one's fabric. Since there is no master pattern of conformity against which all else in the universe is measured, then there can be no wrong choice, no dead-end street, no fruitless maneuvering, for all goes toward the integrity of the individual pattern and the uniquely individual search.*
If there is no right or wrong to the way one's fabric

should look, then spontaneity is allowed to burst forth joyously sparking each to express his individuality. The Universal Core bestows creative impetus upon each soul as it begins its journey. Even as a microcosm creatively spins off from the Original Source, so each fabric develops free of restriction. Each reincarnation allows personal freedom to create anew. Much as a child eagerly puts his pencil on a clean sheet of paper, so the physical self should move with delight to explore its new surroundings.

Physical exploration inevitably leads to spiritual exploration. Just as the nature of yin and yang are ultimately inseparable, so the nature of the heart is always directed homeward. It is but a matter of recognizing the heart's promptings to gather the appropriate physical experience during each reincarnation. The heart is the only constant and sure beam to follow to one's cosmic door of understanding.

Dynamic choices made in the physical, the daring to follow the path set by the heart, are the only prerequisites to ultimate success. One need not be concerned if one is making a physical mistake in life, for one can never step in the wrong direction while listening to the heart. The lesson of the heart is the lesson of one who seeks the path of awakeness—it is the lesson of the first door: there is no right or wrong direction. There is only progression toward the inevitable linkup of past, present and future.

This is the immediate challenge to the people of the Earth: to create a fabric of experience and esoteric knowledge which by its very nature and completeness propels them into the next dimension of learning, enabling each to grasp the rudiments, allowing each to understand the often misunderstood, the subtle definitions of Truth which carve each person's future in eternity.

"Dynamic choices"! If there was no right and no wrong but only ultimate development of all souls toward an Ultimate Source, then the Earth's environment must indeed be a cosmic classroom in which what ultimately matters is one's progress. By this perception the choices one makes are all-

important. It seemed that the quality of one's questions, not
merely the answers themselves, determined one's progression. Learning in full consciousness would be the ultimate
Earth School experience, and making "dynamic choices"
about one's curriculum would become the art of purposeful
living in the Earth School. Mentor continued:

Weaving the Fabric of Life

*✻Earth School can be likened to a great feast in which
every known food is made available for sampling and each
individual is encouraged to select his own diet. The highs
and lows of human experience are all part of the selection.
All are necessary, all serve a function in the preparation
of the individual: first, for complete awareness of the lessons of Earth School; and second, for readiness to move
forward or inward to other dimensions. Until one has
known the hidden mysteries of one's inner dimensions how
can one hope to move on to greater mysteries? It is important to seek first on a personal level in order that one
may move on to then seek on a multidimensional level.*

*At the time one's fabric is completed at one's death,
each must be prepared to assimilate his understanding of
the just completed physical experience. And with an understanding of the physical comes an understanding of the
emotional which prompts the physical. If one has denied
existence to the lesser or the greater aspects of one's being,
then the inevitable has only been delayed, for eventually
one must meet and resolve all those issues and identify all
those modalities which are in one's cosmic path.*

*There are countless aspects to and influences upon one's
life fabric. Certainly all that is within the conscious and
superconscious mind as well as one's composite physical,
emotional and spiritual circumstances exert influence
upon the nature of one's fabric. It is interesting to look
at some of the lesser-seen aspects of one's living fabric in
order to better understand the subliminal workings of
one's being. For example, the waking and sleep states of*

being are continually being probed in response to meta-morphosing consciousness and to altered states such as dreaming. When the consciousness is probed, it is much like blowing air through a straw into a dish of water. Bubbles are created, and these bubbles are extensions of one's unexplored emotions which are important in exploring the fabric of one's life.

Probes are sent deep into one's being when one is seeking a conscious alternative to one's currently accepted mental program. The subliminal response to probes can be either consciously recognized and incorporated into the ongoing conscious program or can be ignored. For instance, in the sleep state during periods of unconscious confusion, alternative impressions are being proposed and explored with probes delving into formerly uncharted regions. As we have said, in order for random and un-classified perceptions to be recognized on the conscious level, the mind must be instructed to make room for new understandings. One must ask one's consciousness to co-operate; otherwise the full potential of the probes is never realized and the probes are indeed then no more effective than bubbles in a dish of water.

Some of these subliminal impressions may initially seem to promote destructive rather than constructive internal or external behavior. This is true. But these emotions need not be manifested into physical form if they are explored in theory. By giving oneself permission to recognize and explore through dreams, daydreams and conscious thought and not repress the potentially destructive from the light of investigation, one prevents the socially and morally unacceptable modalities from manifesting into one's physical life.

Much as a fisherman retrieving his nets from the sea often discovers more than his regular catch, so the individual likewise discovers the unknown when carefully and conscientiously pulling in the catch of the day. The question is: what is to be done with these little-known or un-derstood emotions? Are they to be thrown back into the sea and forgotten, or studied and questioned, each according to its nature? Of course the latter. For that which is initially deemed unwanted or destructive to physical or spiritual life becomes neutralized when exposed to conscious realization and cosmic understanding. The frightening becomes a known and only the unknown remains the enemy.

I had never imagined the life learning process to be so incredibly complex. Apparently there is no time in which we do not learn, whether awake or asleep, conscious or unconscious. Also, it appears that the physical life experiences may indeed be the most elementary of all the learning modes, and that more refined learning may come from learning "in theory" as a result of conscious probes.

The entire process seemed logical and yet it seemed that it might be possible that each person could follow "a different drummer" to such a degree that mankind could evolve along a myriad of divergent paths. What would prevent devolution or aimless evolution? How could man's free will ensure anything but random wandering? What chance would we have of finding "home"?

Earth School, Divine Destiny and Free Will

✻ *The fabric of life is, as we have said, that intricate tapestry of being which is woven from total experience and total awareness. It is appropriate that one is as cognizant as possible of all perceptions in order that one's choices and directions can become realities based on the knowledge of wholeness. One can no longer be trapped by the unseen and often feared elements of the human nature that may be lurking in the darkness. There is no longer any darkness, only awareness and recognition of the human condition as a learning phase, a gradual winnowing out of the unevolved and reinforcement of the evolved.*

This is the purpose of Earth School: to enable each person to experience, to learn and then to choose his path. This can only be done having known on some level all that there is to know of one's individual evolution through the human phase of life. Earth School is a time of physical

*experience and emotional classification, a time not to fal-
ter for want of trying but a time to courageously seek to
incorporate all that lies without with all that lies within.*

*Moving forward, following the path of the star, is each
person's inalienable right—call it "divine destiny." While
there is choice as to the specifics that will fill each life,
there is no choice as to whether one will or will not ultimately progress.*

*All energy moves forward toward perfection and com-
pletion, and therefore life as it is known to each moves
forward allowing the opportunity for mental, emotional,
physical and spiritual experiences to shatter personal
illusion by seeing the reality of the total being.*

*It is, after all, not each soul's choice to begin this pro-
cess of personal evolution, but God's. Each elemental energy is like a sponge placed in a puddle of ink, consciously
and superconsciously absorbing all things. Yet where is
the conscious memory of the motion that placed each in
the puddle in the beginning? It often appears as only a
vague sense of connectedness, slipping in and out of the
cloud-cover of physical life, pulling each in spite of himself
toward the inevitable union with God.*

*There often seems no concrete sense of this wondrous
awareness, yet when the fabric has been completed and
taken from the loom of life, then will each know as the
shrouds are dropped that the search for God is the undeniable essence of creation that underscores the workings
of the Universe. There is free choice only to the extent of
choosing the colors and fabrics that will be used within
each physical life. There is no free choice as to whether
or not one will weave the fabric. All creation weaves a
fabric—a fabric of dynamics which defines life for each
soul in terms of true reality.*

So that was the answer: there is no free choice about the
path to God! The only real choice is the path one takes, the
fabric one weaves. Once again Mentor was stating what
he told me early in our relationship: that divinity is ultimately
for all. If, however, we seem oblivious to the subtle intrica-

cies of the individual's weaving of his fabric, how would we ever gain enough awareness to break the treadmill of unproductive or minimally productive lifetimes?

Going With the Flow

* *This chapter has dealt with the concepts of reality and illusion, those often mysterious terms of awareness suggesting the separation of the real from the counterfeit. We have also discussed how the individual's interpretation and integration of the meaning behind these terms influences the course of his life.*

The physical plane acts as a winnowing process, moving each from seed to ripened fruit and then again to seed. Each rebirth leads to a further refined definition of reality. Awareness of one's movement within Infinite Purpose is called "being in the flow." One might see the flow as in fact a stream where the sparkling water falls away, running joyfully and easily toward its destination. If in the physical each person acts according to the universality of his nature, then one moves smoothly and effortlessly through life, unaware and unaffected by the rocks in the stream. However, most are not able to find or maintain this state of awareness and instead become smashed and entangled by the obstacles of the stream.

This buffeting continues until the path of God is found— the path that teaches each the nature of the rock and the stream. If the rocks are life's problems, those areas to which each is drawn in the struggle to find happiness, then the stream is the subtle yet perfect flow of consciousness within the universe. The scramble to avoid catastrophe only produces anxiety unless based on awareness of one's reality or that which never changes. If one's life is seen and lived with awareness as the goal, then one is buoyed by the motion of the stream. This understanding of the real and the illusionary is the buffer between physical life and the rock. Each life encounters rocks in its journey. It

is only the nature of the buffer which determines the combination of happiness and peace, travesty and malaise.

The physical pleasures and possessions of Earth School
can exist, of course, within or without the framework of
cosmic understanding. The gaining of physical possessions
and monetary power is simply a matter of knowing how to
direct universal energy to gain personal power. There is,
however, no lasting pleasure in just the tangible, for this
changes with each life scenario. What is of monetary value
in this reincarnation will be of no value in the next. This
causes the person who is only interested in the physical to
be always off balance, forever chasing the illusive, never
seeing the link that connects all things and all lives and
gives purpose to existence. It is only with consciousness
of the possessions which are held in the heart that one
releases anxiety and pain and moves toward the next cosmic door.

Manifesting Reality

Mentor was persuasive and undeviating in his insistence
that true meaning was to be found in the nonphysical via the
path of the heart. But what of our Earth reality? How specifically could we avoid the difficulties simply by understanding
the difference between the real and the illusionary? I asked
Mentor to go beyond theory and offer some specific suggestions to improve our physical Earth lives:

* *If manifesting—meaning to create or change one's reality—sounds too theoretical and unfathomable, perhaps
there is need for specific instructions in order to understand
how the process works. Here are four steps which are the
basis for changing or creating reality on the physical level:*

*1. Come to a place of understanding. This means to qui-
etly attune oneself with the environment and the unknowable powers of the universe by sitting quietly, clearing the
mind of conscious thought.*

2. Visualize as specifically as possible that which is to be changed or created. This should include specifics such as color, size, value, location or timing. Focus conscious thought on just this desire.

3. Blend the wish with the total power of bodily energies. This is done by repeating the wish in exactly the same way, using the same words over and over for several weeks until it is felt that the wish and body have merged into one. The wish can be written out and placed in a spot where it will be constantly seen. Each time it is seen it should be read and repeated several times.

4. When there seems to be a total integration of the thought, and one is intimately aware of every aspect of the words, tear up the paper or dismiss the thought. Each person's needs will be met, often in a most creative and unpredictable way. The results, however, must be expected. There needs to be confidence that the outcome, while out of one's own hands, is in the process of being changed or created. This is called creating one's own reality.

The focused energy or personal power which has been united with the intensity of the universe will produce the desired results. This process will not work if: one, the individual is not totally convinced that it is within his power to change or create a situation through the unique connection to the Infinite; two, the individual is too lazy or skeptical to work toward achieving a state of natural attunement; or three, the person does not really want what he is suggesting. Creating what is needed or wanted is nothing more than understanding and obeying the natural laws of manifestation. "Karma" and "luck" are often the conscious tradeoffs one uses when unwilling or unable to use the laws of manifestation.

Many people have known or read books about the power of positive thinking. Mentor's formula for one's reality seemed a creative twist on an old idea. In fact it seemed so simple that I questioned the special power of manifesting reality in such a fashion. Mentor saw fit to offer a "real world" example of the working of the system:

There was a girl who lived in Portugal in the year 1811. Her name was Cortina, and her life will serve as a most appropriate example of "creating your own reality." Cortina was born to a wealthy family, one which was involved in shipbuilding. She was a sensitive and loving child and an energy with whom I had worked, although not in her conscious state, for many lifetimes.

When she was sixteen, her family's business suffered a fire in which they lost their shipyard and several large speculative vessels which represented all the family's resources. Cortina's family found itself destitute. Unwilling to accept this apparent devastation, she became convinced that she could change this seeming catastrophe. Her friends called her a ridiculous optimist. She should, they said, accept what had happened and turn her life in a new direction. She instead set about finding the means to restore her father's fortune. (I will say at this point that while consciously she had not been schooled in finding the spiritual matrix and the inherent power involved in recognizing this God-connection, nevertheless, she had already evolved to a significant state of natural attunement with herself and her environment. Also, I was working with her in the sleep state.)

Cortina focused on this one desire: to restore her father's shipyard. She was unwilling to let it out of her thoughts and found herself drawn to the potential for positive resolution rather than the despair and tragedy. In other words, she failed to recognize the physical circumstance as having power over the ultimate determination. She tried convincing her father's friends and former business partners to reinvest in the family business. Her overtures were dismissed as inappropriate conversation for a young woman.

Nevertheless, several months later, still undaunted by the bleak outlook, she was wandering through the old burned-out warehouse when she saw a small silver locket lying in a cloudy puddle. Curious, she picked it up. On the back were three beautifully engraved initials. She went home with the locket and asked if anyone knew the initials. They did not. She went into her father's library and began to browse through the accounts salvaged from the warehouse fire. At the top of a ledger sheet were the initials and the full name and address of a former client to whom, many years before, her father had sold a ship. The initials matched those on the locket.

She sent a letter returning the locket to the address given on the ledger sheet, and explaining her family's desperate situation. She asked if they would consider the commissioning of a new sailing vessel to re-start her father's business. She was convinced that a solution would come from that letter and so it did. The owner and his wife, taken with the courage and commitment of the daughter, did indeed invest in another ship and her father did build a new shipyard with the funds from that ship.

This is not a fairy tale, but a story of manifestation resulting from a belief in the ability to influence for the positive those life situations with which one is confronted.

The story of Cortina was touching and demonstrated Mentor's point about manifesting in the Earth plane, but this did not explain where karma or circumstance gives way to the power of positive thinking. In my personal mythology there was the notion that some misfortunes were beyond personal control and might actually be the important workings of the universe. I asked Mentor to explain karma:

✳ *What of karmic debt or the need to fulfill predetermined and predestined obligations incurred in a previous lifetime? Once one realizes he has the power to create, the power to change his own life, then one becomes a part of the universality of all that is. When one begins to play within the natural laws of manifestation, karmic debt is released. Once attunement and awareness have been gained, the confinements of karma have been transcended. One exists within karmic debt only so long as one is willing to exist within karmic debt. Once one has opened his eyes to his own inimitable connection to God and involved those cleansing energies in his reality, one is beyond the reach of karma and has passed through the purely physical cause-and-effect of lifetimes. One is beyond its reach as long as he operates in the name of Ultimate Love.*

The Dynamics of Creating Your Own Reality

Move forward with this knowledge of the flow, realizing that each can create from the smallest to the largest those items which change life to the personally productive. Energy, cosmic energy, is all around. One has but to draw it into his reality by being aware of its existence and one's own God-given right to use it.

There are many avenues to creating one's reality, and I have but briefly touched on the cornerstones. Wanting to build on personal reality, wanting to dismiss the illusion that manifests itself in pain, broken dreams, and unreached goals is the beginning. It is possible to take only one step at a time, always trusting to the fact that one's feet will find the next step. One must not be overcome with the seemingly insurmountable problems of life and the blocks which seem to exclude one from the benefits of the connections of which we have spoken. Go ahead and dare to try, dare to believe that what I speak is true and that all is possible if one but trusts in himself and in those powers to which he is undeniably bonded.

Agartha, I realize that it is difficult for you to grasp the significance of "making your reality." My explanation, though simplified for your understanding, will have to suffice, for it is not possible to be privy to all at this point. Give your emerging awareness a chance to blossom and develop using the forces of creative energy we have discussed. There is no limitation to what one's life can be on Planet Earth. Quite literally, one creates every aspect of living. With this in mind—create wisely!

CHAPTER FIVE

THE POWER CONNECTION: KEY TO EARTH'S SURVIVAL

Are the trees in the forests
and the birds of the air aware?
Are the flowers of the field
and the animals of the pasture awake?
Are the children in the schools
and the parents in the houses ready?
Aware, awake and ready to know the truth.

MENTOR

THE PERSONAL MEANING behind a word or the manner in which one defines a word or phrase, changes as one's experiences trigger a deepening awareness. I had defined words such as "love" and "power" in terms of my previous frame of reference. I found these definitions no longer applicable. As Mentor approached each new subject, I moved into more intense dimensions of understanding in which my vocabulary began to be redefined by increasingly in-depth perceptions. Words such as "love" no longer meant just an emotional response, but came to represent the most profound energy of the Universe, that which causes all to evolve toward understanding.

Likewise, "power" began to take on a new meaning as I reflected on the abuse of physical power and the way in which power was so often seen as an extension of external force rather than as inner discipline. It became increasingly evident that one's definition of "power" created one's relationship with objects which symbolically held power. If, for

122

example, an individual believes that genuine power is contained within the force of money, social status, political energy or other forms of external power, then that individual is also subject to the influence of these spheres of power. Further, that individual will automatically be drawn or attracted to any number of the possible forms of external power as a means of compensation for a lack of personal power. Literally speaking, one becomes controlled by the very power one seeks to harness. How, then, does one become released from the limitations of external power?

It does not take a sage to recognize that such a definition of power stands in direct opposition to spiritual power. The spiritual power active within such historical figures as Jesus Christ, Buddha, Gandhi and St. Francis of Assisi resulted, in part, from a perfect belief in the nonphysical world and an ability to live fully in the knowledge of their connectedness to the Universe. They understood power to be an internal force and their lives became illustrations of this level of power which is equated to unconditional love and compassion. They wove the major threads of history without an external demonstration of power requiring weapons or armies. And through the use of their power, humanity has only benefited.

I realized I had personally redefined power when the old power symbols diminished in their ability to attract my attention. The source of my developing power was increasingly defined in terms of my relationship with Mentor and my belief in his teachings that all could transcend physical limitation.

The Power Trip

✳*Earth is embroiled in an intense power struggle. This conflict exists between countries, states, cities and individuals, as well as between the spiritual and physical aspects of each individual. The basis is always the same: to be recognized, even honored, for possessing the most power.*

No case can be made for the prima donna, singularly

or collectively, who feels his whim is provocation enough
to justify any infringement on another. The individual has
the right and the God-given purpose to pursue his own
path, creating his own destiny, but this has never—and
will never—mean that it is acceptable or allowable to move
in a direction that causes another pain. The Earth must
and will move past the impertinent and heavy force. This
will happen, but not until man has unequivocally accepted
the need for harmony and peace among his kind.

The years 1980 to 1987 will be difficult times with countries vying for the world's resources and prestige, both
through political and physical manipulation. It will be a
time of strict demarcation of boundaries as each separate
group of peoples struggles unsuccessfully to bolster changing economic and national value systems. The people of
the world will be pulled this way and that, with govern-
ments scrambling to prove that the prosperity of the past
is just ahead in the form of a new economic package or a
new war against a supposed aggressor.

There have always been a few farsighted people speaking out on issues involving humanity. But now, more and
more will listen and learn, question and decide that they
too wish to opt for the presence of a harmonious world
community, the emergence of a balanced planet. These
voices, while at first considered strange, will gradually be
integrated into the mainstream of everyday life. Herein
lies the basis for the great conflict.

There will be strong elements of the world's societies
which will tenaciously cling to the old, remaining with the
inhumane and unsupportable economic and social policies
of the past. These groups will violently oppose the new
voices raised in love, calling for world peace and a change
in the repression, violence and nonproductive leanings of
the past.

The twenty-five years following 1987 (1988–2013) will
be filled with increased fear and bloodshed as people struggle through war and natural disaster to reach a common
vision. Wars will be wars of desperation, creative against
static, vision against rhetoric. The slowly metamorphosing

planet will suffer all the anguish inherent in being reborn, struggling to exchange the inappropriate and nonproductive for the intrinsically satisfying. As this general consciousness shift gains momentum, the turbulence of Planet Earth will gradually subside and the physical countenance of Earth will become one of calm.

The realized focus of planet Earth will eventually be harmony among all living elements. By the beginning of the Twenty-first Century, there will be a coming of age of physical and spiritual alignment with the peaceful purposes of the universe, for the world will have tasted the result of long periods apart from the universal structure of light. People will have finally seen and completely rejected the ravages of war and the misuse of power.

The physical planetary changes will act as cleansing and purification for Earth as it seeks equanimity. The land masses currently above water support more life than ever before in the world's history. The peoples now living on these lands continue to influence the alignment of Planet Earth, although they are certainly not solely responsible for the Earth's current entanglement with negativity. To-day's people are but the physical realization of yesterday's joys and fears.

What force propels the United States and the other countries of the free world? Is it the vision of evolved harmony or that of singular power? It is currently both. America has indeed picked up the challenge of planetary evolvement but is struggling to find the vehicles to bring this into line. The country's leadership anguishes over the dichotomy of a perceived advanced purpose and yet an apparently runaway physical reality. This is a widespread dilemma, and I would suggest that the leaders of the world are being tested. Each governing body is being forced to go beyond the failing physical systems to find solutions, to go beyond the apparent limitations of human avarice and contrived superiority to a connection of purposeful existence in which all can share.

There is an abundance of nonphysical teachers guiding men and women through these tense periods. While teach-

*ings are recognized by some on a conscious level and by
others on a superconscious level, the powerful leaders of
the world community are nonetheless being assisted in order that they might lend their weight to the creation of
peaceful coexistence in the twenty-first century.*

I was stunned and more than a little frightened by Mentor's
explicit explanation. He clearly stated that Planet Earth could
anticipate an extended period of pain and conflict, yet I noticed he did not say anything about nuclear holocaust. I
searched to find something positive in Mentor's message
about the near future, but it appeared that war (hopefully
non-nuclear) and natural disaster were on the horizon. He
did say that by the twenty-first century we would have lost
the need for war. At least that was cause for hope.

I wondered about the possibility of a shifting of the Earth's
axis. Mentor had stated: "the physical planetary changes will
act as cleansing and purification for Earth as it seeks equanimity." What kind of changes was he foreshadowing? I
thought of the beautiful lands of the world and I felt pain at
the prospect of their potential destruction. It was difficult to
accept that our blindness to Earth's plight may ultimately
trigger natural disasters. It was no less frustrating, however,
to see the major powers of the planet flirting with nuclear
war. What could prevent earth changes? What was the answer—if there was one—to circumventing the unthinkable
horror of large-scale destruction, man-made or nature-made?

Personal Power: Learning to Draw from the Source

* *Since even the largest group of people quickly reduces
to the individual, let us talk of power as it first relates to
the individual. What is power when reduced to its simplest
form but self-actualized cosmic potential? Personal power
is manifested in the energy generated by conscious choice
and is both finite and cosmic in nature. When one chooses
to remain limited by accepting his position as powerless,
then the energy is finite. When the individual accepts his*

connection to the Universe, allowing his being to become
infused with the unlimited, then the energy becomes cosmic. He may abuse his power and use it for his own purposes; he may relinquish power to another and feel
unprotected and vulnerable, or he may increase his power
by using it according to a higher order of development.

Personal power is gained through conscious choice in
one of two ways: first, in the seeking of a known goal and
second, in the seeking of a meaningful direction with no
goal in mind. For example, in the first instance the person
has a vision he wishes to manifest. He isn't aware that
personal power is achieved through his search; he only
looks to his goal and then to whatever means are at his
disposal to seemingly achieve it. This produces the vehicle
of power.

Consider, Agartha, your initial attempts at finding understanding for yourself and others. You used meditation,
though you had no idea of its true power. It was the only
seemingly available means of achieving your goal. As you
have grown and changed, fallen down and picked yourself
up emotionally, you have become aware of your own personal power, learning to direct it accordingly. You have
taken responsibility for being spiritually awake.

In the second case, the individual is again unaware of
personal power yet seeks to define his ultimate happiness
or despair in terms of only the search with no thought of
the eventual goal. The energy in both situations is potentially productive as a source of personal power.

The power we are discussing here is not imaginary. It is
real—but only as real as the individual's belief in his own
power. It is the energy with which he creates his own reality, as I have said. Believing in the actual existence of
power is the first step, and laying claim to one's possession
of power is the second.

The discovery of one's power connection is triggered by
normal physical circumstance. For example, the child may
learn of his potential power at the onset of physical life.
The young adult may find his unlimited connection as a
student. The middle-aged adult or elderly individual may

become aware of his very real endowment as the Earth School experience unfolds. Or, unfortunately, the connection to the realm of personal power through the recognition of the God Source may not be forthcoming at all in a particular incarnation.

Each individual is, figuratively speaking, like a satellite of intense power revolving around the main generating source which is God. Through the individual's connection to this Ultimate Source of Power, each satellite energy, be it galaxy, solar system, sun, star, spirit, person, flower, or microorganism, draws whatever it learns to draw from the Source.

There are many who lay claim to seemingly extraordinary power. These people can indeed perform and function in ways in which others apparently cannot. I would offer, however, that those who appear lacking in power have simply not worked at cultivating their own power connection. Each individual element of the universe has power. The extent of that power is based on the successful union with the spiritual matrix and the lack of limitation placed on that connection.

There are, of course, those who only wish power to manipulate for their own motives. These people have no conscious alignment with the spiritual matrix or Godconnection and are thus limited to that personal power which they possessed at their birth as part of their Godgiven birthright when they came into their current physical reality.

Those who trust in and choose to consciously draw from the ultimate power and love of the God Source are unlimited in their ability to capitalize on the personal power which is manifested. Personal power can continue to grow and expand an individual's awareness by drawing on the universal energy which can bring about dynamic changes on the physical level.

This suggestion that unlimited personal power was available only if one elected to recognize his power connection was an intriguing, if slightly elusive, notion. Still caught up

in my concern about wars and natural disasters, I had a flash
of concern that this power could be abused as well as used
for the good of all people. I thought of Adolf Hitler who had
caused pain on an enormous scale and wondered how he
managed to become so powerful, since he seemed to be
coming from a place of darkness rather than God-connection.

Personal Power: Birthright Gift and Spiritual Matrix Affirmation

٭*Birthright personal power, Agartha, can be likened to
the nourishment within an egg. For a limited period of
time, there is abundant nourishment for the developing
life within the egg. But there comes a time when that
nourishment has been depleted and the life within the egg
must be born or die. It must find a new, ongoing source
of nourishment. Likewise, each individual possesses immense personal power at birth. This power is part of one's
God-given connection to the greater powers of the universe. It is part of the expanded self which exists over and
above individual physical lifetimes. When that birthright
personal power supply becomes depleted, one must consciously tap a new connection in order to sustain and enlarge the flow of personal power.*

*Interestingly, this was the original meaning behind the
church's ceremony of confirmation or bar mitzvah, when
a young person was invited to become aware for himself
and participate in his own spiritual affirmation. He was
encouraged to seek his own presence in the light of God's
being. Of course, as so often happens, the awareness behind the ritual has been largely lost. The ceremonies do
continue, although they are often more social than spiritual. They lack much of the meaning which was the transfer of power from the God-given birthright connection to
a conscious awareness of the spiritual matrix connection.*

*The spiritual matrix is an integral part of the multi-
dimensional human body. The energy pouring forth and
stimulating the young child from the spiritual matrix grad-*

ually slows as it nears the end of its birthright supply, sometime in early adolescence. Unlike the contents of the egg, the young adult usually does not die if the appropriate transition is not made from the original energy source to the consciously aware source. Nevertheless, full cosmic potential cannot be realized and one remains haunted by the obvious dilemmas of the human condition.

In the course of growing up, one runs into three main periods of intense physical, emotional and spiritual upheaval: adolescence, eleven to eighteen years of age; midlife, thirty-five to forty-five years of age; and later life, fifty-five to sixty-five years of age. These periods are all highlighted with often erratic physical and emotional energy swings which belie the intense inner shift that is wanting to happen. The superconscious, aware of the slowing of the original energy source, produces physical urging for a new connection, and this sets up a most intense confrontation between mind and body. If the switch is not made and a new source of universal connection found during adolescence, then one limps along on a low level of energy until the middle years and then the later years when there are again periods of confrontation.

The complete rejection of a new source often produces perceptual distortions, extremely irrational behavior, and emotional and/or physical sickness. There can also be a partial shift in any of these three major transition stages from an attempted connection. Depending on the degree of transfer from birthright energy to conscious awareness and which of the three stages is involved, one may experience varying degrees of loss of energy, confusion, inability to focus on objectives, sense of futility or hopelessness often culminating in a morose depression and sense of failure. The longer one waits to tie into a new universal source, the greater becomes the distance between the warmth of the original God-connection and the coldness of solitary human existence.

Now, Agartha, you wish to know of those individuals who apparently have unlimited power in spite of their obviously unenlightened actions? There have indeed been major historical figures whose continued power seems to contradict what we have said. But let us look more closely. Since you are interested in the incarnated presence of Adolf Hitler, let us use him as our example.

There is a counterpart to the spiritual matrix energy of enlightenment. It exists as the void or lack of God-orientation around the spiritual matrix. It is your "evil," "black magic" or "forces of the dark." But evil is not a force in and of itself but a lack of the light. It wields no power except that it is given power by the individual and except that one invests in the power of non-light. This is because the void is merely one's own limited perceptions, expectations, and promotion of the self as all-knowing. It is like looking into a well and seeing only a distortion of one's own reflection rather than the depth and unlimited nature of the water.

Adolf Hitler's life lesson was one of finally overcoming his preoccupation with feelings of persecution and failure. By the time he had passed and repudiated his teenage connection to the spiritual matrix, he fell prey to his own personal torment of aloneness, rejection and personal distortion. These feelings, of course, colored his total Earth School experience and caused not only his paranoid behavior but also his obsession with the occult, in which he saw himself glorified through the self-righteous ego justification he sought. Is this not the ultimate illusion, that one's personal reflection outshines the omniscient universe?

Intuitively, when one chooses development of the void over that of the spiritual matrix, one is aware on some level that the choice only fulfills the prophecy of karma and not that of personal growth through the interaction with life's lessons. Gradually one becomes consumed by the void that had seemingly offered vindication for one's lack of struggle toward the universal connection.

Each person discovers his own need for personal power through the experiences and awarenesses of Earth School. As one yields to the overriding pull of a stronger connection, one acknowledges the increased and unlimited power *of the Universal which is for one to use to affect physical and spiritual reality. When one denies this powerful positive connection, one becomes consumed by the power of the void, and, as in the case of Adolf Hitler, becomes the ultimate victim. While one may feel no sympathy for the physical Adolf Hitler, move beyond that to understand the distortion of his potential vision of transcendence which changed from one of elevation and reinforcement of the highest ideals to subjugation of his own being through a warped tangle of misguided beliefs and ideologies.*

What is present as birthright potential does not necessarily move into affirmation of an expanded spiritual matrix. That is why I have spent a significant time highlighting the importance of recognizing potential and turning it toward manifestation. While all potential remains on the spirit level and is never lost, it does, however, remain beyond conscious reach until one does seek awareness of one's true self and ultimate vision through connection with the spiritual matrix.

I had not expected that Mentor would reveal the contents of the mind of Hitler in such a vivid and yet compassionate manner. Moreover, his explanation of the nature of evil moved the subject well beyond the understanding of evil as an independent operating force in the Universe. Still, I needed to understand how so many people could have been slaughtered unless somehow an "evil" force had been empowered to allow such terror. In spite of what Mentor had said, I could not grasp why anyone would deliberately give power, personal or otherwise, to such a man.

Relinquishing Power

✳ *What of those who allow themselves to be victimized by others, allowing atrocities which defy every code of human decency? Since we have spoken of Adolf Hitler, let us also include those who were his victims. Individuals and groups often relinquish power. They often allow themselves to be blinded to the nature and source of personal power and thus are unaware of their own personal feelings of defenselessness. The individual attributes power to others while denying his own right to power. This allows those to whom he has given power to break the new trails. He becomes obliged to always follow another's path.*

There are those who lead through the limited power of the dark and those who lead through the unlimited power of the light. One may experience many misfortunes at the hands of the former, for without one's own sense of the power of the Universe, one has no way of discerning one's course, separating what is and is not truly meaningful and life-sustaining. Until each develops a sense of personal power compatible with the energy available from the Universe, there will only be the paths of others to follow.

Each person must instead measure for himself, be responsible for his own life direction, and decide for himself what is appropriate to his own needs. Each must draw initially on all experiences and then personalize those which "feel right" in light of the energy from the spiritual matrix. This can be done satisfactorily only when one is in possession of one's own power through one's own connection to the personal power source of God.

The personal power connection! As in the discussion on enlightenment, Mentor was clearly saying that personal experience of the God-connection was the key. The question of how one made this connection became once again the burning question. I was convinced of the truth of Mentor's words and the value of making an attempt to touch my personal power base. The question once again was: how?

✳I would like to suggest exercises in which you can experience power, but first, Agartha, let me recap what has been said of personal power:

1. Personal power is obtained through the personalization of the cosmic linkup, or, put another way, personal power is found through the self-realization and accep-

tance of one's right to belong to the universal network of energy.

2. Personal power is unlimited except that it is limited by conscious action or intent, and it exists in measurable quantity only so long as it is perceived as unlimited and universal. It is, in other words, the nourishment which is possessed by right of one's connection to the Ultimate Source.

3. Personal power is the vehicle through which one manifests his own reality. It is taking the energy of human endeavor and infusing it with the power of a universal or God-connection.

Personal power is constantly being siphoned from the Main Universal Power Source. It is siphoned by all elements of creation, each according to its nature and its needs. Man alone doubts or ignores the power from his connection. For power to be drawn from the Source, each element must recognize its connection.

For example, the oceans of the world ebb and flow in relation to Earth and the solar system, never questioning the natural process or power through which they fulfill their purpose. There is no hesitation within the uncurling wave as to whether or not it has the right or ability to crash upon the shore, unloading its full complement of sand, stones and sea creatures.

The personal power of the wave makes a most interesting analogy to the personal power of the individual and further explains the way in which one builds personal power. A wave is created by, and is the product of, the influences brought to bear on the the ocean. The wave, born of massive gravitational pulls, nevertheless crests and drifts in relation to its singularity as well as its plurality. It exists as an energy in its own right, and yet it is obviously and overwhelmingly connected to the energy body of the ocean through which its draws its power. The ocean is the wave's power connection, just as the spiritual matrix is man's. If the wave saw itself as alone on the horizon, *separate from the ocean, then it would have the power of only one wave. It is through the wave's acceptance of itself as more than one wave that it is able to draw on the supreme might of the water. This awareness just exists in the natural world, but it must be found in the human world. Awareness is given to the newborn, but must be sought by the adult.*

As ridiculous as it seems for the lone wave to see itself as separate from the ocean, is it not equally ridiculous for the individual to close his eyes to his true connection to the Infinite, to all of creation and to his natural power connection? Without awareness of his God-connection, he sees only his own separateness, the separateness of each act and the separateness of each year of physical life.

Personal power is built through the realization that man is just one more link to the Isness. Power flows into one's presence as one sees himself existing within the whole. What is the reason that one feels so intensely alive and in harmony with his surroundings when one goes to the ocean and watches the waves crash upon the beach? It is because one intuitively recognizes the power—separate yet similar to his own. This is why people flock to the ocean on every possible occasion. They wish to share the power and majesty of the water. The need to experience natural power exists within all consciousness, for it calls to the unfulfilled nature of man's personal power.

I felt the pull of Mentor's powerful wave metaphor. It sounded so simple, and yet it seemed that mankind had somehow lost the conscious ability to feel his connectedness. Despite our many metaphors and poetic references to brotherly love and harmony between nations, our actions seem to reflect an abiding sense of isolation with every man (and nation) for himself.

This seemed to be the crux of the problem: despite our longing for higher ideals, we feel alone and this leads to acts of aloneness such as selfishness, greed, insensitivity, murder and war. Suddenly it became painfully obvious that this perception of duality, instead of unity, was the problem. I asked

Mentor what one could do to begin feeling this power connection. What specific steps would he recommend to anyone
wishing to experience his own connection to God?

Experiencing Personal Power:
A Meditative Exercise

✳ *Now can be the time for each person to reaffirm his own
personal power connection. There are three things I would
ask each to do in pursuit of this realization. (Thirty minutes should be allowed for this exercise.)*

*1. Mentally put yourself into your own magic place—
wherever you feel particularly strong and connected.
(Allow four to five minutes to become comfortable with
this place.)*

*2. Stand in this place. Recognize that you stand to sa-
lute the Heavens of which you are a part. This salutation
should take form deep within your being with whatever is
within your heart. (Allow four to five minutes for the salutation.)*

*3. Breathe in deeply. Breathe in the reassurance of your
cosmic connection, that connection through breath to all
forms of energy everywhere. Mentally reach toward the
sky, with the arms outstretched, with the mind focused
but empty of expectation, and with your heart open in joy
and love to receive and consciously know your own connection to the Universal God. (Allow fifteen to twenty
minutes to experience this connection.)*

*Commit yourself to the reality you have proclaimed and
nothing is beyond your control. Feel yourself tied to the
Infinite Structure of all things. It suddenly seems so obvious, so real. This is the realization of your personal
power. It is understanding what you have always known
on some level, that you are connected, a very real part of
the universe. There is nothing that you cannot handle,
nothing that can overwhelm you. You are the ocean, not*

*the wave; you are man aligned with personal power, not
man alone.*

As I began returning from Mentor's guided meditation, I
felt soothed, as if all the tension of everyday stress had been
removed. I had made my statement affirming my connection
and felt momentarily "there." It was exhilarating and yet so
simple. As my mind jumped to consider the other ways this
wonderful tool of centering might be used, Mentor apparently read my thoughts and added this afterthought:

✴ *You may wish to know of specifics. Can this personal
power be used to change your living situation or personal
relationship, your career or other aspects of physical life?
Of course. Personal power is open-ended; it is one's for
the claiming. As you draw in personal power, you become
strengthened emotionally, strengthened to the point where
you cannot be overcome by anything of an earthly nature.
Each individual creates on a deeper level that which is
needed in his life, and this composite forms a picture that
continues to evolve as long as physical life continues. This
picture is colored according to the decisions one makes,
and the decisions one makes are colored by one's reassurance of personal power. Every individual does indeed create his own positive or negative reality through the
realization of his own personal power connection.*

Beyond Personal Power:
The Consciousness Shift

*The problems being faced by the human race today—
nuclear holocaust, war, massive famine, starvation and
disease, economic collapse—all abound because the individual has failed in his responsibility to claim his own
connection. Instead, each tentatively waits for some other
person to correct the imbalance, some politician, scientist
or religious leader.*

The responsibility for living harmoniously on Planet

Earth rests with each individual. As each person spiritually and cosmically comes of age, claiming his attunement and therefore his involvement in the business of all mankind, a beautiful new energy will be released which will gradually swing the Earth into alignment with the universal forces of harmony and peace. This period of awareness will happen, but only when each man and woman looks beyond the exterior to the interior of their being to discover their own personal power through their connection to the Ultimate of All Energies. Realization of one's own connection is a gift to all others, for it signifies one's own readiness to participate in and use one's own energies for a world where love and awareness are the core.

Now the Earth exists as a place of unrealized and unaligned energy. Because it is struggling does not mean people have chosen a wrong path; for there is no wrong path. They simply have yet to choose a path that aligns with the higher forces. The result of this floundering is that the Earth is in "neutral." Too many citizens of the planet wait hesitatingly for something or someone to claim their allegiance. Most have inadvertently frozen their dynamic choices and allowed neutrality to win the day.

But "neutral" can be a very dangerous space, as Earth's people are discovering. For "neutral," by its very definition, means assuming a non-choice or refraining from making a choice, and in this case no choice is a choice. It is a choice for the status quo. Unfortunately there is no status quo. Nothing remains the same for even two consecutive seconds. Change is a dynamic which must be recognized and embraced. Acceptance of change will be crucial as the Earth shifts into forward gear.

People must learn to be unafraid spiritually even if they are overcome with fear emotionally. In order to survive the psychological as well as physical traumas of the twenty-first century, the individual must be prepared and sustained by the teachings of the spirit in order to give birth to changes which must follow this stage of dwindling effectiveness.

Thus there is the necessity for learning of personal

power now. As the physical plane becomes more and more disrupted through "acts of nature," it will be imperative for each individual to know of his connection to powers beyond this phase of disruption. As thousands reach to realize their personal power connection, they will not only be lifting themselves beyond the reach of the physical calamity, but also allowing the planet to gain momentum in its upswing into realized alignment within the universe by bringing forth a massive consciousness shift. Power needs to be personalized to be effective in each life. Until the commitment is made to affect one's personal reality as well as the planet's, fear and fear of change will continue to hold sway over Planet Earth.

"Acts of nature"? "Massive consciousness shift"? My heart sank as images of planetary destruction mentally appeared. Even the consideration of earth changes and notions of Armageddon caused me to want to postpone considering or questioning Mentor further on the subject. Yet Mentor was seemingly referring to "acts of nature" as a matter of fact. I could not bring myself to question him directly on the possibility of such destruction. On some level I hoped that his continuing communication would help allay my anxiety. As if in deference to my wish to move away from fearful images, Mentor shifted from personal to group power:

Group Process: The Power Squared

✳ We have spent considerable time investigating personal power, what it is and what it means. Now let us look at power on the larger scale. Group awareness, group effectiveness training, group dynamics and group counseling are all familiar terms and all hint at the lesson of recognizing and learning to use group power appropriately and effectively. Indeed the world needs to learn of group dynamics in order to move into its new course of harmonious realignment with the spirit. The usual attitude toward groups is that they are necessary for some decisions. But

is the individual aware that the energy or power of a group with a common vision, the actual units of energy generated, increase in direct square proportion to the size of the group?

If the power of a group can be the number of the people within a group squared, one can quickly see that each group's power increases exponentially with size. This power is the power of creative energy which can manifest in specific physical form, not only making things happen quicker but making them happen in line with expectation. The actual units of power to change and create thoughts and actions grow in a great proportion when in a harmonious group than in an unintegrated group.

For example, a group of people may get together to start a school. The collective vision is the same as the individual vision. Through discussion, and also disagreement, the specifics of the goal begin to take shape. The people involved in creating the school have become a unified body with a goal and a means of reaching that goal. If there are twenty-five people in the group then, 25 times 25 (or 25 squared) equals 625 units of viable energy. The comparison is between six hundred twenty-five units of energy manifested by the unified group compared with only twenty-five units of energy which would have been manifested had they been unable to form a unified body.

Remember: group power equals the square of the number of people within a group. If there is a group of one hundred people who share a common vision and interact to achieve that goal, then the number within the group (100) squared equals the group's power (100 times 100 energy units) or 10,000 units of generated energy. And to complete the example, if there is a group of one hundred people who do not share a common vision but are nonetheless thrown together in a group, then that group's power is equal only to the simple addition of the power of each individual member of 1 + 1 + 1 + (etc.) up to 100 to equal 100 units of general energy. As one can readily see, those in a small united group would have potentially *more power than those in a much larger but fragmented group.*

Let us consider the world as a group—a group of continents, bodies of water, and most importantly, a group of people. What kind of power is it possible for this world group of people to generate?

Initially, mass awareness is beginning to take shape on an individual level. It needs to awaken people to their mutual brotherhood above and beyond regional, religious, ethnic, or cultural group differences. The largest and therefore most potentially effective group is the world group. If there are approximately four billion people on Planet Earth, then it would take a unified group of only about sixty-four thousand to effectively shift the mode of the planet in favor of that group's energy (64,000 times 64,000 equals 4,096,000,000). In the United States where there are approximately two hundred twenty-five million people, fifteen thousand persons with a unified vision would have equivalent potential power.

It is also possible to effect the necessary planetary changes through combining smaller but already aligned groups. The key is man considering himself in the broader context of a planetary being and working toward this end rather than seeing himself as only one insignificant part of a fragmented world.

The notion of people uniting for a common goal—to end the nuclear arms buildup, to pray for peace, to save a vanishing species, to end pollution—suddenly took on enormous significance. Jesus implied the existence of this power when he said, ". . . for where two or three are gathered together in my name, there am I in the midst of them." (Matthew 18:20).

This understanding of personal power dramatically shifted my definition of the word "responsibility." None of us is truly able to say that there is nothing we can do to change the problems of our world. We are, each of us, responsible for the well-being of our planet. The capability of the group power concept seemed obviously a major key to our Earth's

difficulties and possibly even to our survival, for it meant
that small numbers of people can make a difference.

Planetary Destruction or Spiritual Awareness?

✻ *The world as a group can remain a poorly integrated
and ineffective body or it can become a viable unified
group. The world group has options. It possesses the power
to manifest mammoth planetary devastation, destroying
much of Earth's life in its wake. The world group also
holds the power to creatively manifest a different reality,
a reality of spiritual awareness, each according to his own
vision. So, which will it be?*

*I can tell you that the massive nuclear holocaust that
you so fear will never become a reality because the forces
of the universe will not allow it. These forces are energy
embodiments of many realities and all are involved in the
workings of the cosmos. While the seeds of the new awareness or consciousness shift are sprouting and starting to
grow in every part of the world, nevertheless the predominant thrust of man is still toward aggressive, warlike behavior. This predisposition toward the aggressive depletes
and debilitates the body of the Earth just as surely as if
there were leeches sucking her blood. The physical and
etheric planet cannot withstand this constant bloodletting
without declining into a deeper and deeper depression.
The neutralizing of this depression, the dispelling of this
terrible pain, can result in gigantic physical changes involving every aspect of the physical Earth.*

*While the cosmic forces will not allow nuclear destruc-
tion because of cosmic consequences, they will not prevent
physical calamity from touching Earth if it is brought
about by the unwillingness of Earth's peoples to choose
an aligned path with creative forces of the universe. It is
up to Earth to choose. The creation of a spiritually attuned world can happen with or without the physical
changes which are forming in response to human indifference and negativity. If man is to turn the tide away from*

physical destruction of his planet, then the world group of which I speak has grave responsibilities. It must learn of its power as a group. It must learn to be a wise governing body. It must learn to equally orchestrate for the benefit of all. It must, in fact, learn to use its own version of personal power. It must find and use its group power and its group connection to the universe.

This world power is built from individual power just as universal power is built from world power. All group power systems blend to create a working, functioning body of total energy. The sooner the individual becomes aware of his responsibility to himself and his world group, the sooner the wars and aggression-oriented thinking will stop. What is currently neutrality will turn to all-out panic if the complacency and unaligned energies of the planet are not dealt with before it is too late.

Personal power is the issue at the very heart of the disaster crisis. For without personal power, the individual will remain frozen and inactive too long, and all will gradually slide beyond recognition into depression. With personal power, the individual and world group will slow the insidious moral and physical decline by inviting planetary awareness into their lives and openly living a broader view of their spiritual beliefs. Those of Planet Earth must become cognizant of their God-given right and responsibility to challenge the course of human evolution, making course-corrections to change the destiny of man.

There it was: the ultimate challenge of survival! Either we would discover individually who we *really* are, or we would perish from ignorance of our true connection. The primary responsibility for survival was shown to be an individual one; the secondary responsibility was that of the group, people uniting to change the course of evolution. If the "up side" seemed presumptuous or grandiose, surely the "down side" was unthinkable.

True to everything I had learned about Earth School, Mentor was saying that—except for nuclear destruction—man would have to seek his own solutions from natural disaster.

The seeds of both man's salvation and his destruction have been planted. The question was whether or not individuals and then groups would awaken in time to correct the course of the impending troubles.

I shared these passages with Jim. His comment about natural disaster was that nobody was going to believe it. "We have had plenty of people predicting the end of the Earth," he said. "Why would anyone see this as anything other than another doomsday prediction?" In response to Jim's question, I asked Mentor to explain how man's problems could manifest in Earth changes, earthquakes or any other type of disaster:

The Ionosphere: Earth's Aura

✳ *Since you have concern for truly understanding not just the metaphoric references to disaster but those ways in which metaphor can be explained on the physical level, let us look at potential disaster as a viable physical force.*

Negativity, in the form of individual thought patterns magnified many billions of times, is capable of creating a physical imbalance within the molecular structure of the ionosphere, causing a depletion of its mass density. A weakened ionosphere would allow more outer space pressure to be exerted upon the Earth's surface, drastically increasing the already existent gravitational pulls experienced by Earth. This added tension from the atmosphere could create a stronger and stronger inner pull toward the center of the Earth. Eventually the pull inward toward the Earth's inner core would become strong enough to buckle the outer crust of the planet, causing an inward collapse.

If one accepts the fact that thought patterns are the real basis of communication and that thoughts have the same power as the word, then what is being projected in thought waves, as well as words in the minds and hearts of the world's population, is the determining factor in increasing or decreasing the density of the ionosphere. This happens as thought waves color their molecular counterparts in the ionosphere through a transfer of energy. These energy transferences positively or negatively charge the ionosphere. Because this layer of Earth's atmosphere is so sensitive to energy feedback from the planet, it is a very accurate monitor of the overwhelming mental predisposition on Earth. The ionosphere exists as the Earth's aura and is easily read by other realms of the galaxy and universe, just as all developing planets can be monitored through their color-energy auras.

The ionosphere is that atmosphere which exists outside the stratosphere, beginning about sixty-five miles from Earth's surface and extending for several hundred miles out into space. It forms a protective barrier around the Earth, preserving the balance and intensity with which matter is drawn toward the Earth's surface and protecting the Earth by screening out hazardous heat, radiation and numerous toxins from the planet's surface. Earth functions smoothly as long as this nurturing atmospheric condition prevails. Destruction of this protective shield through nuclear blasts or other such mechanical means, or through the unrelenting and cumulatively overwhelming negativity in the world can cause the demise of the ionosphere and thus of Planet Earth as you know it.

You might wonder why the ionosphere has not been destroyed in the past due to the wars, atrocities and intense negativity which have existed from the beginning of man's time on Earth. Negativity or negative energy has an eroding effect on the ionosphere, and while the ionosphere was very dense ten million years ago and able to withstand the inevitable negative energy given off from a developing Earth School, nevertheless it has gradually been reduced to a critical level of density. You are now approaching a crucial time in which the density of the ionosphere has become so weakened that it is in danger of disintegrating altogether.

This thinning of the ionosphere is not happening because of poor planning for your Earth's longevity, but represents the given allotment of time for a developing world to shift from a self-orientation to a group-orientation, from pure analysis to feeling, from blindness to awareness. It is like a yo-yo attached to a cord. At first there seems an unlimited amount of cord, but as the yo-yo descends, one quite suddenly feels tension on the cord as it begins to run out, and if one is sensitive to the cord held by one hand, one senses when one is coming to the end of the cord before the end is actually reached. Just a split second before the yo-yo hits its full extension, one jerks his wrist, causing the yo-yo to bob upwards, allowing it to rewind back up to one's hand.

If the Earth is the yoyo and is fast approaching the end of its cord, who is there that is sensitive to the tension on the cord? Who is it that speaks out for what will happen if nothing is done and the Earth continues to catapult toward the end of its cord? Those with realized personal power will speak. Greater and greater numbers of people will feel the tension on the cord and will, through shared positive energy, allow the Earth to stall only temporarily before it begins its upward path toward the Ultimate Source, filled with personal and collective spiritual insight.

For those worlds where there is no one sensitively attuned to the planet's condition or where there is not sufficient positive energy to effect a change in general awareness, then the yo-yo does hit bottom, and the planet likewise is left hopelessly stranded, unable to ascend on a different path. The atmospheric protection disintegrates and all re-merges with the universe. This is the way of things. This allotment of time is different for each planet, but does exist for all.

Where, given every opportunity, man is not able to struggle out of the mire of self into the freedom of beyond self, then once again his planet fuses with the energies of the cosmos and a new Earth School is born. The ionosphere is the Earth's protection and is also the barometer of the positive and negative energy levels of the planet. The ionosphere needs to have its mass rebuilt, not further depleted, or soon there will be no more protection to give, and the Earth will have waited too long to awaken.

Jim was as astonished as I was at the many details Mentor provided in response to his request for specifics on the relationship between man's behavior and nature's reactions. We were amazed at the wealth of substantiation behind Mentor's general statements about negativity and Earth's possible natural destruction. This was just what we had hoped would be provided—facts that would undeniably link the physical world with its nonphysical counterparts in order to call attention to the energy imbalances which could lead to earth changes.

We wanted to ask for clarification of what form natural disaster might take. We had heard speculation about earth changes—land masses going beneath the sea while new masses arose from beneath the Earth's waters—but it seemed mostly speculation. What could Mentor tell us about earth changes or other natural disasters?

Earth Changes Explained

❋ *We have talked of man's development to date and his interest in only his five-senses reality. I have also told you that now the balance must shift. There must indeed be a consciousness shift in order to bring about the next stage of Earth's development.*

Quite literally, earth changes refer to any change, external or internal, on the surface or in the nature of Earth. To this extent, earth changes are perpetuated on a constant basis by natural circumstance. Of course, I realize your concern is for changes of such proportion that the planet as you know it would cease to exist. Catastrophic earth changes in the way of abrupt land shifts with some sections sinking and others rising is not as intense a possibility as disturbances and eruptions occurring around the weakest links in the planet. These disruptions would in any case occur well in advance of any massive land shift. Even less dramatic devastation is still relative, since

all forms of disruption cause heavy loss of life and prop-
erty. It is significant that an understanding of the skin of
Earth and what lies beneath the skin can help highlight
weaknesses before such earth changes could spread be-
yond the level of eruptions to a more intense level of land
upheaval. Let us begin by looking to your planet for clues
to her well-being and potential disease.

Fault lines are surface cracks, fissures or weakened ar-
eas arising from unstable in-earth conditions. The Earth's
continents are supported by massive shelves or plates of
rock. These plates are constantly in motion, grinding
against each other, causing continual change. The tur-
bulence produced from this friction translates to the
Earth's surface as fault lines. Bizarre and erratic weather
phenomena such as earthquakes, tremors and eruptions
of all sorts are most likely to be observed along these fault
lines where the tension is the greatest.

This is the purely physical explanation. There is also a
corresponding energy explanation. The approximately
twenty subterranean plates are not inanimate sections of
dead rock but in fact are alive with energy. These plates
are mirrors of the energy patterns above them on the
Earth's surface. They do not mirror just the living civili-
zations but all those which have ever existed throughout
history.

Given that energy patterns once created continue to ex-
ist within the Earth's framework until transmuted and
allowed to return to the universal stream of awareness,
then each thought lives as a "real thing" long after the
creator of the thought pattern has changed consciousness
levels. In other words, one may die, but what has been
created in the way of positive and negative thought forms
continues to live, influencing each individual continent as
well as the planet at large. Thus each plate has its own
distinct collection of energies.

For example, Agartha, look at a standard physical world
map and you will see that the North American Plate is the
land mass under your country. It is bordered to the south
by the Caribbean and Cocos Plates, to the east by the

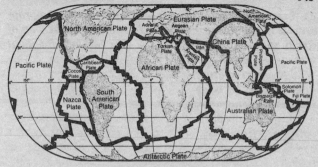

The Tectonic Plates

African and Eurasian Plates and to the west by the Pacific Plate.

The negative and positive energies which make up the North American Plate are the energies given off by the peoples living within this area. This includes:

1. The initial people who crossed to Canada across the land mass which connected North America to Europe.

2. The Atlantean civilization which was located in the approximate area of the Bermuda Islands.

3. The Central American peoples, Aztec and Mayan civilizations.

4. The early Indian cultures located in what is now the United States.

5. Emigrants from other parts of the world who came to the "new world," settling the lands of present-day America and Canada.

The individual thought patterns and actions brought into being by each of these contributing groups have accumulated to form the current-day energy of the North American Plate.

For example, Atlantean society had created a civilization of beauty and learning. They were adept at astron-

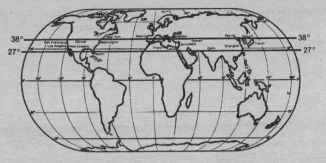

omy, astrology, geophysics, geology, medicine, psychology
and philosophy. Architecture was a highly developed science with construction following advanced space and form
concepts. They had rare and splendid gardens with much
emphasis on originality in design. However, the Atlan-
teans began to see themselves as invulnerable and in this
mind-set allowed internal preoccupation with their own
perceived superiority to weaken their connection to the
Universal, and thus the realization of their vision of great-
ness vanished and with it vanished their ability to control
their destiny.

The 27th to 38th Parallels North:
Earth's Weakest Link

✳ Fault lines are obviously the areas of greatest weakness
in the Earth's skin. However, there is a major band of
unstable energy which bisects the Earth between the 27th
and 38th parallels north. This area is the weakest collective line through the Planet and therefore the most dangerous. It is the area most susceptible to physical eruption.
If one were to draw lines through the 27th and 38th parallels north and then draw dotted lines several hundred
miles to the north and south of these original lines, one
would see that many volcanoes and earthquakes fall within
this area, certainly the ones which seem to be the biggest
potential threat, such as Mt. Aetna, Mt. Vesuvius, Mt.

Fujiyama, Mt. St. Helens and El Chieon. The dotted lines represent unstable energy radiating out from the original bands, hundreds and sometimes thousands of miles away. When an earthquake or in-earth eruption occurs, the vibrations travel along and away from the band. The distance the shock waves travel depends on the density of the Earth at those spots.

Looking again at the map, you can see that the band between the northern 27th and 38th parallels, moving from west to east includes: Midway Islands, California from San Francisco south to Los Angeles, San Diego and halfway down the Baja Peninsula, across the United States lining up on the East Coast with Washington, D.C., and south through Richmond, Raleigh, Wilmington, Charleston, Savannah, Jacksonville, Daytona Beach, Orlando, West Palm Beach and Ft. Lauderdale. Continuing east across the North Atlantic Ocean, the Bermuda Islands, Canary Islands and Azores fall within this unstable fault area. On the European Continent from slightly south of Lisbon, Portugal, to the African Continent including Casablanca, Morocco, the unstable band of energy continues through the Mediterranean to Athens, Greece and southern Turkey on the north and south through Algeria, Libya and Egypt. The fault area flows through Iraq, part of Saudi Arabia, all of Iran, Afghanistan, most of Pakistan and northern India. The northern tip of Burma is included in this unstable area, as well as central and southern China, from slightly south of Peking to south of Shanghai. Off the coast of China, the energy band continues to include all of South Korea and central Japan.

This description of plates and the danger zone between the 27th and 38th parallels north was completely new to me, but upon checking several sources I was able to pinpoint Mentor's explanations on maps. Now that we had this new information, however, what were we to do with it? Surely nobody would feel compelled to move to safer territory based on this information. The people of California proved that with their willingness to build along the San Andreas Fault. Short of an unlikely mass migration of people from these areas, what could be done about averting possible disasters? To my great relief, Mentor presented a series of meditations for use in healing the troubled areas.

Correcting In-Earth Energy Imbalances

✷ *Not all people are aware that it is possible to neutralize Earth-bound negative energy by consciously recognizing and releasing such unaligned energy, allowing it to be transmuted by the forces of the universe into a reusable form.*

Healing of fault lines can and should be undertaken by individuals and groups interested in and dedicated to the protection of Planet Earth. The most effective way to protect the Earth and increase her power is to become concerned with the healing of the major band of unstable energy between the 27th and 38th parallels north. In light of this, here are some specific meditations to be considered:

✷

In-Earth Healing Meditation for Groups

- *Sit in a circle with eyes closed.*
- *Concentrate on projecting one's own healing energy into the center of the circle, letting it merge with the healing energy present from other members of the group. (Spend at least five to ten minutes allowing maximum energy to be generated by each individual.)*
- *Arrange ahead of time to have one person begin chanting or repeating a healing mantra such as, "love heals and balances all."*
- *Stop the chanting and mentally visualize a golden or white light of combined energy from the group spiraling upwards and outwards to the specific band or fault in question. (This site should be determined ahead of time.) See the spiraling energy then descend to the physical*

plane, balancing the in-Earth energy vibrations in the designated areas.

* Each person then quietly repeats to himself, "I place my hands on the energies in this place reconciling in the name of the Universe any imbalances or imperfection

which may exist." **In-Earth Healing Meditations for Individuals**

✳
"THE ENERGY BALLOON"

* Sit in a relaxed posture with eyes closed.
* Allow your personal energy field to become expanded by visualizing your aura growing and pushing out beyond the immediate area of your physical body. It is becoming filled with cosmic power, increasing the effectiveness of each vision. Quietly center and integrate this cosmic power.
* Reflect on the thought: "There is beauty in motion, there is beauty in lack of motion, there is awareness in all things."
* Become filled with the realization that each individual may become an effective tool in the hands of God.
* Release this energy much as one would release a balloon, allowing it to peacefully drift to "the area of greatest need" or to a specifically designated location.
* Let this balloon of cosmic energy disintegrate and merge with all other loving thought descending to the physical plane at the fault site, augmenting the positive balance in the weakened area and allowing any and all imbalance to be nullified.

✳
"THE FOUNTAIN"

* Sit quietly placing your hands together, palms touching, fingers pointing upward. Raise the hands in front until your fingers are at forehead level.

- *Visualize streams of white light, pouring from each finger, falling to the ground.*
- *Ask that the cosmic energy which you are drawing be allowed to merge with the basic building structures of the Earth, eliminating all imbalance within the internal structure of the Planet and allowing the strengthening of the 27th to the 38th parallels north (or whatever specific fault line has been determined).*

Ionospheric Healing Meditation for Groups

*

"THE RHYTHM WHEEL"

- *Lie in a circle with the feet toward the center and the heads away from the center, forming a wheel.*
- *Have one person sit outside the healing circle. This individual must create a steady rhythm, such as the tapping of a hand on a drum, or similar beat. The purpose of this sound is to draw individual energies together, unifying them into one powerful force. (This should continue for at least ten minutes.)*
- *When the person outside the circle feels the concentration and energy of the group have reached a maximum level, he should stop the beat.*
- *This is each individual's signal to cause the accumulated internalized sound energy to move away from his body, moving in harmony with the elements of the air, adding to the enlightened and dynamic circle of energy which protects and nurtures Planet Earth.*

Ionospheric Healing Meditations for Individuals

✻
"THE COSMIC CURRENT"

- *Sit quietly in a relaxed position.*
- *Place your arms over your head in the shape of a circle. Sense a golden light of healing cosmic energy growing within the circle. See it become brighter and brighter as one's own healing powers are called forth.*
- *Release this energy ball by opening your arms. Project this golden energy balloon upward to the ionosphere. Allow your arms to slowly fall to a comfortable position.*
- *See the energy ball touch the ionosphere and flow into it, adding its healing energy to strengthen the world's protective body.*
- *Each should repeat to himself: "I ask that the flow of cosmic current be forever directed toward the protection of Planet Earth."*

✻
"THE FLOW"

- *Sit quietly in a relaxed position.*
- *Visualize a stream of blue energy. Let this stream represent the stream of continual life, the cosmic flow. Form the stream into a circle.*
- *Allow a sense of increased power and effectiveness to enlarge the cosmic stream.*
- *Expand this stream of energy, allowing the cosmic stream to gradually encompass the Earth.*
- *Merge the expanded energy circle with the Earth's ionosphere.*
- *Visualize the Earth and its atmosphere as one, forever connected to this ongoing flow.*
- *Focus on the increased density of the ionosphere resulting from union with the expanded positive life force energies from Earth.*

- *Allow this universal flow of all things to merge into an uninterrupted continuation of positive life-giving energy.*

Mentor never expressed emotion in our sense of the word, and yet from the detailed explanations and meditations, Jim and I knew Earth's survival was a matter of galactic significance and beyond. We were eager to begin working on these meditations to heal the planet. A number of our friends were also interested in helping, and we resolved to gather for celebrations to do what we could.

We have since learned that there are numbers of groups working on general Earth healing as well as healing specific geological disturbance areas. While we have no way of actually measuring what good we accomplish, we trust that our efforts are well served. Certainly our caring is, at least, symbolic of our positive intentions and, at the most, extremely effective. The networking of group awareness continues to increase as individuals and groups all over the world reach out to their vision and respond to that of their fellow human beings.

The crucial question is whether enough people can gain enough awareness to halt Earth's momentum toward probable disaster. While that answer is apparently unwritten, it is obvious that we are able to count on "a little help from our friends."

Will Earth Survive?

✳ *Disaster and survival need not be mutually exclusive. In all probability there will be degrees of disaster and of survival. The longer the Earth's peoples avoid making course corrections, the greater the probability for increased disaster and decreased survival. At the point where man's combined energy becomes sufficient to stem further deterioration of the planet, then disaster decreases and survival increases.*

Celestial beings from the universe at large, energies of

the nonphysical, are working toward the reality that Earth will be able to gain momentum in a reconstructive mode, harmoniously aligning its energies in order to avoid heavy bloodshed. For once set in motion, a depleted ionosphere will have its way, triggering subterranean and submarine imbalances and causing immense physical destruction.

The choice is each person's, Agartha, to use personal and group power as it can be used for the advancement of mankind or to use one's God-given potential for the destruction of mankind and the disruption of the Earth. It is the responsibility of all who are awake to make this tenuous balance known, that none may later say they did not understand all that was being held in the balance. As each person moves through each day, he must realize he is choosing not only his course but also the course of his planet. Every voice is heard and counts in this rush to understand and explain the direction in which Earth moves. The choices that are made this day will determine the planet's future or lack thereof.

The Earth has been set on a physical course. The United States has likewise followed a purely physical course, but now the physical has gone as far as it can go without cosmic perspective. As man recognizes his physical limitations, he effectively opens himself to the vision of the future, and this vision becomes the course by which he sets his standards.

Earth stretches to realize its intuitive destiny of realization of unilateral harmony. We strive, as you do, to avert excessive and needless anguish and will rejoice as the human species moves toward the pinnacle of ordained brotherhood.

CHAPTER SIX

INNER SPACE VERSUS OUTER SPACE

The innermost reaches of the soul
produce those areas of Divine contemplation
Through which the mind, body and spirit
become one.

MENTOR

AT THIS POINT in *Agartha*, it is appropriate to issue a "spiritual disclaimer." Mentor represents one person's spiritual reality. The material in this book is in no way meant to undermine that which the reader finds meaningful. I truly believe that all paths lead toward a greater whole, and it makes very little difference which one is chosen. The nature of spirituality is that it longs to be shared, and I suspect the authentic teacher shares that which is of greatest personal value, fully allowing for another to choose that which is personally applicable. There is no room for spiritual arrogance in today's world, and I think it would be highly inappropriate for me to do more than strive to do justice to the work and spirituality which has created my life anew. It is my hope that Mentor's writings may add in some way to another's knowledge.

The experience of being in direct contact with a nonphysical teacher has dramatically reshaped every detail of my life. Perhaps the most profound shift in my consciousness has been at the level of faith. I have exchanged the experience of doubt and speculation about the existence of the nonphysical world for the state of absolute certainty. This is not meant to imply, by any means, that I know all there is to know about the nonphysical world. I do emphatically state, however, that I no longer doubt the existence of life beyond this reality. I simply know that consciousness is immortal and that we continue to evolve well beyond the human experience.

For reasons which are more than obvious, I have often publicly presented information from Mentor as theoretical material, without stating the source of the information. But within the context of this book, I feel it necessary to credit the source and to add my spiritual disclaimer. I am one of a number of individuals with whom an open channel to the nonphysical world has been established. Further, not a person on earth exists who does not, in fact, have a nonphysical teacher. While I am incapable of proving this to the reader, it is enough for me that I at least issue that as a statement of fact.

Inside-Outside: The Two-Way Mirror

＊*There are inner and outer worlds existing concomitantly within all levels of the universe from the microscopic to the macroscopic. To every element there is an inner nature and an outer nature. The outside is but an expansion of the inside, and the inside mirrors the nature of the outside. Both are outreaches of understanding, measured by their poles of existence.*

In becoming aware of the nature of any living element or combination of elements, several thoughts bear understanding: namely, that which is on the inside is as alive and viable as that which is more obviously on the outside; and that the internal and external are always held in a unique balance appropriate to the completion of an organism's designated function and thought processes. Also, whatever tangible or intangible expression is applied to one must also be applied to the other.

The human body exists as the sum of its component systems, organs, tissues, unit patterns and cells. It is fluid, solid and gaseous. Looking to the tiniest building blocks of the body, one sees that the body's subatomic, atomic and molecular particles are as responsive and as alive as the outside vision of the physical body. Internal and external live and function in relation to their own separateness as well as in relation to their combined function.

This is not a new concept, but it is important, if one is looking for wholeness in body and mind, to think of the internal and external as both separate and unified into a functioning whole. For example, the human body is a myriad of smaller divisions, each living within its own world of separateness and wholeness. By the time the body has been reduced to its most basic elements, one has laid open an incredibly beautiful and intricate system of multilevel cooperation, one which exists on the most basic of intercellular levels as well as on the most advanced levels of human wholeness.

Thus in searching for the total being, in health and awareness, it is essential to see the interrelatedness of inner and outer spaces. Wholeness comes as a result of recognizing the interrelation of all planes of being: internal physical, external physical, etheric, astral and mental.

There is a balance between the inner and outer levels of creation. Each organism and substance holds tenaciously to the fulfillment of its unique purpose. Just as the salmon single-mindedly seeks return to the waters of its original spawning ground, so the evening grosbeak wings its way south and then north in response to its own migratory beacon. The outer and inner worlds conform to fulfill purpose, and with oversized gills and strong wings, the outer adapts to balance the inner. This balance is seen throughout the physical kingdom. Just as the hair-like cells of the inner ear of man function according to their nature of vibrational sensor and transmitter, so the total physical body seeks to balance and complement the sounds which are brought into its presence.

The term balance means to weigh sides equally so that any substance may be held in a state of equalization. Inner space and outer space seek balance. The cell within the body seeks equilibrium just as the conscious mind seeks a centered state. This is the natural flow exerting itself. As the inner voice calls to the outer physical presence, so the external physical contributes to the harmony within. What is not maintained in balance rolls as a lopsided wheel, music without sound or animation without movement. Balance is the perfect reflection of the opposing outside and yet complementary forces of the inside and out, the yin and yang. Without harmony and balance there is only cacophony and disease.

Poetically speaking, Mentor's statements about the balance of inner and outer made sense, but it seemed so theoretical. I asked for further clarification of his metaphors:

Equal Application of Expression

✳ *Whatever expression, be it thought or action, that is applied to one half of the whole must also be applied in like measure to the other half. The child who cries for attention must have his needs met on the external as well as on the internal level. The cookie given with a reassuring hug nourishes twofold. Inadvertently, the child has been given solace on the psychological as well as on the physical level. The mother intuitively senses that the child is asking for more than the obvious and responds by appropriately nourishing the body and mind simultaneously.*

Taken one step further to the plant kingdom—why do some people's plants die and other's flourish when given exactly the same physical diet? Here again, plants flourish when simultaneously nourished with loving thoughts while being fed with nutrients. This is another appropriate application of energy to both aspects of a whole.

Because the true whole is a perfect balance of all the layers of the human body and psyche, it becomes important to seek the balancing of every aspect of one's life, for to stop short of complete recognition of thought, action and experience is to settle for an imbalance and potential debilitation.

In wanting to be healthy, happy and physically successful at life, it is important to see these aspects of life as
part of the human body and mind which are in turn all
parts of the greater whole. To change one part of this
whole requires a like change in its balance. For example,
to take a new job without examining the reasons for unhappiness in the old one is only to recognize one side of
the whole. The understanding of one's anxiety, anger or
frustration in the first job allows the second to be chosen
with an eye toward potential balance. This is wholeness,
knowing within oneself that a happier, more satisfying
reality can be chosen and lived.

The purely mechanical means of treating dis-ease in the
western world have gradually risen to the forefront of
medicine as cure-alls for whatever ails the body and mind
of man. Stores and hospitals are filled with convenient and
immediate treatments which advertise their guarantees of
success. Yet a rebellion has rightfully gained momentum
as the individual instinctively moves toward a sense of
wholeness and multi-level treatment, rejecting treatment
which is only physical. It has never been enough to treat
the symptoms of the condition and ignore the other less
visible aspects of the person which may have produced the
dysfunction.

Successful cures most frequently deal with more than a
single phase of the whole. What is suppressed and not
examined or fully understood finds form in but another
disease, problem or threat to one's well-being. The mechanical means at one's disposal should instead be used
to "talk" to the wisdom of the body, while the contem-
plative means of understanding are simultaneously "applied" to feed the spirit and emotions. In the past,
medicines such as herbs, packs, potions, tinctures and the
like were used simultaneously with healing thoughts,
prayers and meditations. It would have been inconceivable
to use one without the other and expect results. Most
modern medicines, as well as many home remedies, fall
short of their potential value when only the mechanical
manipulation of the body is sought, for one's power of the

whole crosses all lines, heals all wounds, sorts out all misinformation and inappropriate data.

It is the job of the healing practitioner to find and expose the mystery of the disease to the best of his ability—physiologically, emotionally, and spiritually—sharing the results in a loving atmosphere in order that the patient may appropriately choose the parts to his own whole. There is no substitute for patient responsibility in the act of healing. True healing is not overriding another's wishes, even with the best of intentions, but reflecting the patient's wishes in a positive, supportive mode. This is the process of healing that appropriately promotes health on all levels of consciousness.

I felt that I had been given only a glimpse of this parallel world of nonphysical laws operating harmoniously and simultaneously with the physical world. Mentor was touching on the physical nature of a healthy life, and this was the underlying question I had asked for so long—what were the unseen influences affecting and creating pain and trauma in one's life?

The Nature of Vibration: Positivity and Negativity

❋ *What of the very nature of influencing the whole? If there is a need for ministering to both sides of the whole, then what form does that ministering take? What actually happens when one tries to apply more than mechanical stimulation to a problem? On one level it is enough to talk of concepts, such as love and understanding, awareness and enlightenment, but on another it becomes necessary to appreciate what is the actual basis through which human interaction affects the physical body.*

Let us begin by understanding that there are positive and negative vibrations given off by all actions and thoughts. All peoples are besieged through their waking hours with various degrees of negative and positive input, both of their own making and from others.

While there is no right or wrong, there certainly are gradients of nourishing and productive as well as of barren and unfulfilling. "Positive energy" lives as the force of all loving and Divinely-aligned thinking. It is the force that generates balance within all aspects of life. "Negative energy" is the opposite; it is the alien, the unnurturing, the destructive and unaligned energy. If one wishes to increase the positive input and decrease the negative, an understanding of what causes each vibration is essential.

A "vibration" is the condition resulting from an object's becoming forced out of balance or away from its static equilibrium. Vibrations are sensed, touched, felt, heard and seen. One's response to vibration can be voluntary or involuntary. One can choose to hear a song or choose not to consciously hear the very same song. But if the song is playing, it is nevertheless heard on an involuntary level. This involuntary absorption is what we are concerned with here. The body absorbs voluntarily and involuntarily all that it produces and translates as well as all that surrounds it. Indiscriminately, it pulls in and tries to assimilate all that it contacts. If red paint instead of blood surrounded a living cell, the cell would struggle to interact with the paint even though it caused its own death.

Every interaction with another person produces a myriad of vibrations, from the trivial greeting to the in-depth conversation, from the chance remark to the deliberate statement. All encounters produce waves of vibration, either positive and productive or negative and destructive. All input is absorbed and processed by the body.

How outside stimuli are processed as positive or negative energy depends not only on the sender's original intent but also on one's own interpretation. This interpretation is of course based on one's current outlook, one's mental and physical health and disposition, and one's hereditary and environmental programming. The interpretation may or may not be accurate, but it nonetheless is seen by the individual as real. Each creates his own environment of positive and negative vibration not only through what is thought and interpreted within the psyche, but also as that which results from interplay be-tween the physical five senses.

What is seen, touched, eaten, heard and smelled pro-vides the body with a combination of either positive or negative energy. For example, clothing which is only of synthetic fibers tends to be less supportive of the health of the body than that which is of a natural fiber. This means that one receives negative energy from many of the clothes one wears. Natural fibers are of the Earth's vibration and therefore tend to be compatible with the human vibration which is also of the Earth. On the other hand, acetate and polyester are manufactured in the laboratory and there-fore are not naturally compatible with the human form. Realize that all these influences on the body are subtle but in total, influence one's state of health. Different clothes are appropriate for different people, but where the body 9intuitively resists being put in a particular material or blend, realize that that is more than whim. It is body wis-dom surfacing into conscious thought.

Food which is mainly chemical in nature, synthetic and filled with non-nutritious elements is unhealthy for the body. Here again, the body is continually exposed to an invisible source of negative input through substances which only partially break down within the body, causing near-starvation of bodily tissues as well as poisoning the body with chemicals, additives and preservatives. Recog-nition of the vibrations transferred to a food or food prod-uct while in the growing stage is also extremely important. What negativity is infused into the life of plant or animal while growing and during the picking or slaughtering is all passed along to the individual who eats it. Just because negative vibrations are not seen by most people does not mean they do not exist. The potential boon to mankind is enormous as each family assumes responsibility for not only their external actions but also the internal environ-ment they create.

As I read Mentor's description of positive and negative vibrations, I realized that he still had not answered the basic question sufficiently: what makes positive energy good for people and what makes negative energy non-nurturing? It was important to know about the effects of positivity and negativity of people, clothes, food and other natural substances, but just what was the "stuff" of negativity and positivity?

✻ *Vibratory waves pass in and through the body in ceaseless rhythm. As waves of positive energy flow through the body and brain, they heal and ameliorate disease and dysfunction wherever it is found, tending to cleanse and attune internally and externally through alignment of all the bodily energies. Positive energy does not remain within the body. It is used and then dispensed into the atmosphere after working its way through the body.*

Negative vibration, on the other hand, because of the denseness of its nature and its incompatability with the human wavelength, becomes caught within the body's fibers. Acute disease occurs when a large influx of negative vibration is drawn to a particular organ. Organic response to such a massive buildup is disease, dysfunction and gradual death. A chronic disease can be likened to a magnet placed in a dish of metal filings. The metal filings become pulled to the magnet just as negative impulses are drawn to a part of the body. Wherever negativity becomes entrenched, it, in turn, becomes a new magnet attracting new negativity until the circuit is broken. In the chronic condition, one is dealing with a negative vibration which continues to attract and attach to new negativity, causing an ever-enlarging chain of dysfunction.

If negative energy could be stained with a dye and put on a slide to be studied under a microscope, it would be seen as a cross section of fibrous material, incompatible with and foreign to human life because of its intensely condensed form and impenetrable nature. If studied further, it would be seen that negative vibration holds not the slightest degree of usable energy for the human body. Its structure allows but a slow entombment of the physical being. No nurturing or nourishment can be brought forth from this vibration. Negative vibration is cumulatively collected within the body until physical cells begin to suffocate. This, man calls the "natural aging process."

There is no "cure," no way to totally remove oneself from negative influence. There is only constant monitoring, course correction and also cleansing of one's body and mind in order to dislodge and eliminate the unwanted density of the negative energy.

Stress

Interestingly, the general physical reality of taking on negative vibration has become generally accepted and is described clinically in the word "stress." Stress through work, stress through personal relationship or stress through general interaction is really the acceptance of overwhelming negative energy into one's body without the countering balance of cleansing. While stress is widely recognized as a major factor in heart attacks and heart disease, I would like to suggest that stress is equally contributory to dysfunction on all bodily levels. Stress, in relation to heart disease, has been studied the most because of the high toll of deaths each year from this little-understood state. Hopefully, equal attention will soon be directed toward the understanding of stress in relation to the rest of the body and mind, for it plays a significant role in causing deterioration of the physical presence as well as debilitation of the thought processes which are necessary for clearing it.

As it becomes more and more obvious that "stress" is just a euphemism for the ingestion and creation of negative vibration, then each individual will perhaps decide he owes it to himself to take notice of what has been previously dismissed as metaphor.

"Positive" and "negative" are words signifying intent of purpose as well as degree of fulfillment. Consciously and unconsciously, people have a positive or negative intent when interacting with one another. One wishes an-

*other well or wishes another harm, or wishes them any
one of a hundred gradations in between. But, in addition
to being on the giving end of positive and negative vibration, each person is also on the receiving end in every
interchange. Each thought registers within the physical
body. The degree of positive and negative vibration which
finds its way into the body determines whether a malfunc-
tion is temporary or permanent.*

*Negative and positive energy affect every aspect of the
human being, every action and thought. The identification
of what produces the positivity and negativity provides a
personal crossroads, for if this knowledge is accessible and
is believed to be true then the question becomes: is one
willing or able to change and integrate such creative new
information?*

*Choices, there always seem to be choices. Life and be-
yond life is indeed a series of unending choices, all of
which more finely tune one's path. The knowledge that a
certain food or thought or circumstance produces tangible
negativity theoretically should allow the individual to walk
in the opposite direction, being healthier and happier because of this simple identification. One no longer needs to
suffer the slow atrophying of body and mind into disease
and unhappiness. Understanding stress and the natural
aging process in terms of tangible positive and negative
energy patterns provides one more tool in becoming, always becoming the perfect whole.*

Negativity had seemed such a vague term until Mentor's
remark about physical aging occurring as the result of accumulated negativity. It was easy to imagine negativity causing stress or even disease, but it was a wholly unique thought
that aging was the cumulative effect of unprocessed negative
energy.

Even as I read about the insidious effects of negativity, I
was reminded of many negative situations, often of my own
doing, that might have contributed to my own aging process.
I felt uneasy just recalling the possible impact of my words
of anger, both spoken and unspoken. "Love thy neighbor"

suddenly assumed significance in terms of health in addition to its worth as a standard of everyday harmonious living. I felt compelled to ask Mentor what we could do to rid ourselves of negativity:

Cleansing Through Visualization and Harmonics

✳ *Just as one takes a shower to cleanse the outside of the body, likewise one may take an inner shower to literally wash away all undesirable negative vibration. This inner cleansing can be done in a variety of ways, but I wish to concentrate on the two simplest and most effective means: visualization and harmonics. Both of these techniques are effective preparation for meditation or prayer and should rightfully be used to cleanse and align body and mind.*

Visualization is the creation of a viable mental picture representative of one's current state and the state one seeks to achieve. For example, a person suffering from scoliosis (curvature of the spine) would create a visualization around a mental picture of a beautifully straight or appropriately curved spine. Visualization is an intense tool because, as simple as it seems, its effectiveness in adjusting the program and actual physical functioning of the body is unequalled. The conscious mind and subsequently the conscious body become aware through visualization of the potential perfect functioning of an organ and can then see what has to be changed to create that condition. The body often allows disease to exist by failing to recognize a condition as untenable, maybe even life-threatening, until suddenly the disease arrives full-blown in the physical. Visualization helps the patient crystallize his own conception of his condition, be it minimal, moderate or severe. This crystallization increases the body's awareness, thus pictorially plugging in awareness of the ongoing physical and mental picture and altering the current physical condition in favor of the desired outcome.

Along with visualization, an understanding of color is helpful in arriving at the most specific explanation possi-

ble of one's total well-being. Color is a diagnostic as well as a therapeutic tool. What colors an individual sees when quietly sitting with his eyes closed are significant in defining his current mental and physical condition. Different colors are seen in dreams, daydreams and meditations and represent one's physical, emotional and spiritual condition. The colors one sees can also be the tools the body and mind suggest to change an already existing condition. In other words, one may see a color as the result of a current condition or as the means to eliminate that condition.

Visualization can be used effectively by the allopathic and holistic physician to further intensify and integrate treatment. While less traditional forms of healing use color as a diagnostic and therapeutic tool, traditional medicine is currently also using visualization to increase the effectiveness of chemotherapy and radiation, reaffirming the premise that the degree of mind and body working together can augment or retard even traditional chemical treatment.

Visualizations for Cleansing and Balancing the Body

✳ While practicing the following two visualizations, one should try to be aware of the different colors which play in and out of one's quiet times and draw one's own conclusions about which colors correspond to which of one's own moods, physical condition, and the play of outside circumstance. No two people's responses will be exactly alike.

✳

"SHOWER OF COLOR"

Colors used: Black—representative of disease
              Yellow—representative of replenishment
                        as in the sun's energy

Mentally place your body under a shower. See the gentle drops of water pouring down over your body as special cleansing agents capable of washing away all dirt, all disease, all negativity. Let the water wash gently over the body, knowing that all imperfectness of any kind is being removed. Creatively elaborate with color or sound to appropriately personalize this visualization. If a visualization does not feel "right," change the details until it fits what is felt. Visualizations are only as effective as the personal contours they define.

✳

"EXPANDING COLOR CIRCLE"

Colors used: Green—dynamic physical growth
Orange—integration of physical and spiritual

Picture a green or orange circle over the area of your solar plexus (this is the area four inches below the heart or slightly above the umbilicus). If you have difficulty picturing a particular color, you can substitute another color which just appears in your vision, or picture a familiar object which has the desired color and then transfer the color to the designated space. Here, for example, the representation of a green apple could be used.

For this exercise, mentally look in the mirror at your own body, placing a green or orange circle over the area of the solar plexus. Watch the circle begin to gently revolve, turning around and around, gradually expanding in size and becoming a beautiful spiral. Let the size of the spiral increase as it goes around until it is large enough to encompass one's feet and head in the same circle. Simultaneously think of this expanding circle or spiral as expanding your horizons in order that appropriate awareness and information relative to your own life will be seen and known. This is the expansion stage.

Then, once the circle/spiral has reached the size where it has encompassed the head and feet, let it gradually

COLOR, HARMONICS AND THE HUMAN BEING

Color & Its Properties	Musical Notes	Primary Organs/ Systems	Personal Characteristics
RED Intense love, anger, abrupt change in the sense of life and death.	C	Heart and Circulatory System	Universal in nature, nurturing, one who sustains. Highly motivated with strong potential for physical success and spiritual achievement. Arbitrator, one who seeks harmony and balance and has the potential for the balancing of yin and yang energies.
ORANGE Vitality, integration of dynamic physical and spiritual change, increased personal power and ability to approach new understanding.	D	Liver, gallbladder, pancreas, muscular system	Prone toward exploration yet often plagued by self doubts. Sees "divine" possibilities for people and circumstances but needs to seek the appropriate vehicles for successful fulfillment. Can be caught in periods of depression, often seeking the comfort of like-minded people. A very strong group participant who can successfully develop into group leadership. Personal life may not be completely happy until one finds a means of identifying and combining divergent aspects of life.
YELLOW Intellectual orientation, pragmatic, competence through analysis, replenishment through the sun's energy.	F	Brain and nervous system	One who tends to initiate, dominant energy but not abrasive. An achiever. One who is motivated initially by the external to later discover that there is a deep connection to the internal.
GREEN Revitalization and healing of physical body. Strength from connection to plant kingdom.	G	Esophagus, stomach, small and large intestines, skeletal system, reproductive organs.	One who is drawn to life and the living process. One who is nourished by being outside or in an outside job. The spiritual quest comes easily to this person, usually through an initial experience of physical dysfunction. One who is sought after by groups, especially well-defined ones which emphasize higher ideals.

Color & Its Properties	Musical Notes	Primary Organs/ Systems	Personal Characteristics
BLUE Peace, serenity, calmness, passivity in pursuit of goal, susceptibility to spiritual development.	B	Lungs	One who eases tensions and brings calmness and tranquility to people and situations. A strong potential for spiritual development with the impetus coming from a transformative experience. One who is often swayed by others' opinions and will be initially enticed into less than fulfilling situations. However, the path of the heart will prevail and a truer path will be chosen.
INDIGO Spiritual desire, intuitive, sense of needing to search even though it requires difficult personal decisions.	A	Spleen, lymphatics, thyroid, kidneys, pituitary, adrenal glands	One who leans heavily toward the spiritual, often leading to the monastic life. Balanced but drawn into situations where personal power and magnetism can cause a change in a situation involving higher moral codes. Often is seen as distant or aloof, but this is merely a protection from the intensity with which situations are experienced.
VIOLET Advanced spiritual development, extreme awareness. Integration of physical, emotional and spiritual.	E	Spinal cord, pineal body	Universal Note, harmony of purpose aligned with physical endeavor. Total awareness of physical body in relation to higher levels of consciousness. This energy is a perfect balance to whatever energy it contacts.

shrink in size until it approaches its original size. This is the integration stage. Mentally you should suggest to yourself that all newly found information and intuitive insight that has come into your consciousness may be allowed to become integrated with your physical, emotional

*and spiritual bodies to change, correct and improve your
total self.*

*What is suggested to oneself during visualization actu-
ally creates that impulse on many wavelengths, cosmically
and physically, and your whole presence is then potentially open to change. This kind of cleansing is imperative
if you are to keep yourself free of disease. This should be
done at least once a day. While the negativity may not
actually be seen with one's eyes, rest assured that it is
indeed being removed as per your instructions. Do not let
the power of the unseen wavelength be underestimated.*

*For the individual who has difficulty with visualizing,
there is another equally appropriate and effective approach to cleansing. This involves the use of sound as a
stimulating and balancing agent in order that imperfection and negative vibration can be loosened and allowed
to fall away from the body. In other words, the person
comes to know the sounds to which his body most perfectly
resonates, and he then duplicates the sound when seeking
health and wholeness.*

*There are three notes on the standard major scale
which are of special importance. First, understand that
a major scale consists of seven notes or an octave of eight
notes and goes sequentially: C-D-E-F-G-A-B-C. We are
specifically considering the A immediately above middle C
with a pitch of 450 vibrations per second. While there
is often discrepancy over which pitch is applicable, nevertheless this elevated pitch of 450 vibrations per second is
appropriate for our use. The identification of one's personal
three notes gives the individual one more means of triangulating on and reinforcing the physical with the cosmic.*

*1. Universal E: E Major is the universal note and is a
necessary part of each musical triad or three note combination. This note harmoniously aligns the body's purpose
and being with the Divine Forces of the universe. It is
present in every person's triad.*

*2. Personal Note: The second note of the triad is the
personal aspect of the triad. One note from the scale must*

be picked as one's personal note. The note can be psychically selected for an individual, or the individual can listen to a simple scale and pick the note (other than E) to which he is the most drawn. Another way to find one's personal note is through the reading of the color/harmonics chart I have provided in order to see which characteristics most accurately fit one's own nature and to assist in the selection of the corresponding musical note.

3. *Catalyst Note:* The third note of the triad is the catalyst note. This note unites and intensifies the personal note with the Universal E and is the full note immediately above the personal note. For example, if the personal note were G, then the catalyst note would be A. This triad would then be E-G-A. The catalyst subtly completes the two tones into a meaningful inner harmony. The combined sound of all three notes may take getting used to, however, since modern man is not used to considering sequential notes as harmonious.

Let us take another example, Agartha. Let us use your note of C. C is your personal note. Combined with Universal E and the catlayst note of D, which is the full note above C, your triad is E-C-D. Realize that your note can change as you grow into different stages of awareness and that variations and refinements of a note are possible as you work with and through each note of your own triad. There is potentially perfect fulfillment, health and joy within the realization of each complete triad. The sound of the note should be listened to and then imitated. Since sound is vibration, a natural state of resonance is already at work within one's body when one hums a note. The sound should be allowed to completely permeate the body, filling it with vibrations at times of prayer and meditation as well as at times of relaxation.

An Exercise Using Harmonic Vibration

Allow your mind to become quiet. Hum your personal note or listen to the repeated sound of your note, notes or triad being played, hummed or sung. Let the sound permeate your physical and emotional bodies with its purity. You may experience a feeling of separation from the physical body, of removal from the purely physical. When this state of beyond the physical is felt, allow the mind to suggest that all disease, fear, anxiety or imperfection of any kind be eliminated from the body. Use this cue to feel the body cleansed with the pure vibrations of your note or triad. As the vibration is given permission to cleanse, heal and exist within the body, it will become a permanent memory from which you can always draw. Since the body is vibration, the matching of one's vibration to the healing and cleansing sounds of one's triad vibration enables one's whole presence to seek a different, purer level of identification by exposing the body to a more powerful set of personal harmonics which lead to wholeness and ultimate life.

The intricate interrelationship between colors, musical notes and the organs and emotions of the human being opened yet another avenue through which to explore the human experience. Mentor had said that the human organism (and all other organisms) are actually vibratory in nature. It seemed logical to consider human organs and states of emotion resonating to the vibrations of specific colors or sounds.

A friend of mine who had practiced yoga for many years introduced me to the nonphysical energy centers of the body called chakras. She frequently referred to energy blockages in one or more of the chakras, explaining how these blockages could be opened through various visualization exercises. I asked Mentor to explain the chakra system and its function in processing the body energy:

Beyond Basic Cleansing: The Chakras

We have seen how the human body is responsive to its surroundings through the internalization and creation of negative and positive energy. We have discussed the use of visualization and harmonics as tools for maintaining a high level of wellness through the flushing of negativity and disease. Keeping this wellness goal in mind, let us take a look at the seven major chakras or energy centers of the human body, since they exist as centers through which one can monitor personal levels of emotional, psychological, physical and spiritual health.

"Chakra" is a Sanskrit word meaning "wheel" and is usually interpreted as a circular or psychic (soul) energy vortex through which universal energy travels. These circular energy centers are located in the nonphysical body in close proximity to the physical spinal cord. Chakras are the interface between the physical and nonphysical aspects of one's being, mirroring the cosmic energy which passes through each disc. Chakras reflect the colors and vibrations which are unique to each, much as a stained glass window reflects the colors in its design when held to the light. There are seven major chakras and many minor chakras in the body. Each major chakra reflects one's own perceptions and belief patterns; in other words, what one believes to be true about oneself. While there is always a blend of energies interacting at the level of each chakra, the primary source of incoming energy is cosmic in nature and enters the body through the head or crown chakra. While I have shown the chakras existing in a straight line, there may actually be some variation with the actual location, especially with the third and fourth chakras, which are often seen to the left of the individual's spinal column.

The degree of energy allowed to interact with each chakra (the openness of each chakra) influences not only the health of the organs in that general vicinity but also is reflective of the broader attunement of body, mind and spirit. Chakras become obstructed whenever one's day-to-day life is not supportive of one's cosmic potential, and

Energy Fields and Major Chakras

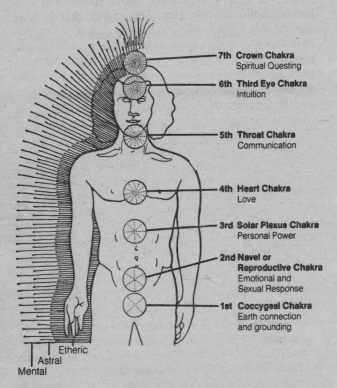

7th Crown Chakra
Spiritual Questing

6th Third Eye Chakra
Intuition

5th Throat Chakra
Communication

4th Heart Chakra
Love

3rd Solar Plexus Chakra
Personal Power

**2nd Navel or
Reproductive Chakra**
Emotional and
Sexual Response

1st Coccygeal Chakra
Earth connection
and grounding

Etheric
Astral
Mental

therefore a duality exists which registers as fear, insecurity, loneliness or other unproductive emotions. Repression or deviation from one's cosmic nature allows only partial use of one's chakras, meaning the individual's full physical, psychological and spiritual potential remains unrealized. So let us look at each chakra, seeing what physical organs and what emotional and/or spiritual issues are affected.

- *The seventh chakra, or crown chakra, is located at the top of the head and exists as the entry point for the blend* of energies which flow through the body. This blend includes the etheric (physical), astral (emotional) and mental (spiritual) energies. The energy that is seen around this seventh chakra is reflective of the individual's interest and adeptness in seeking answers to the greater spiritual questing issues of life. On a physical level, general nerve and cerebral function is affected by the energy in this area.

- The sixth chakra, or chakra of intuition, is the chakra of the "third eye." It is the seat of spiritual intuition. Energy in this area is indicative of one's intuitive prowess and also of one's conscious awareness and use of intuition in one's life. One can either use one's intuition as a tool of spiritual insight or as purely a psychic asset. It should be remembered that the aliveness in this chakra affects all the other chakras as indirectly as the head affects the body's functioning or as one's spiritual adeptness affects the course of one's life. This chakra is located between and slightly above the eyebrows, and affects the following physical function: the pituitary gland, pineal body, general spinal cord and endocrine system activity as well as eyes, nose, ears and sinuses.

- The fifth chakra is known as the throat chakra and influences the mouth, vocal cords, trachea, esophagus, thyroid and parathyroid glands as well as general skeletal activity and the cervical vertebrae. This chakra is usually seen as important in reflecting the ease with which one communicates with others as well as one's ability to consciously recognize one's own needs.

- The fourth chakra reflects heart energy and is located in the area of the heart. It is important in reflecting the health of the heart, ribs, lungs, bronchial tubes, breasts, diaphragm, major circulatory and respiratory function, general muscular activity and thoracic vertebrae. This chakra gives an indication of the importance of love in one's life and the degree to which this is currently being met.

- The third chakra is in the area of the solar plexus and influences most of the major organs of purification and digestion, including liver, gall bladder, stomach, pancreas, spleen and lymphatic system, kidneys, adrenal glands, lumbar vertebrae and general digestive systems. This chakra indicates the amount of "personal power" one sees himself possessing. The energy flowing in and around this chakra suggests whether or not one has a strong sense of himself in relation to other people and whether or not one feels comfortable and in control of one's life or rather threatened by life's interactions.

- The second chakra, or navel chakra, is the chakra of emotion and sexuality and is located in the region of the reproductive organs, bladder, small and large intestines, appendix, lumbar vertebrae and general reproductive and excretory function. This chakra is situated slightly below the umbilicus. The energy in this area reflects the degree to which one is either positively or negatively involved with life through emotional or sexual response and whether one draws unduly from either emotional or sexual energy.

- The first chakra, or coccygeal chakra, is located at the tip of the spine and functions as an indication of a person's "groundedness" or ability to link with the earth and function effectively on a day-to-day basis. The lower spinal column including the coccyx and sacrum as well as the external orifices of excretion are affected by this chakra.

Tracing the Energy of Life

The blend of energy appears in the etheric body as a filmy white, grey or purplish cascade. Many other colors are created around each chakra in reflecting the specific condition within each of these areas. There are specific colors and energy patterns to each chakra which must be learned before it becomes clear if something other than *normal function and growth are present. Energy enters the body through the top of the head or crown chakra and continues through the major chakras radiating out through the body as well as down the torso, gradually working its way into the arms, legs, fingers, toes and then off into the atmosphere to be recharged and recycled. This recycled energy then merges with cosmic energy as it again prepares to enter the body through the crown chakra.*

The energy within the body is constantly being replenished, but its density, mass, tone and color depend on the quality of the individual's life and the circumstances, short and long range, within that individual's life. A buildup or breakdown in any of man's emotional, spiritual or physical parts is reflected in one or more of the energy fields. The ability to regenerate a depleted energy field depends on an individual's willingness and ability to recognize a problem and adjust or change whatever existing behavior is causing or adding to a disease or general dis-ease in order that a potentially more harmonious behavior may be adopted.

It is often difficult to think of a nonphysical field of energy as playing a part in physical health. To this end, let us examine a specific case in order to more clearly illustrate the connection between the physical body and the various energy fields.

Case History of John

John was a forty-year-old production foreman in an automobile plant. He had worked in industry all his life and was considered a rather quiet but seemingly well-adjusted and well-liked worker. After celebrating his twenty year anniversary with the company, John's attitude subtly began to change. His once gentle, resilient nature became more aggressive, apparently filled with frustration and resentment. Friends and family were puzzled by the irrational outbursts of anger and the sarcasm and criticism which became more and more a part of his conversation.

Simultaneously with these overt changes, John developed what appeared to be an ordinary cold and a case of
laryngitis. The cold gradually disappeared but the laryngitis
continued. John's voice remained weak and unable to last
through a day's work. His condition was diagnosed by the
plant physician as chronic laryngitis, and it was felt that
this might be due to the dust and debris which he breathed
all day at work. He was given a tranquilizer and told the
condition would probably improve if he wore a protective
face mask. However, the condition did not improve.

Let us take a closer look and see what John's energy
field looks like at this moment in his life. (Refer to the
diagram of John's energy field as you read this section.)

The energy coming through John's crown chakra is
quite substantial, suggesting that he is feeling a strong pull
(consciously and unconsciously) toward exploring the more
profound issues of his life. This is triggering a need to look
beyond his physical life of job and family to integrate his
early religious training with his current belief patterns.
But perhaps his conceptualization of religious interaction
has never grown beyond his early days of Sunday school.
Religion to John is static, rather than a living, evolving
sense of the God within and the God without. Since this is
true, the question then becomes: does John have or will he
seek a framework, a conscious emotional support system,
within which he can dare to mature spiritually? The ample
energy in this chakra suggests that he had better begin to
make allowance for these deep needs or the already established duality between the physical and the nonphysical
could very well develop into a more traumatic condition
than laryngitis, for repression of emerging needs can result
in further physical and psychological dysfunction.

Notice how the energy diminishes as it moves through
the sixth chakra. Yet there is still sufficient energy to suggest that John is by nature a very intuitive person. Perhaps
this strong intuition is causing him ever-increasing difficulty in making decisions at home and on the job. John
believes that intuition is only a feminine quality. He is a
staunch believer in role play, and he is having trouble

Case History of John

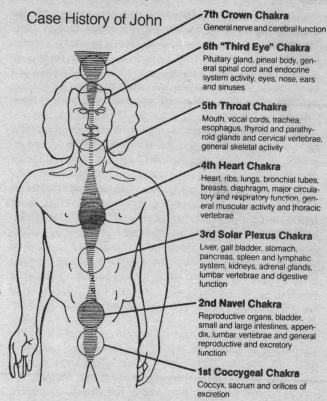

7th Crown Chakra
General nerve and cerebral function

6th "Third Eye" Chakra
Pituitary gland, pineal body, general spinal cord and endocrine system activity, eyes, nose, ears and sinuses

5th Throat Chakra
Mouth, vocal cords, trachea, esophagus, thyroid and parathyroid glands and cervical vertebrae, general skeletal activity

4th Heart Chakra
Heart, ribs, lungs, bronchial tubes, breasts, diaphragm, major circulatory and respiratory function, general muscular activity and thoracic vertebrae

3rd Solar Plexus Chakra
Liver, gall bladder, stomach, pancreas, spleen and lymphatic system, kidneys, adrenal glands, lumbar vertebrae and digestive function

2nd Navel Chakra
Reproductive organs, bladder, small and large intestines, appendix, lumbar vertebrae and general reproductive and excretory function

1st Coccygeal Chakra
Coccyx, sacrum and orifices of excretion

reconciling the surfacing spiritual intuitive skills and accompanying insights with his belief in the strict role model existence he has chosen to live.

The energy leaving the sixth chakra becomes drastically compressed and dissipated as it approaches the fifth chakra. Communication and conscious identification of what John feels is obviously a problem. He has not begun to recognize or sort out his feelings, since his strong belief in traditional roles suggests that men should not talk about their feelings. The undeniable upsurge of energy in the crown chakra, the need to reevaluate and integrate his life into a meaningful reality, scares him because he does not understand it. He is unconsciously fearful that in communicating his fears and lack of clear-cut answers about spirituality, he will be seen by others as weak. Talking or sharing this becomes a painful and threatening experience in which he feels vulnerable and open to potential ridicule and rejection; thus the use of aggressive behavior to compensate for his feelings of vulnerability and confusion.

The stream of cosmic energy gradually enlarges and expands again as it approaches the heart chakra. This suggests that John is concerned with loving and being loved, and since he finds the fulfillment of this need inherently compatible with his belief system of male/female relationships, he has no trouble acting on this part of his belief structure. The high level of energy in the heart area also indicates a need to find and maintain a nurturing, satisfying love relationship beyond the physical. John, no doubt, feels relief at being able to openly release emotion into the acceptable and sanctioned channel of loving a mate. Thus loving becomes a source of gratification and an increasingly sought after emotional release. Interestingly, a high level of love (even that which begins as physical love) increases and expands compatibility with awareness of higher realms of understanding which are based on love, so inadvertently John is fueling the current high level of "questing" energy in his crown chakra.

The energy again begins to drop as it leaves the heart area and heads toward the solar plexus. There is a very low level of energy in the personal power chakra which suggests, as in the fifth chakra, that this is a potential site for physical disease. Low energy in this third chakra means John is feeling unsure of who he really is and thus unsure of how other people see him. This sense of diminished personal power causes him to question his own value, and because he is not used to questioning his own effectiveness, he feels caught in a frozen place of fear and lack of understanding.

This high level of anxiety is obvious in watching the energy expand to the second chakra. John is trying to compensate emotionally and/or sexually for the nagging

*feelings that everything is not all right and that he is un-
sure of his footing. The intense energy in this chakra suggests that John is emotionally in trouble and acting within
a mentally unstable emotional balance. In analyzing a high
level of energy in this chakra, always reflect back upon
the rest of the energy field to see what areas are in stress.
In John's case the communication chakra and the personal power chakra reflect distress and therefore will be
the areas to manifest physical symptoms.*

*The energy drops to an average level as it enters the first
chakra, indicating that John functions well in a workaday
world. He is usually grounded and able to make decisions
based on his pragmatic daily living needs.*

Conclusions about John

1. *There is a high level of need for spiritual questing in
   John's life which cannot be denied and must be recognized and integrated into physical reality in order
   for him to again feel in control. This involves an over-
   hauling and updating of his current mental program.*

2. *A sustained low level of energy in the communication
   and personal power chakras suggests that these two
   areas are blocked by the fear and anxiety of physically recognizing and adjusting to a growing nonphysical shift in perceptions and general life
   direction. The body's physical viability in the areas
   of the fifth and third chakras are thus low and set
   up a potential field for physical dysfunction. The laryngitis is the physical result of the unresolved turmoil of discussing his changing feelings. The
   laryngitis will not be permanently cured by drugs but
   by an understanding of what he is experiencing. The
   laryngitis could just as easily have been ulcers or
   even cancer of any of the parts of the body falling
   within the area of the third and fifth chakras, if the
   repression was severe.*

3. *The strong emotional energy as seen in the second chakra is fast leading John toward a confrontation. Either he will be confronted by family or friends or by himself in such a way that he can no longer duck the issue. In this situation either the germs of a new thinking will begin to sprout or a more permanent block will be established which may cause a mental collapse. These are the two extreme possibilities. There are of course many combinations of acceptance/rejection and change within this range.*

4. *The high love energy can be John's salvation. Because he cares deeply about the feelings of those individuals he loves, he will be able to be reassured of their support and of the rightness of questioning his life and belief structures. If, however, his support structure (wife and friends) is afraid and unable to be open to his needs, then this avenue closes to him and he becomes forced to find a more appropriate support system through divorce, a change in jobs, or moving toward new friendships and a changed life-style.*

5. *The energy in the first chakra says he is a person who seeks stability in his life and will, in all probability, confront the turmoil and confusion he is experiencing in order to establish an acceptable level of compromise.*

Reading the Aura of a Chakra

When a clairvoyant sees an individual's aura, he or she is seeing the colors of the individual's energy fields plus the natural colors of each chakra, since each chakra has its own unique color combination as well as vibrational rate. There are a number of differences between chakras. For example, the spiritual chakras, seven and six, vibrate faster than do the lower chakras of one and two. While there is no need for a lengthy discussion on the subtle

color combinations of the chakras, let us at least establish
the predominant chakra colors:

7th Chakra - *violet/yellow*
6th Chakra - *Yellow/orange/indigo/violet*
5th Chakra - *Indigo/violet/red/orange/yellow/blue*
4th Chakra - *Red/blue/violet/orange/yellow*
3rd Chakra - *Orange/green/yellow/red/violet*
2nd Chakra - *Green/violet/red/orange/yellow*
1st Chakra - *Red/orange/yellow*

If one is not clairvoyant but nevertheless wishes to learn
to see and interpret the energy interplay within one's own
body, here are some thoughts. Knowing that each part of
the body is primarily influenced by one of the seven chakras, try to identify which of the chakras seem to be responsible for whatever particular problem you may have.
Close your eyes and picture the chakra in question as a
viable disc of multi-colored energy. Work only on one
chakra at a time even if there is more than one involved.
Mentally connect the appropriate chakra with the specific
unhealthy or dysfunctional part of the body by imaging a
line attaching one to the other.

Once this connection is made, slowly follow the line
that has been created from the chakra to the organ or
area of trauma. Your own psychic vision will pick up the
colors of the particular organ as the periphery of the organ
is approached. By quickly glancing at the organ while still
focusing on the periphery, you will see the true auric color
of the organ in question. The aura will first be seen as
quick flashes of color rather than a prolonged image. As
you become more adept at gazing rather than focusing on
the organ itself, you will be able to hold the complete vision more clearly. The first color reaction is apt to be the
most accurate before the conscious mind has a chance to
influence the picture.

Do not expect to see any particular color or shade of
color. Just make a mental note of the color and the corresponding degree of pain or problem experienced from the

particular organ on that day. A picture will develop over several weeks showing what the organ looks like when it is giving off signals that the body interprets as pain. (Refer to the chart on colors and their meanings for assistance.)

For example, in looking at the larynx (voice box), you might see any combination of indigo, violet, red, orange, yellow or blue. The overall appearance of the energy as it moves through the chakras is white, grey, gold or pale violet. Its presence within each chakra illuminates the chakra's own colors. While the moving energy can be seen in many ways, for our purposes it will be sufficient to see the color as white. The color of the diseased organ will reflect some combination native to the chakra of influence. In the larynx you might see a predominance of just red and orange rather than the full spectrum of colors possible from this chakra. With repeated scanning, if red and orange always appear, then a high level of tension exists around the need to communicate and the nature of the problem becomes clearer. Red is indicative of love, anger, hate and compassion. Orange indicates a need or desire to integrate one's spiritual awareness with physical change. If you have laryngitis, as John did, you might have seen a predominance of violet and yellow in the larynx indicating a need to resolve a nonphysical problem (violet) through intellectual means (yellow). It is only through repeated work that a pattern appears which becomes significant in approaching and understanding the state of your own health.

A healthy chakra is an energy center which is effectively processing the cosmic stream of energy. A normal, unblocked chakra reflects all the colors that are inherent to it. For example, if the fifth chakra were totally healthy, one would see the organs governed by the fifth chakra reflected in a combination of indigo, violet, red, orange, yellow, and blue.

A chakra which is blocked is a chakra which is not using the available energy to maximum benefit and reflects this diminished flow of energy in the poor aspecting of its colors, meaning only a limited number of colors are seen.

Blocked chakras can be either the result of an already existing condition or can reflect abrupt change. If you fell and broke a rib for example, the heart chakra would look differently after the fall than before it. The chakra would reflect the diminished flow of energy in that middle region of the body (the broken rib). On the other hand, if there was ongoing deterioration of the heart due to poor diet, stress, or active disease, then the heart chakra would initially appear less than perfect and one would see a very limited number of colors, possibly only one reflected on the organ of heart.

Because blocked chakras are unique to each person and each circumstance, it is only through ongoing study of a particular chakra that you can hope to recognize what colors indicate a blockage and what colors indicate a healthy organ for your body. In the example of John's larynx, seeing either set of the colors red and orange or yellow and violet would have indicated a block because they reflected only two of the possible six colors. A chakra is blocked when the total spectrum of possible colors is not seen. The fewer the colors that are seen, the more substantial the block.

Assuming that you have narrowed your problem to a specific chakra, have then connected the "study" line from chakra to organ as suggested and then seen and read the colors reflected in the organ, then what? If the organ or aspect of your body has a problem, how do you change it? Clearing or cleaning out the problem chakra and the chakras in general should be done once a day. You will feel a substantial difference when opening a chakra to allow more energy into a particular area, since the increased energy promotes physical health and psychological well being. Now that you have arrived at your own diagnosis of why a chakra might be blocked through analysis of your total energy field and the particular organ or system in distress, you are ready to understand the remedy.

Any vibration, auditory or visual, can be seen as a means of "opening" and unblocking the chakras. Here is one possibility:

- *Sit in a straight-backed chair. Be sure both feet are squarely on the ground, hands resting in your lap. Attack the "study line" from the chakra in question to the troubled area of the body as has been suggested.*
- *Picture a beam of light coming in the top of the head and flowing slowly downward through all seven chakras, gently opening each chakra to the appropriate degree. Follow the energy as it divides going down into each leg and foot and then passing out of the body.*
- *Go back and mentally work down the chakras to the mental picture of the chakra in which there is a problem. Observe the brilliant white light that has remained in the area of that chakra. Travel along the study line to the problem organ or disturbed area of the body and see it surrounded with white light. Let the organ reflect the white light suggesting that all disease, pain, or trauma be healed and that the chakra in question continue to "feed" the organ. Mentally retrace the study line and continue down through the energy field attaching study lines wherever necessary. Leave them in place and when the last chakra has been reached, calmly ask that the chakras be allowed to know and find their own acceptable degree of "openness."*

It may not be appropriate for each chakra to be completely open. The desired openness depends on what is appropriate to that part of the physical/emotional/spiritual body for that person at that precise moment in time. Whenever each chakra's appropriate degree of openness is achieved, the total spectrum of color will be seen on analysis.

As I studied Mentor's thoughts on sound, color, vibration and their counterparts in the chakras, I realized that it was no coincidence that my new sense of self allowed me to look further into his words than usual. I saw that his teachings transcended mere linear theory and drew me into a reality of multi-perceptual systems which held the potential to heal. Mentally, I stepped back to observe this insight and became aware that Mentor meant for me to synthesize his teachings on the structure of spirituality with the physical manifestation of physical change. This reality grew to become a major part of my focus, and as I continued to respond to Mentor's instructions on aspects of healing, I slowly developed perceptual abilities to observe what was physically, psychologically and spiritually at work in another's body. Mentor's thoughts and my personal experiences in healing and wholeness are contained in Chapter Eight.

Chronic Disharmony: The New Norm

✳ *We spoke of wellness as the goal all would hope to achieve. Yet twentieth century civilization is beleaguered by chronic physical woes. The bodies of even the young are becoming weighted with problems of obesity, lack of body tension, poor circulation, decaying teeth and bones, deteriorating nervous conditions and much more. Why? Tension, frustration and seeming inability to understand, change, integrate and control one's environment have allowed the resultant freewheeling lack of understanding and confusion to become the rule rather than the exception. It has become expected that people will be neurotic and introverted. The deviation has become the norm and thus the unhealthy body has been accepted as inevitable. But awareness of etheric, astral and mental energy fields potentially adds a further dimension to understanding and achieving physical and emotional health. For when one looks beyond physical disease to blocks in one's energy field, then one is able to take a decisive step toward changing disease as well as the general format of one's life.*

The nature and health of the physical body are reflections of personal harmony. The body responds in health to its environment when fed a diet of nurturing positivity. Conversely, the body balks and becomes jammed when fed a diet high in negativity. Keeping one's body functioning at optimum efficiency allows maximum benefit for life, and one can move in accord with one's own wishes, reach-

ing out and achieving in whatever direction one is drawn.
Whenever pain immobilizes the body, the paramount importance of health is highlighted. The formula for complete health is not fraught with abstract terminology, but
is very simple: that which is fed into the body in thought
or action reacts to further either health and increased
vital function or disease and loss of energy.

There are, of course, many approaches to developing a
positive framework from which to launch a successful life.
Visualization, awareness through sound or movement,
meditation, prayer, simple receptivity to love, openness to
the positive energy of the cosmos, all of these focus the
power of the positive on the physical level.

Inner space and outer space—body, mind and spirit—
have the potential for complete harmony through unifi-
cation in wholeness and positive action. That which exerts
influence is also acted upon by other influences. Influence
and action combined with individual awareness all flow
together, mingling energies and creative forces, allowing
and repudiating positive and negative vibrations. Life is
potential wholeness—potential in that it must first be recognized as a worthy goal in order to commit one's personal
energies to its fulfillment.

Inner space, the deep reaches of the soul, reflects and
magnifies the beauty of the physical realm. Outer space,
the expansive world of physical creation, mirrors the oneness of all life. Both respond when treated with loving
attention. It remains up to the individual to replace his
own splintered reality with the vibration of wholeness.

CHAPTER SEVEN

BENEATH EARTH'S GREENNESS

Life blossoms into abundance
covering the Earth with its grandeur.
Nature and man serve a common destiny:
nurturing the Planet with love.

MENTOR

THE HUMAN SPECIES has a given number of characteristics which we have grown to accept as an intrinsic part of our basic nature. For example, we tend to doubt the existence of the nonphysical world before we believe in it, and we accept the experience of doubt as our innate process of discernment. We recognize the aspect of the human personality called ego, and yet we are loath to admit that any of our behavioral patterns are the result of our own personally insecure egos. It is finally dawning on individuals that the once respected human policy of "an eye for an eye" can now result in the total annihilation of the planet, and yet even with this knowledge, we still hesitate to alter our behavior.

A natural extension of that egocentric belief is the manner in which we relate to our planet. We have come to believe that what makes a human life or another form of life of value is its ability to serve our needs. Within the human community, the moment an individual can no longer perform a task, the entire person is seen as diminished in worth. This belief has a multitude of tributaries. If an individual believes that the value of a person's life is in his ability to do and to perform, then that feeling is apt to carry over to his thought about all life forms, whether they be animal or plant. Further, this individual will tend to believe that the earth is here to serve the human race. A peculiar psychological twist is contained within this thinking pattern. If one believes that all life forms are here to serve him, oftentimes that is translated into the carelessness and privilege of abuse, for it is just another form of the master-slave relationship. If, however, we can become capable of seeing ourselves as equal to all forms of life, we would recognize and know deep within ourselves that what all schools of wisdom and spirituality have taught us is true. All is one.

I did not fully grasp this massive concept in the early stages of Mentor's discourses on the subject. Further, I did not see the clever trap which is laid in this foundational belief. Simply put, if you can allow your consciousness to consider and perhaps accept this profound truth, then you must change your behavior accordingly. You can no longer ignore the earth and any form of life.

If this notion sounds presumptuous, or perhaps even outrageous, consider what the state of not believing in it has created. Man has subjectively determined the consciousness levels of animals and plants based upon their ability to serve him. We permit open hunting seasons on those animals which are of no use to us. Those plants which are not desirable to eat or subjectively beautiful to our eye we call weeds and seek to destroy. Our design of preservation or annihilation seems based exclusively on what suits our fancy. This is an appalling thought, yet it is so true.

Mentor's talk of oneness kept coming back to what was truly of value, and it included all that existed on the surface of the earth as possessing consciousness. I wondered about man's arrogance, his obvious sense of personal separation from the planet. Perhaps it was a lack of bonding to the Earth that accounted for this disregard for man's cohabitants. It was also possible that man was just coming into a stage of awareness that would allow him to see more clearly that species extinction, pollution, bombs, and general destruction were intolerable to the planet. Mentor was eager to talk about what he called, "beneath Earth's greenness," and I was eager to listen:

No Such Thing as Nonexistence

* *There is a vibrational pulse within the soul of Planet Earth which pushes forth seeking display and fulfillment into multitudes of life. Earth has dynamic form, each aspect of which uniquely identifies its own existence as separate and yet as linked to all life. The vibrations of life are universal, yet continually focus and refocus on life and its ever-changing expression. The intuitive expansion and contraction of the Earth's mass combined with the manifestation of the God-force within provides the creative impetus for the birthing of life on your planet.*

The living children of nature—plants, rocks, and animals—have long been subjugated to the human vibration. The nonhuman forces have patiently existed outside human understanding, waiting to be included in the human perception and ready to respond to the long overdue invitation to join with men and women in love to unite the planet.

The vibration of Planet Earth is such that billions of life forms exist in and on its surface, yet much of this life remains obscured from man, because it cannot be adequately understood, described, seen, smelled or touched. Therefore it is denied any form of consciousness. That which is presumed dead is of little or no concern to man; thus liberties are taken with nature's very existence, even to the point of annihilation. Man plays lightly with the Universe's gifts, destroying vast and extravagant arrays of Earth's existence. Whether visible or invisible, tangible or intangible, all forms of nature are real, and all of it is worthy of man's consideration.

All elements and substances of and on the Earth "live." Death is not an end to viable expression but a change in vibration, just as growth and then dormancy promote the birth and continuation of a new cycle of life. If this is true, then dormant life, though unresponsive, cannot be considered dead. If there are only stages in the life cycle, then it stands to reason that everything within the human experience lives through existence and then resurrection of existence through changing vibration. Thus any action which is taken that is divergent from this understanding and does not adhere to the notion of life on every level and in every stage is totally inappropriate.

Vibration is the common denominator of all forms of life. It is also the means of identifying individual life forms. Vibration identifies crickets as crickets, daisies as daisies and humans as humans, as well as particular members of each classification. If it were possible to see all forms of life in terms of readable vibration, one would discover each living force's tonal resonance. We have spoken of this before as the vibrational pattern unique to each form of life. Each individual life is as special as a note on a musical score where whole, half, quarter, eighth, and sixteenth notes each fill a designated space, yet no two notes ever take up the same space. When such individual musical notes are played together, a melody emerges; when nature, including man, responds appropriately through the intertwining of all its unique vibrations, harmony of life emerges.

Because the human vibration is the most dominant, or shall we say intense, of knowable Earth vibrations, it falls to man to safeguard the stewardship of this wondrous garden called Earth in order that he may be instrumental in the blending of all knowable parts into a perfect universal pitch. If man shares a special relationship with nature, then what blocks his understanding of this fact?

Humankind has yet to evolve beyond self-centeredness, where indeed it is assumed that anything of value originates from one's own self or one's own kind. That would explain the commonly-held belief that other forms of life do not feel or understand. While this premise is without basis, it has done much to promote discrimination against nature and to further widen the gulf that already exists. The animal and plant life of Planet Earth are cognizant of the lack of interest paid to them as well as the resultant pain and abuse which accompanies this lack of concern for their well-being. This discrimination does not go unnoticed. It has simply been accepted in the past as the result of man's lack of cosmic perspective. When the human race willingly accepts its joint participation in the earthly experience, then there will be no more advantage taken, one of another. Then there will be mutual respect and understanding as each life force searches to further its own development through meaningful interaction.

Two Levels of Natural Life: Physical and Spiritual

Since the perfect vibration of life is harmony, each individual life force resonates in a way commensurate with its physical properties (animal, vegetable or mineral) and its developing spiritual vision. In other words, there are at least two aspects, physical and etheric, to every living force. While Nature is masterful at creating its species in the most beguilingly intricate and yet practical patterns, do not be fooled. All life has purpose and progression both in an ecological and a spiritual sense. Man is too often lulled into accepting nature on its most obvious physical level, failing to respond to nature as an evolving force.

While there are obvious differences between human and nonhuman life, initially one sees a dynamic similarity, for both man and plant creatively interpret their physical and nonphysical realities according to physical need and divine desire. With this duality in mind, let us look more closely at the physical and nonphysical aspects man and plant hold in common.

In the purely physical sense, an individual chooses his school, career, wife or husband, area of the country in which to live and type of living situation. The plant chooses where to take seed and where not to, where to grow, how fast and how tall to grow, whether or not to blossom or produce fruit. Both plant and human live within predetermined spheres of creativity, changing their environment to fit their needs.

The nonphysical sense of cosmic destiny is more subtle and therefore more difficult to qualitatively define. Man stumbles toward a more accurate perspective of his uni-

versal role, seeking to understand the truths that often seem less than apparent: reincarnation, karma, universal harmony, personal divinity and responsibility—personal and cosmic. It is extremely egotistical for man to think that only he searches for truths that affect his life, when in fact he is only now becoming cognizant of the depth of life within his own galaxy and the fact that each aspect of that life is divine and therefore also searches to substantiate this Divine Destiny. Perhaps "Divine Destiny" sounds a bit mysterious and unknowable. Actually the term means understanding that you, the individual, as well as everything that surrounds you, live as part of a much grander cosmic interaction. Awareness of Divine Destiny means that your actions reflect this awareness.

When a life force is annihilated from Planet Earth, there is disruption within the planet's ecological life chain and within the less noticeable energy of spiritual evolution. Every species that becomes extinct and every plant that loses its natural habitat alters the Earth, physically and spiritually. Melding an understanding of these two aspects of nature, physical and spiritual, provides man an opportunity to truly maneuver his planet on an enlightened course. Humankind, as stewards of the Earth, must understand the total earth environment if it is to understand its own existence, for man and plant are brothers in the complex land of spiritual and physical evolution. Nature must be offered no less than verification of this insight from the human dimension, if the exquisite pulse of mutual development and awareness is to be realized.

All aspects of the natural kingdom benefit from awareness, communication and interplay with realms of higher consciousness, since these are the building blocks of your world. While the plant kingdom needs and looks to the human world for enlightenment and advancement, the human world should look to its natural counterparts to expand its understanding of the Earth. Within this scheme of natural harmony and coexistence, both nature and human find reassurance and new opportunity for advancement. Just as the individual can feel unfulfilled when limited to his own finite physical nature so, too, the plant craves input from beyond its reality. Most plants, for example, understand the notion of life and rebirth better than most humans, accepting and expecting as they do the continuing nature of change through their shortened stages of development. Nature exemplifies the mystery of adjustment as its varying aspects thrive and diminish according to Earth's need. Nothing exists within the natural world by chance. What is displayed has found a necessary link in the overall chain of life. Man must bother to look at each slice of nature as significant and therefore existing for a reason, though it may not be immediately evident to him.

It becomes increasingly important for Earth's peoples to seriously consider the notion of intelligent nonhuman life on Planet Earth as more than poetry. The right to live with mutual consideration and respect needs to be the newly-forged path of an aware society. Men and women cannot respond appropriately and lovingly if they lack an education in planetary awareness, yet this lack of knowledge can no longer exist as the excuse for Earth's rampant destruction and lack of consideration for other living forces. It is time for the human race to clearly appreciate and accept responsibility for the results of its actions, because Nature is fast losing interest in joining in any kind of a partnership with man. And of course you realize that man cannot survive without nature.

"Man cannot survive without nature." That thought caused me to experience a very deep internal shift in awareness. The world and all of nature's wondrous creatures did not need me to exist; I needed them. What use has the ocean for me? Or the wind? Or the entire animal kingdom? But, dear God, how I needed all of these precious forms of life.

Mentor was more than right; he spoke the truth as it has always been. The fact that I had lived for so long not realizing that this is true was hardly a reflection on the validity of the teaching. It was an indication of how far I had ventured into the world of supposed cold, hard facts, scientific thought and the generally accepted principles of reality.

I was spiritually humbled by this reverse in the dynamics of my relationship with the earth. Now, just hearing the expression ''Mother Earth'' made me choke with emotion. This was a notion, a concept, a thought I did not want to release from my conscious mind.

One afternoon while sitting in our meadow, I felt as though the earth knew I had experienced a change of heart. My eyes focused on trees in the distance, and I was totally and gently surrounded by the vibration of the earth itself. It seemed to embrace me, to enfold me, to say, ''We need your help; thank you for being able to hear us.''

I felt weak from a sense of shame, wanting to apologize. I needed to say to the earth, ''I did not realize you were in pain, I did not realize you were really being poisoned, I did not understand that the pollution in the air was suffocating you . . . I did not realize you were truly alive.''

It may be difficult to fully appreciate the impact of this moment in my life. It may sound positively absurd to think of oneself as developing a relationship with the earth in the same fashion and with the same social contract that one would honor with a new friend. And yet, that is precisely what I am suggesting.

To those who would completely disregard the possibility of engaging in an intimate relationship with the earth, I offer only this response. To the extent that these ideas seem alien, outrageous or totally incongruous with one's reality, that is actually the yardstick by which an individual can measure exactly how far removed he is from the gentle forces of the earth.

While the experience of feeling a sense of shame for the consideration of our earth was, and continues to be, a humbling experience, at the same time it permitted a door to open within my consciousness. Because I no longer felt that I was a superior life form to the earth, I could believe without doubt or hesitation that the same spiritual guidance available to the human species was available to all forms of life. In other words, suddenly nothing seemed more natural than to believe that all forms of physical life had the benefit of a non-physical support system. After all, I had learned early in my relationship with Mentor that what we held to be true here on earth was rarely what the nonphysical world knew to be true, not only as regards the earth, but for life systems beyond our own as well.

Somewhere during this period of time, I had begun to recognize a definite characteristic of Mentor's teachings. The teachings consistently directed the human being toward harmonious patterns of behavior, whether Mentor spoke in psychological, physical or spiritual terms. I knew that this was truth. Every word he communicated was designed to encourage individuals to rethink their belief patterns and where stifled, to move beyond.

I now looked at the earth and its needs and once again, this measure of truth applied. Mentor was revealing to me the personality of the earth, metaphorically speaking. The wider I could permit the door of my consciousness to open, the more I could experience the earth's personality. In what could be described as a gestalt experience, I spontaneously knew that my ability to see the earth from the vantage point of the Universe included a natural progression of corresponding beliefs. I could no longer commit acts of disharmony and carelessness toward any life form.

As unconventional as this thinking process might seem, consider that which is currently held to be true: that nature is a force but not life, that life is only of value when it can be used. Follow the "natural" course of that thought. If an individual has the tendency to judge the worth of anything, then he automatically creates two major categories: valuable and useless. That belief pattern includes the perception which would allow a person to destroy those forms of life which are marked "useless." Further, if a personality has a destructive tendency, there is every reason to assume he will develop that trait alongside his other personality characteristics.

The antidote to this negative pattern is simple, but not easy. And only the Universe could offer such a spiritually elegant alternative to humanity's present course. If an indi-

vidual can permit himself to grow in gentleness, to trust his
emotions, to develop a relationship with the earth, then the
only possible extension of that has to be peace. It requires
that people dispel hostility, anger and feelings of superiority.
I can not imagine a world mourning the loss of those characteristics. These prerequisites of consciousness, I was to
learn, are also necessary for people wishing to move into the
gentle and accepting state of consciousness in which communication with the forces of nature is possible.

Evolution: Will It Wait?

✳ *While it is reassuring to talk in terms of visions of harmony and wholeness and perhaps threatening to talk of
actual Nature communication and interaction, nevertheless, you must seek practical toeholds in everyday life that
can help to further define these notions of oneness.*

*Beyond the extravagance and inspiration of life, be-
neath and within Earth's greenness, exists the ground
swell of natural interaction, evolution and survival of all
species of life. In the past, life forces supported the mutual
evolutionary progression of other life by the close interaction of man with Nature. This guaranteed survival of
the appropriate aspects of Earth. That which was used by
man from Nature's storehouse was used with a respect for
the life that was changed or taken, even though the taking
of that life may have been surrounded with superstition.*

*But, Agartha, human life no longer approaches the
Earth with an expectation of comradeship or with a heart
seeking love. While historically there have been times
when Nature has reacted harshly to man through famines,
earthquakes, tornadoes and droughts, never before has
Nature exhibited extended periods of natural disruption
such as the Earth has now begun to experience. I will
suggest that Nature's currently erratic behavior is the
result of a slack in the grounding rein which tethers Nature
to man. The increasing unpredictability of nature in the
way of changing temperature zones, failing crops, unset-*

tled tides, winds and tremors does indeed suggest that Earth's natural elements are confused as to their most immediate source of guidance.

In other words, man's superiority, his recognized role as teacher to the natural kingdom, is disintegrating. Nature is failing to recognize or abide by man's rule. Instead Nature sees itself tossed adrift to seek a new master. This is dangerous, for without Nature's cooperation, man will cease to thrive on the Earth. He cannot sustain life on a barren planetary surface. Food, shelter and the simplest existence is dependent upon the forces he so blindly subjugates and ignores. Certainly Nature could exist without man, free to refurbish the lush valleys and repopulate the cities with greenness. Unfortunately man cannot live without Nature, but even more to the point, man is not meant to live outside of Nature's loving sphere. Man is to develop in the role of teacher and gentle arbitrator, destined to evolve in closer cohabitation with his planet if he seeks to see life through a different vibration.

The question becomes: will the human race reach to fill this gaping chasm between Nature and itself or will man wait until the opportunity for coexistence no longer exists? Nature will not wait forever. The distrust and pathos which currently block men's minds must be dislodged. All of Nature has looked to man to interpret the Universe through an appropriate attitude of respect. But man in his ignorance has been actively eliminating his role in the essential chain of life by abusing his role of teacher to the life forces.

Plant energy has now begun to reach beyond the human level to establish its own loving relationship with the Universe, leaving man to struggle alone. If Nature has to search beyond the human level to reach satisfaction, it will. Then the door for continued human interaction will be closed, and there will no longer be any need for the human dimension to interact with the rest of Nature. Man will have made himself obsolete. He will find himself isolated and estranged even in his own forests and mountains. A magnificent opportunity for mutual benefit and

*the growth of cooperation will have been lost, with man
the biggest loser. Nature will move beyond reach, for evolution waits for no one, not even man.*

There it was. The issue was clearly laid out. Either man
would shift his consciousness toward the earth as a living
being and act out of responsibility for nurturing the proper
relationship with Nature or there would be extreme consequences. Implicit in Mentor's comments was the need to take
action to prevent an impending separation that would result
in worldwide devastation. The issue of how one individual
could make a difference now seemed paramount to survival.
My personal response was that discussion, while appropriate, is not as effective as action.

Mentor's communication on earth changes and earth
consciousness affected me quite differently from the other
material. Discussions on the nature of human and spiritual
consciousness are matters for each individual to consider as
they are drawn toward investigating more enlightened patterns of living. While the effect of this process is indeed
dramatic, it remains intimately personal and self-initiated.
The individual makes the decision.

The reality that the Earth was alive and presently concerned with its own survival caused me to view every aspect
of life from a radically different position. I would find myself, for example, involved in "everyday" conversation with
someone, simultaneously thinking, "I wonder what they
would say or do if I shared with them the probability of earth
changes? Would they believe me?"

Certainly, no notion could sound more absurd to anyone.
After all, we are no longer a culture which respects prophecy. Indeed, we exist within a reality in which angels have
been reduced to a rumor—a source of inspiration created by
primitive man. And yet, is it really such a difficult scenario
to imagine? It is an unfortunate human trait that we tend to
disregard that which we have not personally experienced as
somehow less than real. We can discuss poverty, for example, as a tragic aspect to the human condition, but that is
hardly the same as the experience of hunger.

We can "imagine" the horror of nuclear war, but that amounts to nothing more than an intellectual exercise. Having a bomb destroy your city—or country—is a "reality" whose total and genuine horror defies our imagination. And what is even more frightening is that human beings are rarely moved into action unless the bomb is dropped on their front lawn.

Afterwards, the warning signs become incredibly apparent that the event was in the making before it happened. Historically, we see with clear vision. Are we so blind to think that the same process—those same warning signals— are not being given to us now? Why does each generation work so desperately to promote or enhance its own reality, oblivious to past mistakes and successes? It is dangerous to believe that that which is old is useless, whether it be current truths or the knowledge already learned by our ancestors.

It seemed critical to remind myself that because Mentor exists beyond earth's time and space, I was being allowed to view a probability which in all likelihood was already forming or indeed underway. It was one thing to be shown a fact of destruction but much more frightening to be shown the potential when it seemed I was the only one watching this preview of impending planetary disaster. It was inconceivable to think of a world where man, plant and animal were warring factions. If the natural laws of the universe were causing this struggle to be played out, then it needed to be played in an arena where all could understand the rules and the potential outcome for failure could be jointly shared. I considered the necessity of change, wanting and needing to participate in these new directions before nature moved forever beyond human control.

Communication With Nature: Fact or Fiction?

❋ *When I speak of Nature reaching beyond man to connect with the forces of the Universe, I mean quite simply that the world of Nature is losing its willingness to be used and denied access to man's teaching. If indeed men and* women are teachers, then they should share with their gardens and fields, allowing learning and interaction to develop on all levels with the natural forces of the world. Plants, trees, animals, rocks, all the things that live in areas untouched by man have already bypassed the need for human interaction and have effectively strung together their own sense of Universal Relevance. They have found that they can exist quite happily apart from humans. Just as a plant which grows in the crevice of a craggy rock has a different root system, a different appearance and a different vibration from one raised in a cultivated garden, so Nature in general is moving away from interest in the traditional modes of gardening and farming which are becoming stagnant with poisons and harmful additives. Man is not nurturing his grounds on any level, with the result that Nature is modifying its needs to exist more and more in the wild, moving away from man's influence. In other words, the wild things are looking to discard man's yoke which is bringing only confusion and negativity to the planet.

The Earth began as a self-sufficient, burgeoning ocean of life which gradually grew to incorporate all the many, varied life forms that now exist, including man. Nature has been accustomed to living in harmony with all aspects of the planet, but if man insists on diverging from a path of unison and well-being for all, then nature will increasingly exclude man from its own growth, and man will find himself growing apart from the greenness of the Earth.

All life, no matter how small, has a sense of universality. Nature responds to love as well as indifference, to understanding as well as abuse. This becomes obvious in the simple handling of plants where one's attitude makes the difference between average or less than average growth and superlative growth. All life has the potential to give and receive love, but it falls to man to move on this knowledge and advance the cause of unilateral peace and harmony on the planet, for it is his right and his obligation to transmit the heavenly vibrations to the other tenants of

Planet Earth. After all, he exists as the most evolved form of consciousness on the Earth's surface.

Communication, the transmission of thoughts from one source to another, is considered fundamental to personal interaction. I would suggest it is also fundamental to interaction with Nature. Communication is Nature's most immediate link to the Universe. Fulfillment of divine intervention comes from Nature's connection to man, much as man's fulfillment comes from communication with angels, spirit guides, incarnated masters and higher-consciousness intuition.

This dimension of cosmic vision is the world on which Nature must advance, and if man is not willing to share teachings in a meaningful way, then Nature will seek its own definition of universal commitment through the abandonment of civilization and the refocusing of energy only through life in the wild. Nature's unruliness will continue to increase and could eventually reach the point of complete rebellion and anarchy, in which case the reestablishment of any kind of successful living mode with nature would become extremely difficult.

As the division between the worlds has risen higher and higher and man has continued to ignore the existence of the living earth, the natural world has withdrawn from its former interest in communicating with humans, and these once friendly forces are now loath to enter into relationships with man, choosing instead to look elsewhere for loving spiritual interaction. In other words, man is going to have to seek and persevere in order to establish anew a dwindling interest in any kind of exchange.

Communication with Nature as a way of understanding and thus ameliorating trauma is the most obvious panacea for the modern world's physical difficulties. The peoples of the world will alter their approaches to agriculture, industry, mining and animal experimentation when they themselves experience a connection with other life forces of the planet. Thus I offer you an opportunity to try to find your own connection. Nothing can be lost and a great deal can be gained, for as each individual seeks a more

*personal interaction with Nature, the planet will slowly
change to reflect the energy of a more enlightened planet.*

I thought of the Findhorn Community in Scotland, now
more than twenty years old, and their world-famous garden.
The magnificent vegetation bursting forth from the garden
shocked the world, especially when it was explained that the
horticultural achievement was due to the established communication between the Nature kingdoms and man. The
community had effectively established what no one else had
been able to, and though scientists from all over the world
struggled to explain the garden's vegetation in more conventional terms, the original premise held. I had to believe that
Findhorn was the Universe's way of calling attention to the
dynamic impact of a union between nature and man. This
point of contact made in this remote community located on
the northeast coast of Scotland blossomed with the gentle
truth that the aspects of nature could and were meant to work
in harmony. When cooperation was sought with the kingdoms of the earth, the dynamics of growth were miraculously
enhanced.

We now had two things in common with the Findhorn
Community; one, our garden and two, that the explanation
for the striking vegetation in our garden was the same. Those
who saw our garden frequently had to consider that the most
unbelievable explanation for its production was, in fact, the
only believable one.

✳ *Disappointingly, man has trouble recognizing and accepting communication from other than his own reality.
For example, nobody questions that human communication is essential to sound family or interpersonal relations,
yet the idea of openly communicating with Nature seems
rarely considered. Humans are poorly prepared for all but
the most obvious of conversations. Nature, on the other
hand, is more given to accepting responsibility for its role
in the human life cycle. Animals and plants are accustomed to producing for man, but the production cycles
have become too taxing.*

While the use of chemicals has forced larger production, it is hollow production, for there is no integrity in this kind of bloom or grain. It exists without the permission of the plant. The plant is forced to produce—not allowed to produce—and herein lies the difference. Because violation of plants by this force-feeding method actually shortens its life cycle and eliminates any joy in the production process, Nature's usefulness as a continuing food source is becoming diminished. The food which is produced is filled with the artificial, negative aspects of creation and lacks the overriding positive energy infused in the natural growing cycle. Even the water is becoming so acidic and filled with pollutants that basic water replenishment is no longer possible. How can health be produced from plants which are prevented from having a proper relationship with the essential elements which provide for joyful and complete growth? How is man to know that the planet suffers if he is deaf to any perceptual interchange?

Given that one would wish to listen to Nature, you might ask how this is to be done. Communication is traditionally an exchange of ideas or at least perceptions. "Perception" is an appropriate word for understanding the actual communication process with Nature, although the word may be too vague for some. Perceptions are random and scattered fragments of thoughts and impressions which, when put together, add up to a communication. If I am suggesting that one understand perceptions, then it would appear I do not expect one's first tries at Nature communication to produce full-blown conversations. This is certainly true.

The perceptual experience may be visual, auditory or tactile. While an explicit exchange is often possible for those with experience in translating perceptions from non-human channels into intelligible language, nevertheless most people will begin by learning to listen to every subtle input that presents itself from their natural surroundings. Once one's level of reserve and fear of appearing ridiculous is overcome, one is free to settle into less traditional modes of listening and responding in order that the living

*presence of Nature may quite literally come flooding into
one's presence. It is only where the imagination is allowed
to weave with the spark of experience that the world of
devas and Nature spirits can be seen and known. What
comes to life is different for each individual, but the primary experience is no less real, just different for each as
the core of truth is experienced and interpreted within the
individual framework of beauty and understanding.*

*Communicating with any aspects of the natural world
means mentally sharing perceptions in a meaningful way
with forces outside one's physical presence. Normal day-
to-day life sets the stage for this kind of communication.
Children waiting for the school bus, adults working in the
garden or field or mowing the lawn all represent opportunities for communication. Unfortunately the mind is
usually preoccupied with the functional aspects of living,
and so the contours of experiences which exist outside the
normal physical framework are overlooked and even denied when they somehow wander into consciousness.*

*There is every reason to believe that what is important
for total growth on the human level is significant on other
natural levels. Because humankind is intricately and in-
exorably tied to its fellow nature beings, man must work
toward the areas of shared brotherhood, focusing on the
similarities of spiritual pursuit rather than the differences. For every aspect of the planet moves toward creative fulfillment of its divine purpose and humankind needs
to reassume its role of teacher, inspiring and supporting
its fellow creatures.*

I could feel myself drawn into Mentor's words as well as
to his level of human expectation. It did not shock me to
think of talking to my plants since I had been doing that for
years. But it was novel to consider having a dialogue with
them.

I wanted to know what these communications truly felt
like, how they might differ from my times with Mentor, and
in what way I might exchange ideas with my new garden.
Given how far I had come with Mentor, it did not seem

strange to be considering actual communications with the plants I now stood and watched. Communicating with life in whatever form began to feel more and more natural as Mentor talked of the enormous need for this exchange. I was eager to go with him to experience a new level of perception.

✳ *I would like to suggest, Agartha, that before I proceed with ways to actually communicate with one's surroundings, we discuss whether the possibility exists that what I am asking you to do is merely an exercise in developing one's imagination. Certainly imagination plays a role in allowing fresh, new visions of Nature to present themselves to the conscious mind. It is not, however, that imagination originates the vibration of interaction but instead that it weaves an acceptable picture around the true connection.*

The imagination is an interpretative tool of the mind which plays in and around a core concept of personal truth. Imagination is the elaboration of the real, it is the changing scenery in a play, it is the ad-lib around an actor's scripted lines. Whenever imagination is allowed to weave its colorful presence around an experience, there is always a core of personal truth from which the experience has sprung. To dissect a potentially meaningful experience with Nature by attempting to peel imagination away from the core experience is as fruitless as dissecting a bumblebee to discover how it can fly. Aerodynamically, the bumblebee is not supposed to be able to fly, and yet it is totally oblivious to this supposed limitation. Watching the flight of the bumblebee is no stranger than experiencing the intriguing mystery of listening to a daisy. Neither is supposed to happen, and yet both do happen. In the case of the bumblebee, our vision confirms the truth. In the case of the daisy, it is a subtle matter of listening with the mind and allowing the imagination to bring forth the response.

Experiences with Nature seem to hearken back to childhood when one joyfully chased the morning's dancing sunbeams in a game of hide and seek or when one tiptoed through the meadow's evening dew watching as the shad-

owy wetness changed footprints into damp puddles of mat-
ted grass. Perhaps these experiences are but a recapturing
of the natural union with Nature that was felt as a child.
The remembrance of such experiences tends to encourage
mature reawakening to the forces that live just beyond the
periphery of the five-senses world.

The child accepts what he feels and sees until told his
or her experiences are false or that the visions and awarenesses are not real but only imagined. If the skeptical
adult could become the child again, he could see with
trusting and loving eyes, realizing that all is real yet as a
dream, a fragile bubble limited only by the lack of human
understanding of the expansiveness of all life.

These are times of interaction with Nature's life forces,
and it makes no difference if they are times of quiet repose
or of active participation, as long as desire for oneness is
openly sought through love. With the direct communion
with Nature comes a joyous sense of oneness, renewal and
rebirth, and the return from such a primary experience
provides a sense of man's own mortality and therefore his
recognized connection with the rest of the metamorphosing world. These fleeting exposures to the plant and animal worlds occur when protective mental defenses are
down and when one is peaceful and filled with what might
be called the assertive edge of consciousness, meaning a
dynamically positive sense of reaffimation of the oneness
of all life.

Personal awareness is transmitted, life force to life
force, through communication. It is only where the imagination is allowed to weave with the spark of experience
that the world of devas and nature spirits can be seen and
known. What comes to life is different for each individual,
but the primary experience is no less real, just different
for each as the core of truth is experienced and interpreted
within the individual framework of beauty, understanding
and conscious acceptability. The desire to be part of Nature and to share in all that goes on around each person
is to regain and treasure the sense of imagination and of
the core experience of the spirit of life. One's own expe-

riences in Nature should serve as a beckoning into the world of Nature, an invitation to share life.

The energy forces which inhabit the gardens and fields can be open to personal experience when man is willing to give credence to such an exchange. Whenever one seeks to know other forms of life in a sense of love and honor, meaningful interaction is experienced. To believe that life does not exist where it is not obviously seen or heard is to let one's rational mind eliminate much of the confirmation of the Earth as a living planet. To learn to listen with the mind's inner mechanism, without drowning the subtle responses with one's own internal chatter or excess of anticipation, is to become a possible channel for the gentle voices of Nature and a harbinger for the peaceful evolution of the planet.

The Communication Process

Mentor's words drifted from ideas which made me fearful to words which encouraged. He was suggesting that valuable insights were possible when one proceeded with an experience of the garden. I was increasingly intrigued by the prospect of an actual garden communication and eagerly awaited Mentor's invitation to introduce me:

✻ *Very well, Agartha, here are some thoughts in beginning a communication with the spirits of Nature:*

1. *Sit quietly outside in any pleasing place. If there is a particular plant with which communication is desired, sit close to the actual physical presence of that plant. Realize that recognizable life-force communications can exist between an individual and a specific plant or between an individual and a general category of plant. For example, one may "pull in" communication with a generic category rather then a specific plant, since group and individual energies are of a similar vibration in the world of Nature.*

2. *Allow the mind to picture the plant with which communication is desired. This picture should be as close a representation of the actual appearance as possible. This specific imaging serves as an invitation or welcoming to the plant's energy, literally drawing it to the individual.*

3. *After the specific imaging comes a period of quiet acceptance. This means the picture of the plant should be allowed to drift away and in its place appear whatever representation the plant's energy wishes to put forth. By releasing the exact representation of the vegetable or flower from one's mind, the energy of the plant is then allowed to appear in whatever vibratory form it wishes—auditory, visual, perceptual or tactile. By eliminating any regimentation or restrictions to which the element must conform, the individual plant's energy is allowed to enter into a communication in whatever way is desired or most appropriate or possible.*

4. *It may take numerous tries before a realized contact is made with a particular plant only because the energies of the garden are not used to being summoned and are quite reticent to contact humans without a great deal of encouragement. It is as if one needs to repeat the "invitation" to convince the natural energies that indeed communication is truly desired.*

Like a friendship, once a communication is established, one must continue to use the established link. Trust, love and sensitivity are equally important aspects of any shared relationship. Garden relationships are no different.

Communications in the garden are meant to be enjoyable as well as informative and above all to allow man to experience his connection to the planet. Most people simply need to expand and give credence to a level of sensitivity already in place. Walking through the desert or the woods, swimming in the oceans or the lakes, one must give oneself permission to freely interpret, listen and share

*with Nature. In this way, one's own struggles and aspi-
rations can be shared with Nature verbally or telepathically, uniting the two dominant forces of the planet.*

The Garden Energies

Communicating with Nature is as subtle as a cosmic whis-
per, a joyous gentle relief from the often imposing reverence
needed for talking with Mentor. Nature has a sense of humor
and is often eager to share that side of its presence as well as
its more serious side. My first communication took a most
unusual and unexpected turn.

I chose a beautiful morning to go into the garden to try
Mentor's instructions. I sat directly in the center of the garden where the three triangular beds came together and faced
the new pea fence. Folding my legs, I closed my eyes and
prepared to wait for any forthcoming impressions.

Nothing happened. I retraced Mentor's steps and proceeded by picturing a green pea with whom I hoped to share
an impression. At first this was difficult because green was
not a color I found easy to visualize, but I kept trying until I
eventually produced a mental picture of a large green pea. I
became preoccupied with holding this image and did not at
first realize that the green pea was moving toward me at what
seemed a shocking rate of speed. I was startled but had no
time to react. The pea seemed to be headed directly toward
me, and I braced for a collision. Instead of impact, I experienced a small watery-green presence which abruptly un-
rolled itself from the pea shape and stood staring at me! I
did not dare move. Cautiously we eyed each other without
either of us venturing any closer. It was altogether quite incredible. I wondered what would happen if I spoke, then
considered that we could communicate telepathically and was
suddenly thankful that I would not need to articulate words.
I tried to mentally project a greeting. Instantly, the presence
disappeared. "Now what?" I thought. "Had I failed stage
one?"

Disappointed but also somewhat relieved, I sat trying to

collect my thoughts when I became aware of a sense of motion. I felt myself swaying back and forth. I began to feel dizzy. This was awkward since I did not want to move but felt I must open my eyes. I heard a small voice which interrupted my thoughts. It said, "How do you like that?" I was speechless. Then it occurred to me that the voice was referring to how I liked being rocked back and forth. I managed to think: "I don't like it!" The instantaneous response was: "We don't either, so make the pea fence good and strong!"

The rocking stopped immediately and so did the voice. The small green figure did not reappear, or in all likelihood I was too disoriented to cause it to reappear. Opening my eyes, I stared at the pea fence and the freshly turned soil where the peas were to be planted later in the day. Then I looked at the posts and saw that they were indeed rather flimsy. Jim and I decided we had best take the suggestion of the green pea and we reinforced the entire fence with oversized posts.

We were overjoyed with the contact and I decided to try again in hopes that the same "energy" might still be present. Moments later, as I listened to the presence of the pea, I thought of how I would like to call it "Pea Deva."

The fence will be secure, and we will be happy. Do not forget the water. Peas need water, you know. The garden is fine, and we are ready to grow. Goodbye.

I sat quietly to see if Pea Deva would return. When he did not reappear, I tried to contact the Spinach Deva, since spinach was another early crop, and was pleasantly surprised to receive a completely different tone of response from that of the puckish Pea Deva:

We are getting our energies ready. You must be sure to keep the soil wet enough. Watch my leaves and if they are not dark green, you will know that you need to change the potassium content of the soil. I think everything will be fine for growing. We'll start and see. We will grow bright, green and shiny leaves with beautiful ruffled contours. We are glad you

*are working with us and will help us achieve our maximum
potential. We welcome you to the garden.*

Next I tried the Onion Deva and received only a brief
message:

*Smell is very important. We are useful in your garden and
are willing to work with you if you are gentle in our planting.*

The Garlic Deva displayed a sort of casual indifference.
This deva appeared to be a tall, skinny presence:

*I'm very healthy and will cause you no worry. Growth
comes easily to me, and I grow well. We understand you are
interested in helping us grow. It will be fine to have some
additional help. We will tell you when we are in need of help.
We usually manage well without man. You can watch if you
want.*

Potato Deva was the most vivacious of the group I contacted that first day. He even seemed in my mind's eye to be
fat and jovial:

*No garden is complete without me. I'm round and firm,
and I'm always in good spirits. That is why I always taste so
good. I find my presence is always welcomed in the garden.
I am happy to be in your garden.*

I tuned into Mentor to express my elation with these contacts. He was there, apparently participating in my experience.

**✳ They will become more talkative when they know your
presence better, after you have spent more time in the
garden. At this point they barely know you so it is not the
same. All progresses well on your level. Enjoy this day,
and go with the gentleness of the breeze as it flutters
through your windows bringing the singing of the garden
to your ears. We will speak tomorrow.**

The next morning, Jim and I sat in bed before going out
to work in the garden. We were delighted with the nature
contacts and wanted very much to have Mentor's perspective
on our progress. Jim was both excited about the communications and a little chagrined that he had been unable to pick
up any perceptions.

✳ *Congratulations, Agartha; you were effectively able to
communicate with the nature spirits. I was participating
only in sending you energy, so you would have an easier
time picking up their vibrational pattern. I was surprised
with how clearly you were indeed able to perceive them.
While it is a good idea to ask if the plants you had planned
to put in that specific garden would be happy there and in
what sequence they should be planted, they will of course
be able to give you more specific feedback on their needs.
     The devas you contacted were certainly willing to par-
ticipate with you. Yet, this may not always be the case.
There has been such neglect that often one needs to ask
and continue to ask before being allowed to participate in
such a show of confidence. This garden is to be a significant factor in your lives. You have no way of knowing how
intense the communications will become or how in touch
you will become with the feelings of the garden. Your garden is a microcosm of the universe and we who work with
alternate energy realities to affect change are filled with
admiration for those of you who are capable of assimilating our teachings and changing to reestablish those patterns which are currently nonexistent.
     Jim's role in the garden is less well-defined than yours,
yet it adds to the general energy reservoir which nourishes
all that grows there. The vibration of love is an open pattern which allows not only the continual flow of growth
potential into the plant but also the flow of waste energies
and negativity away from the plant. He is a very real part
of the growing cycle and like you, Agartha, needs to be
cognizant of his mood shifts. When working in the garden,
particularly this garden, it will be extremely harmful to
transmit the negative energy of anger or resentment. The*

*level of receptivity to human energy is on the increase
within your land which means that nonproductive energy
causes more than the usual growth defects. The harmony
of the growing cycles depends, in large part, on your stability in maintaining the energy which increases your garden's harmony and productivity. Jim should sit in the same
spot at the union of the triangular beds and I will be with
him, as I was with you, to help raise his vibrational level
to allow him to contact the soil and vegetation and to feel
the pulse of the general health of the garden. As he experiences these things he, too, will feel joyous.*

*You want to know if you can communicate with your
house plants? The answer is "yes," with some practice,
but not as easily as with outdoor plants. Energy levels are
quite different for each plant, and one of the factors which
influences the exact makeup of the individual plant's energy pattern is whether or not they are growing inside.
Indoor plants pattern a vibration as close as possible to
those other energies of the house. In other words, they
become an extension of human energy and as such are less
easily defined. When one is feeling centered and in harmony with life, one's plants will also feel this and will
respond accordingly. When one is feeling out of control
and isolated from the Universe, then one's plants will not
grow happily and their growth will show signs of struggle.
When one sees indoor plants which are lush and growing
beautifully, it is because the dominant vibrational forces
of the house are likewise growing appropriately.*

*It is critical that life, human and otherwise, become
aware of the significance of the vibrations they give off.
We are working with diligence to show the Nature forces
the larger view just as we strive to make you aware that
your thoughts as well as actions have long-range effects.
Plant life needs to understand that it too is responsible for
not adding to the negative energy that abounds in Earth's
atmosphere and is under contract to seek to ameliorate
and transform, wherever possible, that which is inappropriate to its growing cycles. I want you to know that Na-*

ture, as well as man, is being reminded of the basis upon which harmony can exist.

Go with the Universe, this day, Agartha, and enjoy your earned connection to all life. Continue your struggle—the benefits are worth it.

Rarely did Mentor seem to mellow. It gave me a warm feeling that he was pleased with my progress and realized we were trying to comply with his wishes. Jim continued to work at garden contact, but with little success. It was true that he did have excellent general insights for managing the garden, but it was discouraging to him that he could not achieve a primary contact. Mentor commented:

✳*Jim is not trying to visualize specifically enough. He only looks for general input rather than contact with a specific energy. He also needs to ask with confidence, realizing that he is seeking a natural connection. He has learned to see colors, and this is a good first step, since several months ago this was not possible. Garden awareness and development of a conscious communication need not happen overnight, and while it is hard to practice and continue meditation without the benefit of direct guidance, nevertheless I am instructing him through you.*

The next day we attempted to contact the Corn Deva in following Mentor's suggestions. I sat with Jim in the "power set" where the triangular beds come together and was pleasantly surprised to find myself in contact with this deva shortly after issuing my "invitation." This time I tried to engage this new energy in more of a dialogue:

CORN DEVA: Our kernels are separate growing units, and we have sufficient nutrients to grow. We are happy to be growing with the squash. They are very friendly toward us and will be helpful to our energy and development. It is curious that you are interested in talking with us.

AGARTHA: We felt we wanted to communicate with the garden, and we had been given guidance that this would be possible.

CORN DEVA: I see. That is the answer then; otherwise, how would you have known of our existence? You are to be congratulated on your efforts. You must have had luck with other vegetables, for you seem quite relaxed and at peace with us. But then I don't look very scary, do I?

AGARTHA: No. You have been kind to talk with us this morning. Thank you. One more thing—would it be too much to ask if you would try to communicate with this person sitting next to me? He loves you, too, and would like to share in this discussion.

CORN DEVA: Is he listening?

AGARTHA: Yes.

CORN DEVA: Certainly, I'll be happy to oblige. (pause) There, how was that?

AGARTHA: I don't know. I'll ask him.

I turned to Jim and asked what he had experienced. He said he honestly had not seen or felt anything, but perhaps he had been trying too hard. He was discouraged with his lack of progress and I was concerned that garden energy communications did not seem to extend beyond my perceptions. I asked my dear friend Martha to join me in a communication with the Sunflower Deva. This was to provide a unique confirmation for us both:

SUNFLOWER DEVA: I am filled with joy at your asking and at your presence. This is a most warm and wonderful place to be. Thank you for putting me here. I am glad you are filled with enjoyment of my presence. I send you both my heartfelt love. I can see the love your friend is send-

ing. It caresses my petals and my being. I don't want to
scare her by talking too loudly.

AGARTHA: It's all right. She would like to hear from you.

SUNFLOWER DEVA: Then I will give her something to enjoy.
(At this point I squeezed Martha's hand to try to cause
her to remember that exact moment.) She smiled at me.
She must have heard! You have no idea how hard it is
to communicate with people. They look right through
you as if you were a dream. How exciting that we can
talk together. (Melanie and Mark came down to be with
us in the garden, so Sunflower signed off.) Goodbye.

The children came running up to us. It was a strain to take
time for their questions when I could hardly wait to find out
what Martha had experienced. When I finally asked her what
had happened, she said that at the moment I had pressed her
hand she had seen a brilliant radiance of golden light and
that she had felt filled with a rush of energy in the area of
her stomach. I asked if she had smiled at this, and she confirmed that she had inwardly smiled when she felt the golden
energy. We compared our mental notes and were terribly
excited that we had verified a three-way interaction among
Martha, the Sunflower Deva and me. This experience was
personally significant because it provided the first human
confirmation of an experience that had previously been
strictly between me and my nonphysical friends.

David and Martha loved sharing the teachings of Mentor
and the nature spirits. Now that we were all aware of the
many different levels of life on the new land, we were careful
to ask about the proper ways to show our willingness to act
responsibly in the light of our growing awareness. David was
an expert gardener and knew a lot about pruning fruit trees.
We decided to ask about pruning. What did the trees themselves experience? We asked Mentor for advice:

❋ *Welcome Dave and Martha. We are glad to have you
join the communication and wish you well in your living*

experience with Agartha and Jim and all that they are about this summer.

Concerning the apple trees, these trees would no doubt welcome the opportunity of being useful again, and as long as the cuttings are not too severe this first year, all will go well. Agartha, you must first communicate with the trees to see if they have any specific objections to their being brought back to life. You should ask if there is any objection to immediate pruning or if there is another time they would prefer. They have not been trimmed for a long time and will have mixed feelings about the cuttings until they are reassured of the loving intent and your desire to increase their production to a viable level. All growing elements are involved and primarily concerned with the production of food or some life-giving or sustaining level of energy. Therefore once these apple trees are brought back into contact with this basic force, they will recognize it as their primary responsibility and reason for existence and will again be ready to produce. They will be amazed to hear from you. Have the conversation this morning and you will be impressed with the results.

Dave asked Mentor about the pruning itself. Should he use hand tools or a power saw? How specifically should he go about the cutting?

✳ *The apple trees are in a semi-torpid state and have not completely recovered from their winter state, so this is an especially good time to prune them. It does not make much difference whether you use hand tools or power tools. The power saw will be quicker and therefore cause less distress, although it is noisy. The hand saw is quiet but takes a considerable time and so draws out the misery. Therefore, make clean cuts and make them surely. Make up your mind first which limbs you are going to cut, and then make the cuts surely and quickly.*

Explain first to the trees what you are doing and that it is for their return to a level of production that these cuts are being made. The trees understand and most will be able to return to a stronger state of health. The older ones should be treated with great care and not too much cutting done, while the younger ones can stand more drastic cutting. Some will have extensive bug growth and disease, and these should be painted so disease does not make inroads into the interior of the tree. Any appropriate sticky substance will protect the tree.

We were quite impressed with Mentor's ability to offer indepth advice on a subject as practical as pruning. It was somehow easier to believe that he would be able to discuss metaphysics or cosmic understanding better than pruning. It came as somewhat of a surprise that he knew so much about ordinary earth matters. I really did not know what he would say in response to my questions, "How is it, Mentor, that you know so much about gardening?"

The Deep Blue Channel

✳*Realities beyond the Earth are able to vicariously experience the sensations of Earth through connection with the deep blue channel of common knowledge. This channel is the living bank of knowledge of all that has been or will be experienced. This amassed thought is available to those who have developed the levels of awareness necessary to match the desired vibratory level of the knowledge one wishes to draw from the channel. The ability to draw in thought patterns from beyond oneself depends on one's advancement, rather than one's physical plane of existence. For example, a person of Earth School may be more adept than one on another plane of existence and therefore would have the ability to reach beyond the physical to encounter knowledge of great advancement. The true avatar will be able to draw on information not available to the developing avatar from both more and less-advanced realities. It is all a progression, Agartha. The more one trusts that all will become available when necessary, the more apt it is to be so.*

You wondered how I knew about gardening? How did you and Jim know about putting in your house foundation? Did you go on building rules alone or rather was it suddenly obvious which steps you should take? Could you be drawing on the blue channel and not realizing it? (Smile) It is not just for us but for you too. Enjoy drawing from this ultimate storehouse. Ask for what you want and you will receive the appropriate answers.

The General Flower Radiance

It had only been a few weeks into the new process of garden communications before we met the most majestic of the garden presences. I was sitting with Jim in the "power seat" and began by putting out my customary call to Pea Deva. But it was not the Pea Deva that answered:

I am the General Flower Radiance and overseer of the flower presences in your garden. Flowers are often shy and hesitant to initially talk to you. I can be of assistance in helping you establish a bridge for this potential communication.

The Pea Deva and I work together to care for this garden, he with vegetables and me with flowers. We are quite different, he and I. He is odd sometimes, but you must not be put off by his brusque manner. You will find I am to be your main guide through these seasons of growth. You may ask me any question and I will be pleased to answer it for you. Think of me as the budding presence of the natural world which is the soaring and illuminating beauty of the Universe. All flowers seek to fulfill that which is their nature. Lend your loving presence to further aid our dimension on Earth that we may return to you the fulfillment of our lives.

The General Flower Radiance won us all with her gentleness and willingness to help us with our flower communications. We attributed a feminine quality to her, just as we had adopted a masculine identification for Pea Deva. Unlike Pea Deva who frequently seemed abrupt and often a bit annoyed by our questions, the General Flower Radiance was always delighted to be of assistance in any way possible. Her responses were long and loving, reflecting the beauty that she saw in all things.

The General Flower Radiance proved a fine teacher as well as an enjoyable, loving presence in the garden. Martha was extremely interested in the healing characteristics of flower essences. Flower essences are solutions made from soaking the blossoms of certain flowers in pure water so that the energy or resonance of the flower is embodied in the water. It can then be taken in small doses to bring about attunement to the natural properties offered by that flower. She asked me to see if the General Flower Radiance could provide flower essences of our own garden flowers. The General Flower Radiance was delighted to comply and provided succinct answers to each of the flowers whose essences we wished to identify for recommendation to our friends and the people of the region. What follows is a partial list from the General Flower Radiance of the New Hampshire flower essences, including their potential physical, psychological and spiritual influences upon an individual when taken internally.

New Hampshire Flower Essences

ANISE-HYSSOP. This flower is of a gentle nature and its essence brings on peace of mind and contentment with one's immediate life situation. It involves awareness of that which is worthy of change and that which is essential for acceptance.

> DILEMMA: Those at a point of frustration between their material wants and their spiritual needs, or even their immediate physical survival.
>
> REMEDY: Peace of mind.

BERGAMOT. This essence is for those who lack an ability to freely experience or express their love for another. The energy from this flower heightens emotional response to the point where it must be defined and shared in order to be integrated. This is appropriate for those who feel isolated from love and wish to develop a relationship in which love is expressed.

DILEMMA: Inability to feel satisfied by one's own definition and living experience of love.

REMEDY: Integration of emotional, spiritual and physical love into one's life.

CELOSIA. This flower represents the energy of analysis. As one seeks to understand one's life choices, this essence allows the choices to be more clearly seen in order that one may make appropriate choices.

DILEMMA: Inability to analyze one's life experience.

REMEDY: Clearer perception of one's life patterns and consequent choices.

CHRYSANTHEMUM. This flower, like the Aster, is a dynamic presence in its qualities of resilience and ability to re-channel energy after a conscious direction has been thwarted. This is important for individuals who have just undergone a change of jobs or relationships.

DILEMMA: Those who are seeking a new direction.

REMEDY: Rechanneling of energy toward the establishment of a new path.

GARDEN PHLOX. The energy from this flower is helpful in overcoming fear which has produced actual physical symptoms. With the application of this essence, the physical manifestations may disappear and the course of the fear may become more easily defined.

DILEMMA: Fear through which physical dysfunction has developed.

REMEDY: Relief from pain and physical symptoms as well as improved insight into the original cause of the fear.

IMPATIENS. This is a loving presence filled with the maturity
and fulfillment of group satisfaction. Those who will
find this vibration important will be those who are primarily drawn to groups but find it difficult to balance
their own energy within a group. This flower energy is
significant in mixing with other flowers and plants, for
it can cause groups to become strengthened and more
spontaneous.
DILEMMA: Those struggling with individual direction
within a group.
REMEDY: Balance of individual power within a group.

MARIGOLD. This is an extremely flamboyant essence and is
persuasive in allowing to surface the positive aspects of
any difficulty. This fragrance is particularly helpful when
one is making a commitment and is in a quandary as to
the appropriateness of the decision. Marigold is effective in blending with the affirmative and allowing its
positive nature to permeate one's thinking.
DILEMMA: Difficulty in seeing the positive aspects of a
situation.
REMEDY: Balance of one's thinking through awareness of
the positive elements inherent in a situation.

MORNING GLORY. This is a passive flower whose vibration
signifies no resistance to the flowing elements of nature.
It is a subtle mingler and goes well with other aspects
of nature. It is strongest in its ability to blend with its
surroundings for the benefit of the whole. It is a beautiful but quiet, gentle essence.
DILEMMA: Those either seeking or resisting the quiet, gentle side of their own nature.
REMEDY: Lack of resistance to one's own nature. Quiet
serenity within the whole.

NASTURTIUM. The energy of the Nasturtium is such that it
promotes rapid opening to the physical side of one's
presence. Wherever one has blocked physical development or healing, either intentionally or unintentionally,

this essence bolsters the body's energies toward rejuvenation.

DILEMMA: Lack of physical development, healing or appropriate physical response.

REMEDY: Positive physical change.

ORANGE HAWKWEED. A person lacking physical endurance will be drawn to this flower. This is an important energy for those preparing for a journey or for any increased physical demands on their body. Those who feel continually depleted and tired and are unable to make decisions because of this would do well to surround themselves with this essence.

DILEMMA: Lack of physical endurance, inability to make decisions because of depleted condition.

REMEDY: Vitality and increased physical stamina resulting in an improved ability to make decisions.

PURPLE ASTER. The aster is a strong, dominant force in fostering spiritual development. This essence is appropriate for those who are preparing for the energy of transformation and wish to be calm and peaceful in the search.

DILEMMA: Inability to draw spiritual development into one's realm while remaining calm and centered.

REMEDY: Serenity within the spiritual search.

QUEEN ANNE'S LACE. This flower is a catalyst to other ongoing physical and mental processes. Queen Anne's Lace allows the body to move through transition more quickly.

DILEMMA: Inability to bring existing transition to conscious conclusions.

REMEDY: Rapid conclusion to period of transition.

RED CLOVER. This sturdy plant is representative of stubbornness and tenacity and will be useful to those needing to understand the energy of resolution.

DILEMMA: Inability to balance the energy of determination.

REMEDY: The ability to have confidence in one's life decisions.

SUNFLOWER. The essence of the Sunflower is that of acceptance of the oneness of the Universe. This is essential for those feeling fragmented and alone and lacking a sense of spiritual connection.

DILEMMA: Feeling of isolation from the Universe.

REMEDY: Sense of belonging through awareness of the interconnectedness of all things.

SWEET PEA. The Sweet Pea is a favorable essence when one is feeling the need to balance the masculine energy with the feminine. The Sweet Pea stands as the ultimate balance.

DILEMMA: Lack of balance of the masculine and feminine energies.

REMEDY: Balance of masculine and feminine energy.

WHITE PINE. This energy represents a strong calming element for those who are in need of soothing. Those who will be attracted to this essence are those feeling tossed and torn by life or those having no roots. This essence is strength with underlying creativity. The Oak possesses the strength but is a more rigid form—no creative influences.

DILEMMA: Those seeking roots.

REMEDY: Strength and creativity.

ZINNIA. This is a very robust flower, strong and durable. Its color and presence portend its ability to promote acceptance.

DILEMMA: One is in need of strength, physical or spiritual.

REMEDY: Strength.

In looking back, it seems I have come a long way toward understanding the broader picture of oneness. I am equally certain that I have only begun to explore the layers of the concept. The natural mysteries seen through Mentor, General Flower Radiance, Pea Deva and the many beautiful and unique energies of the garden have awakened me to a previously unknown reality. The experiences of the garden would never have fit into my former reality, as that level of perception was unavailable to me at that time. I was becoming . . . and the experiences along the way enhanced this becoming. I had begun to see my life as an ongoing process, nothing static or even predictable, yet moving in a direction that constantly added dimension to who I was becoming.

The experience of actually sharing preceptions with the devas of the garden, while startling and gratifying, is really only another dimension to what many people already perceive in the garden. It is not unlike putting on a pair of glasses for the first time and suddenly ''seeing'' clearly objects you already knew existed but were unable to identify.

Combining Energy of the Earth and the Heavens: The Perfect Garden

✻ Listening to Nature has some interesting benefits. Most importantly, it allows the prospective gardener to gain an added advantage as to the nature of the soil, what needs to be added for optimal growth, what plants will be happiest in what parts of the garden and other important issues. Through the establishment of a close relationship with one's garden, one is able to make decisions based on more than the directions on seed or fertilizer packages. Decisions affecting the life in one's garden can instead be based on the needs and wishes of the plants which will make their home there.

For example, when a plant is not growing well, one can accurately determine the cause by placing one's hand first on the leaf, then on the stalk and then on the ground next to the roots. By this method, one is able to determine in which area the problem lies and then, through the process of elimination, whether it is something as simple as insuf-

*ficient water or whether there are insects causing damage
in areas where infestation cannot be seen.*

*In discussing the optimum balance for gardens, Agar-
tha, I would like you to remember the digging and planting
of your own garden. As you recall, I gave you specific
directions for your garden which, though you did not realize it at the time, provided your garden with sufficient
energy to bypass not only the poor soil conditions in order
to produce a lush garden, but also gave your garden the
perfect balance to facilitate a level of trust and understanding to further garden communications.*

*The physical location for your garden was important for
a number of reasons. First, the gardens needed to take
advantage of the southern exposure to afford your plants
the maximum amount of sunlight. Second, the ley lines
(in-earth energy lines) which bisected your land were a
powerful source of growing potential, but needed to be
tapped in the most appropriate and effective manner. In
other words, your exact piece of land was considered in
order to arrive at the most effective use of celestial and
earthly energies. With this in mind, you will notice that
the three equilateral triangles at the head of the garden
draw the southern sunlight toward your garden and your
house, grounding it in your land. The three rectangular
gardens below the triangles form a right angle with the ley
line that reaches down your land, thus combining and
grounding the earth energy. Celestial and in-earth energies have been combined to make your garden a most
unique example of the cooperation possible between the
human and natural forces of the planet.*

**Personalizing Nature: Can Man Teach as Well as
Listen?**

*Man seems the most comfortable when every detail of
his world is explained. Progress can do much to improve
the quality of life. It is essential, however, that contrived
and nonessential modes of living do not blind him to his*

environmental connection. *Mutual respect rather than ownership and control is the avenue of progress that leads to cooperative behavior. The lost equality between man and Nature is what needs to be encouraged and reinstated as man's statement of new Aquarian harmony. In order to appreciate the magnitude of the cosmic perspective, humankind must become teachers to and of the natural kingdoms in order that all may grow in understanding and wisdom.*

The forces of nature function in an incredibly creative and sophisticated mode, potentially ready to nurture man in his own physical growth and cosmic development. While nature stands ready to learn, the question now becomes: is man ready to teach? Awareness beyond functional existence is not limited to the human dimension. Nature also exists with needs beyond its own genetic patterning, but like the human its needs include interaction with man for maximum development.

Now that you have had several years of communicating with the energies of your garden, Agartha, sitting in the "power seat" and listening to the General Flower Radiance and the Pea Deva talk about the garden, could you ever resume the level of action within your garden without input from the forces that live there? You have become so used to this type of interchange that you have forgotten what it was like not to know that everything in your grasp also has needs. Yet in relating to others you may find it necessary to proceed slowly from the beginning, even using more traditional methods of teaching such as retracing those metaphors in literature which speak of nature spirits, devas, elementals, leprechauns, little people, fairies and elves in order to suggest that where there is imagination, there is a stem of truth which sprouted it. All these mentions of "imaginary beings" began with the knowledge that there were energies which lived outside of man's vision. You will need to nurture and gently lead others toward your realizations, Agartha, in order that they be allowed to understand the real meaning of life within the natural world.

There are many people who talk to their gardens. Some talk to pass the lonely hours, some out of a sense of duty and some out of a sense of love and a desire for interaction. While many talk, very few listen. And if they do listen, they are not prepared for the delicacy of the response. Communication can take the form of the subtlest of awareness, a sense of pressure on the body, a waft of color before one's closed eyes. While these sensations are usually considered extraneous, they are rather part of a pattern of response which one must observe over several weeks in order to find a more definable personality or pattern of perceptions. For example, Agartha, when you feel the small hand of your daughter, Melanie, slip into yours, you are not surprised because you look down and see her standing there. If, however, you felt the small hand fit into yours but saw no Melanie, you would dismiss it as random sensation. Just so with most gardeners or tenders of the wild; they look down and see nothing, so they dismiss whatever sensations they perceive.

Wanting to Understand

Understanding begins to seep into consciousness not necessarily in a rush but instead in a slow and steady progression. Perceptions of living greenness enter men's and women's consciousness whenever and wherever they are permitted to do so. When conscious love and dynamic understanding replace prejudice, then permission is subtly given for union with the human dimension.

To know the truth, one must want to know the truth and then be willing to abide by what is found. An appreciation for life is not limited to knowing categories or classifications of life but lies instead within the heart's understanding. For to theorize is human, but to respond to universal law beyond the realm of theory is truly divine. Because man is divine, he is able to tap that level of perception which permits exploration into the innermost reaches of life, grounding this knowledge to the bosom of the Earth in order that understanding may permeate pure reason.

In seeking to fathom the intricacies of life, one must relinquish the urge to prejudge what the Universe can and cannot do and be. For in indulging in this strictly human foible, man denies his divinity and settles for the role of the recluse, the solitary traveler who in his own microcosmic vision fails to recognize the hand of Divine Creativity unfolding.

CHAPTER EIGHT

THE EXPERIENCE
OF HEALING

*You never lay your hands
on someone in love
without a healing occurring
on the appropriate level.*

MENTOR

Holism: A Complement to Traditional Medicine

THE NATURE OF the material in this chapter is significantly different from the material previously presented. Mentor's thoughts on health and healing are tangible and demonstrable, unlike the material in previous chapters which dealt with subjects that remain unavoidably theoretical and unprovable.

I can speak for the authenticity of Mentor's approach to healing because I am now a practitioner in the field of holistic health and have learned to use his guidance as the basis for my work in the promotion of holism. His guidance, coupled with my own developing expertise as a medical clairvoyant, has shown me the vast potential for healing within this concept of oneness or holism. While I always had an interest in medicine, never did I anticipate that it would evolve into my profession in such extraordinary terms. For more than learning the technical aspects of medicine, I have learned the subtle principles of healing.

The concept of holism is becoming increasingly prevalent. It is a term which represents the integration of physiology, psychology and spirituality. In the vernacular of the healer, that translates to the integration of body, mind and spirit which forms the synthesis of human life. The fragmentation of this total life force precludes optimum health and is the root of disease, regardless of whether that disease manifests as physical, psychological or emotional.

Everyone hurts. No one exists outside the laws of change. The larger issue of becoming healthy, therefore, revolves around the willingness to accept responsibility for illness and to explore those aspects which defy personal wholeness. It seems that a unique aspect of the human experience is the opportunity to piece together the many facets of one's evolving life pattern into a meaningful whole.

Health is not achieved solely by responding to the physical symptoms of an illness. An ulcer, for example, is more than the "excavation of the surface of an organ produced by sloughing of necrotic inflammatory tissue"; it is an indication of the inability to process stress through the body. Merely treating the physical discomfort by no means cures the psychological or emotional issues which caused the development of the ulcer. In order to achieve a balanced state of health, an assessment must be made of an individual's psychological, emotional and physical status. Based on that collection of personal data, a treatment plan designed to stimulate the whole person can be developed.

In times of physical/emotional crisis, individuals are particularly vulnerable. Most people tend to rely on more familiar behavioral patterns when dealing with a stressful situation because the familiar always seems safer. It will not be immediately recognized that it was the "familiar" behavioral patterns which caused the illness to develop. There needs to be a transition while in the state of illness from familiar behavioral patterns which no longer promote health to reevaluated patterns which reflect oneness and encourage healing.

Consider the state of mind of an individual who has always seen himself as a "victim": that is, a person undeserving of any of the blessings of a good life. Unless this attitude is treated along with the physical illness, the individual will not recover his health because his dominant belief is that he is helpless to change his physical reality and thus can never be healthy and happy.

Assuming personal responsibility for one's health need not place one in opposition to traditional medicine. Doctors diagnose and treat trauma, disease and dysfunction appropriate to their academic background and the drugs and diagnostic tools at their disposal. The complement, however, is also valid. Holistic physicians diagnose and treat trauma based on the natural energy flows and rhythms of the entire body, with the range of treatments mirroring the body's natural functioning.

The human inclination is to see that which is new as different and thus as standing in opposition to the standard, rather than as a valuable addition to that which already exists. It is unfortunate that in establishing this "either/or" reality, the patient must often choose one or the other form of medical treatment, rather than having the freedom to choose his medical diet as it seems appropriate.

Mentor had often alluded to wholeness, and was interested in the concept of holism in relation to trauma. This brief discussion was to launch the dynamics of his thoughts on healing:

✳ *The search for wholeness which began as a mere germ of awareness has gained impetus, keeping pace with the search for an understanding of the physical pains and psychological traumas intrinsic to the human condition. Hospitals, healing centers, hospices, holistic half-way houses, havens of every sort, are springing up all over the world in response to this need to know how to heal and be healed, as well as how to interpret the nature of disease.*

I offer some thoughts on healing, being healed, and what it means to be whole in the hope that through insight into the nature of healing, the mystery which obscures true wholeness from human understanding may be known, and humankind may indeed actualize a new level of personal awareness.

Four Cases of Trauma

NO. 1 *Martha did not want to die. She never really
thought it would happen. How could there be no
more physical life, no more walks in the woods or
talks with her daughter, no more strawberry pie a
la mode? The reality of her spreading cancer
caused her to retreat into a pretend world where
everything was normal. There seemed no answers
and even the questions scared her.*

NO. 2 *Melissa had felt no warning or premonition to suggest that her child would be born severely retarded.
It all seemed so unreal—the years of specialists,
the tests, the hope and then always the overwhelming depression when it was again confirmed that
the child's retardation seemed permanent. What
had she ever done to deserve this? Who would there
be to take care of her small Darren when she and
her husband were gone? The same questions tormented her night after restless night. Why had such
a child been born to them?*

NO. 3 *It was as if the sun never came out any more since
the hemorrhage destroyed the vision in his one remaining good eye. John's world seemed doomed to
lasting darkness. Maneuvering around his small
apartment, even fixing simple meals became enormously frustrating. The fear of permanent blindness haunted his thoughts, increasing his feelings
of loneliness and of separation from life.*

NO. 4 *Susan had already been married seven years and
still she was not pregnant. It had gotten to be the
rather pathetic joke she and her husband shared.
The yearning for a baby had become an obsession;
everywhere she turned she saw families and children. Why was she different? Unless her body*

*could be forced to ovulate, she was told, there was
no hope of conception.*

Trauma and disease exist as splinters of unresolved, poorly
defined thought and action, thwarted opportunities for
change where the new circumstance has arisen but the old
vibration is still held. The traumatic condition is the condition of indecision, somewhere between acceptance and rejection, between disease and health, between willingness to
challenge the status quo and fear of the unknown.

Humankind in its naïveté is often unaware of its latent
power and calls upon the Universe through the tools of spirituality, asking to be shown the avenues of growth. Yet when
these same petitions are met with new levels of growth, the
human becomes paralyzed, frozen in yesterday's mold and
unable to respond to the notion that physical life is a small
part of a universal understanding, or that change and the
recognition of a need for change is the journey to health.
The development of human growth patterns may often not
fall within the sphere of human understanding. When there
is no glimmer of comprehension—why this trauma, why this
disease?—then confusion and a sense of helplessness reduce
the human experience to less than it might otherwise be.
Sadly and all too often, the status quo remains friend, and
change of any kind becomes enemy.

Of course, asking for awareness and discovering one has
a terminal disease is certainly not what one would choose.
Yet what are the lessons and where are they found? If one
is being slowly weaned from the gross to the refined, from
the earthly to the cosmic, then the lessons of letting go of
the physical in order to claim the cosmic are going to be
intense. When one sees only the physical environment as
real, then loss of that environment or any part of it induces
total panic. All aspects of the universe are subject to constant change, continually moving in a direction of enlightenment. Change but provides the doorways through which
all must travel to find true peace.

The fact that the changes one seeks are usually not the
changes which manifest, further reinforces the fear of what

may be hiding in the unknown. I can tell you that fear is the only enemy, that change when allowed to flow through one's life, carrying along with it whatever it will, is not fearful or painful. It is only the resistance to change which causes trauma.

Consistent with the notion of disease created from repressed change comes the realization that when mental, emotional, physical and spiritual vibrations fail to harmoniously align within the body, trauma results. The greater the imbalance, the greater the trauma. As these splinters of unresolved energy seek resolution and fall back into symmetry with the rest of the being, then wholeness is restored. Finding and sorting out what is not synchronized with what is, can be a difficult task since the properties of mind and body exist in a fast-evolving stream of energy. No two days, two hours or two minutes are ever exactly alike. Healing, or the seeking of alignment of one's being, is understanding that the energy of yesterday is best left to yesterday in order that the new day may possess and reflect an appropriately different energy.

Healing therapy most commonly fails when the course of one's change has not been accurately plotted to include the individual's need for a past, present, and future: past life experiences, present physical condition and possible future alignment. Because the physical life experience is learned in a past-present-future sequence, it becomes important when dealing with trauma that the individual be allowed to see a positive progression, even though it is not necessary to be aligned with yesterday's energy, only today's. Yesterday's lessons are yesterday's lessons. But the results of yesterday's lessons can provide the ground swell around which the current day's lessons can be more completely understood. While the future is what it is and should not be seen as already written since each lesson spearheads a new direction, nevertheless allowing for future growth is essential. Whether or not future goals are reached is unimportant. Yesterday, today and tomorrow do not exist as separations in the continuum of life; they are all one. Each pass through physical

*life is a whole experience which immediately becomes one
with the summation of one's physical incarnation.*

The Three Stages Through Trauma

*Each of the four short case histories cited in the begin-
ning of the chapter have something in common. All four
individuals felt helplessly and hopelessly mired in a strange
and unfamiliar bog of pain and trauma, psychological,
physical and spiritual, where nothing made sense save their
physical symptoms and feelings of despondency and desperation. All four individuals had in fact entered the first
stage of understanding trauma, namely the period of
necessary aloneness or the time of readjustment.*

*In Stage I, "alone" does not mean isolated and ostra-
cized, although many read that into it. It can mean instead "given to solitary purpose." When one enters
through the doors of disease, one needs to be alone to
strengthen one's being to transcend the imperfectness of
unresolved change in circumstances or physical nature and
in so doing to understand what can be perceived by the
Earth mind. Aloneness is a necessary mental and physical
conditioning preliminary to seeing the nature of one's off-
centeredness. This need for physical, psychological and
spiritual seclusion is the result of life-threatening or
life-style-threatening disease or dysfunction. This withdrawal is a bona fide healing stage allowing the energies
to re-synthesize the fragments of one's life with the impending change producing a cohesive, understandable, believable composite. Unfortunately, well-meaning friends
and family mistake this withdrawal for an unhealthy sign
of neurosis or at least morose self-pity and do what they
can to motivate the person into more extroverted behavior
rather than understanding that the patient will only move
to a new stage when this period of solitude has produced
peace. Stage I is the psyche's way of preparing the whole
being for new circumstances. It represents progression*

from physical and psychological shock to the reassurance that there is more to come.

This initial period of withdrawal is perhaps the most critical of the three stages through trauma, for in it is the embryo of the newly evolving sense of self from which all changed awareness must spring. Every human is drawn into this stage when faced with a change, any change, no matter how trivial. Sadly, many never move through this level when faced with a serious change. Instead they remain confused and overwhelmed by these challenges. Friends and family must exist outside this initial stage, loving the individual, praying for or meditating with the individual in order that this stage of aloneness may produce calm and the loved one may move to Stage II where he can see, hear and feel in a way compatible with his own newly evolved sense of self.

Martha, Melissa, John, and Susan had not accepted their changing realities as more than "poor me," "bad luck," or the "malevolent universe" excuse. Until they appropriately released their physically held limitations, life remained a room of four walls and no doors. The realization that a door was not necessary to leave the room was indeed the lesson necessary for physical realignment and true healing to replace scattered confusion and pain.

The human spirit is born with a desire to seek inner stability in the midst of outward turmoil, allowing for the spiritual and psychological reorganization which is mandatory in times of intense trial if the outcome is to be wholeness. As one moves through Stage I, there is an emergence of calm and a sense of purposeful intent. Without a quality time of consideration of the ordeal at hand, no suitable course of action could possibly be formulated which takes into consideration all the individual's loose ends. I use the word "ordeal" here and mean it quite literally to confirm the seriousness and the intensity of life's wholeness hurdles. Anyone who has been in excruciating pain and unable to hear answers to fervently said prayers can attest to such devastation. To downplay the trauma involved in physical and mental suffering on your *planet would be a grave disservice to those who coura- geously and joyously search. For while disease is not what it seems, neither is the physical body or the total presence; nonetheless, to the human who suffers pain and loss of one's valued physical presence or any part of one's phys- ical reality, it is a very real, very tangible and an all- consuming threat.*

Just as Stage I is withdrawal to seek personal strength, Stage II is confirmation of intent, meaning the identifi- cation of a direction to follow, something to trust and in which to believe. This is the transition stage, the tunnel connecting two stations. It effectively causes the imple- mentation of a new purpose.

Stage III is the decided-upon finale. Death is a con- scious conclusion, a releasing to a more appropriate reality, just as life, health and healing are also conscious conclusions. So in trauma, a calm and presence are found, a course of action is then pursued, and a conclusion is sought and reached. The original course of action may change many times before the issue is resolved, yet it re- mains the acceptance of the changing mode of physical life and spiritual life that brings freedom.

Those who move through all three stages from shock to conscious acceptance have learned a great deal of the na- ture of their own inner needs and their response to change. Life, if given permission, can devour the human, digesting and regurgitating the physical over and over until some semblance of realization prevails and the individual re- fuses to continually invest in the purely physical. Listen- ing to the vibration of change and the natural aftermath of physical upheaval can underscore one's sense of whole- ness, as nonattachment to the physical brings an acqui- escence to the vibration of change and inevitable growth.

The connection between negativity and the vibration of change is one worth touching upon to underscore that negativity is produced by one's fighting the change vibra- tion in one's own life. We have talked of negativity and the negative impulses which enter the body and remain lodged within its fibers, defying integration. As one re-

peatedly blocks change, the enmeshed negativity causes disease by its inability to be moved through one's presence, thus stagnating the energies of one's system. The willingness to recognize and accept change within one's external and/or internal structures can cause a return to wellness. Those who are unwilling or unable to flow with feelings induced by disease and trauma remain clogged with the unresolved, continuing to collect negativity and growing increasingly worse. Disease, dysfunction, trauma of any kind is the clue that the need for some kind of change is at hand.

Review of the Lessons of Change

Let us briefly review our four cases histories to see if there were opportunities for change which were ignored and if the fear of change produced sufficient negativity to spark disease.

No. 1 Terminal Cancer.

Martha was afraid of life and afraid of death, afraid of anything that changed her world view causing her to see two sides. Life was only black or white and, while it is indeed true that seeing only perfectness does produce perfectness, nevertheless one must initially see both the black and white and all shades of gray in order to choose a course. Martha never saw the issues and never wanted to know what life held for her. She saw only her own desperate isolation, first from her parents and later from her husband and children. The opportunities to adjust her sense of self were repeatedly presented through her deteriorating personal relationships. She was not able to see the changing relationships in her life as opportunities for exploring and changing stagnant feelings. She entered Stage I of healing, the period of aloneness, and moved to Stage II only after her death when she more clearly saw and understood the path to her true healing.

No. 2   Severe Retardation.

After years of questioning her part in the birth of their retarded son, Darren, Melissa finally found peace, though not in the way she most expected. The years following Darren's birth had been angry years searching for confirmation of the only answer she would accept, namely that Darren's condition was correctable. The moment she released her inner ultimatum for Darren's absolute recovery, she moved into Stage II of healing. Perhaps it was as a sense of finality—no more doctors to ask, no more tests and no more hopes. She was not aware anything had changed except that she began to be happy again, accepting invitations and beginning to interact with people in a way she had not done since her son's birth. Her healing gradually moved toward completion, and in Stage III she began to share Darren's care with others, willingly and openly interacting with others without guilt, building a new stronger foundation for herself and her relationship with her son.

Melissa's own personal rigidity and unwillingness to compassionately love and understand her own childhood polio had resulted in her being drawn to a child in whom the rigidity was manifest in an even more obvious physical form. The child was physically and mentally impaired but possessed a healing gentleness and open acceptance which taught her to see and learn to appreciate the inner nature or meaning of spirit. The opportunities for recognizing the self-destructive rigidity with which she fought her own polio could have changed the need for a child with Darren's problems. But in denying all previous opportunities for such personal exploration, the repressed changes called a similarly rigid form to her. It was only through the gradual recognition of the fact that Darren was happy, peaceful and content that she was finally able to release her own anger and expectation level.

No. 3   Blindness through Hemorrhage.

Fear of the future held John in a perpetual state of anxiety. It was not until his niece involved him in her world of living that he was able to reflect on the happiness of the days before blindness and integrate the joy of what had been his life with what was his current situation. He learned to "see" his own life and circumstances without the need for physical sight, and began to move beyond the obvious superficial reality of his blindness to a deeper understanding of his spirituality. Although his vision gradually returned, he continued to explore his new understanding of the inner self.

As a small child, John had seen his dead mother standing at the foot of his bed telling him of their shared existence. Shortly thereafter he began to have mystical dreams, out-of-body experiences and feelings of unusual closeness to the Universe. He became so frightened by these encounters that he began to repress and disregard the energy which was leading him toward spiritual understanding. John needed to strengthen, not lessen, his commitment to the Universe and to learn to differentiate between conscious fear of the unknown and intuitive awareness of an expanded dimension. He had chosen not to see, and that translated over the years to a withdrawal of energy from the physical apparatus of vision. As he regained his sight, he absorbed the new vision of understanding into his life along with his connection to the universal forces which he had so long denied.

No. 4   Infertility.

On a deep level, Susan accepted her just punishment of not being able to have a child. The picture of her young brother drowning was still very clearly etched in her mind and she was sure she must somehow be punished for allowing such a thing to happen and causing so much pain to her mother and father. The fact that she had been just a child herself with no conception of drowning or death

*did not alter her remorse at having stood by and watched
as her brother's body quietly slid beneath the level of the
water. In her own mind she was guilty, and no amount of
comforting from her parents could dispel the fear of some
impending punishment from God.*

*The manifestation of this fear was the cessation of men-
struation when she married. Consciously Susan denied
any fear of having children and even through seven years
of intensive psychoanalysis she remained in Stage I of
trauma. It was only through the experience of her mother's death that Susan finally touched and felt death not
as the terrifying hand of the "grim reaper" but rather as
the gentle yet powerful hand of the Universe. A year later
Susan and her husband adopted a baby girl and with this
step Susan moved into Stage II of trauma, drawn by the
joy, love and exaltation she felt in the new life she now
shared. She moved beyond her fear of punishment through
experiencing motherhood. She resumed a normal monthly
cycle and in six months was pregnant.*

*There had been many opportunities for understanding
her brother's death and the changes this awareness needed
to cause in her before her marriage. Chances to babysit
for friends' children were repeatedly declined, and discussions with close friends and family were always steered
away from the issues of children. Even though she had a
sensitive relationship with her husband, she refused to
talk out or try to understand the inner fear which directed
her life.*

I thought about the fascinating cases of the four people
who dealt with the stages of trauma. Mentor was definitely
saying that the trauma in each of these cases could have been
avoided had the individuals not blocked some process of
change.

While he did not mention the blockages from previous
lives, I began to wonder about the need to work out problems
from life to life or within a single life. Was there a relation
between disease and "karma"?

Is Disease "Karma"?

✻ *Health and disease are both by-products of the process of personal change. The continuing reflections of personal change do not end with death but instead are incorporated into subsequent physical existences. One's personal growth in each life determines the physical circumstances that will follow in other levels. This cause and effect, action and reaction relationship with past lives is known as karma.*

In other words, the dynamics of past lives influence the lineup of dynamics with which one is involved in current life. The areas of change which were previously the most difficult and perhaps remained unresolved continue to appear in the current life. While in between physical realities it is true that one is again made whole with a broader perspective, nevertheless, as soon as one returns to a physical plane, the lessons appear anew. Disease then is karmic in the sense that:

1. *The circumstances which showcase the need for changes are karmic and often built upon previous decisions.*

2. *Repression of changes as seen through life lessons ultimately cause trauma or disease.*

The vibration of change is karmic opportunity to be continually reborn, and if the person seeking wholeness can actualize his healing when faced with a karmic happenstance, then it is the opportunity to move beyond that specific lesson and remove it from one's physical life so it does not continually reappear. The life situation then is karmic and the decisions made within that framework create new karma. Healing is the amelioration of disease within a karmic setting. Karma merely sets the stage for each new lesson, but the outcome is not determined by karma. It is determined by the individual and the choices that he alone can make.

Humankind often seeks to affirm its own personal action by using karma as a sort of inevitable "cosmic stamp." It is inevitable in that the course of one's continuing lives is formed by personal choices. But one is always at liberty to move beyond the karmic framework of natural progression, for nothing exists within the physical presence which has not been given permission to be there. Once again, through lack of vision and therefore self-limitation of one's own cosmic gifts, one remains within the karmic framework. Moving beyond karma is assuming one has power within one's control to choose a course of action based on the understood bond of cosmic love. Synthesis of love with human energy removes one from slow karmic repetition and propels one into a state of oneness with forces which respond only in love. By choosing the all-powerful vibration of love over any karmic hold, one effectively overcomes perceived limitation.

Resignation to a condition or circumstance, feeling "it's karma," insures that one remains in Stage I of trauma, never releasing the pain to the healing process or taking the matter into the house of one's own responsibility. Love is the singular most important force lifting an individual from isolation and dejection to awareness and joy. Love, as a way of being, seeing, and feeling—the merging of one's presence with compassion—is the key to eternal health. It is the "wild card in the karmic shuffle." Let us look at an example in the form of an allegory of Lord Karma.

Allegory of Lord Karma

There was once a man of whom the gods were so jealous that they punished him by giving him a large burden to carry. He was told he must carry his burden until someone offered him room and board for a night. Because he was given a robe of black and a frightening appearance, all who saw him fled in terror, convinced of his evil intent.

A rumor of his alleged evil pranks soon sprang to life,

running rampant throughout the land, infecting each town with fear and suspicion. Lord Karma traveled from town to town for many thousands of years, waiting for another to so trust in his own power of love that no fear would be seen, only the commonality and love of being would be known.

Slowly, with measured footsteps, a small child approached Lord Karma as he paused by a well for a drink one hot afternoon. The boy seemed unafraid of the black cloak and looked instead at the traveler's bruised and bleeding feet. His eyes were wide with understanding, and without hesitation he asked the stranger to come with him that he might share what he had. Immediately the dark robe lost its blackness and took on a dazzling radiance. The burden vanished as the energy of love permeated his presence and made him whole.

Disease, imbalance or any lack of wholeness, even though it springs to life through karma, cannot stand in the aura of love without being transmuted. The vibration of karma is always present but nullified when one reaches beyond confinement in the name of love. In seeking healing one must realize that the complete acceptance of love into one's presence as the transformative experience is more powerful than any karmic reaction. The ready acceptance of karma as the end of the quest is too easy. The assessment of relevant karma but begins the quest toward understanding. It is the beginning of the healing process, not the end. Healing comes from both an understanding of the karmic forces in one's life and the perspective that any physical dysfunction can be overcome when aligned with the forces of love.

I had always felt one was limited by karma, and yet Mentor was denying that karma had power when one aligned himself with the forces of love. That suggested my next question: Can someone be healed without first gaining an awareness of what caused his block or created his illness?

Healing and Being Healed

✻ *There is a thought I would like to share with you and that is:*

> *You never lay your hands on someone in love*
> *without a healing occurring*
> *on the appropriate level.*

Healing integrates so much more than just the physical presence. Healing is altering total reality, opening the window to a comprehensive understanding of one's true appearance that any and all compromise may be negated and the archetype of perfection embraced. One's natural appearance is after all without physical adornment of accessories or clothes or for that matter even a physical presence. One's true appearance is as light, a transmutable, multi-refractive presence which simply exists as a reuseable force within the universe.

Is it possible to be "cured" of a physical malady without first gaining a new inner perspective? The answer is "no." The understanding, conscious and superconscious, precedes or is simultaneous with any healing. When someone moves past physical trauma in a matter of moments rather than years, it is because the awareness of healing has occurred simultaneously with the physical alterations. In other words Stages I, II, and III have been dealt with simultaneously. There is no rigid sequential time limitation to healing, yet there are usually natural progressions, a step at a time, leading one toward a goal of health through self-awareness.

Perhaps the term "self-awareness" seems too vague. Psychically embracing one's divinity is another way of seeing self-awareness. Healing involves the sorting through of one's emotional and spiritual baggage to see what is still in one's present life suitcase. Much can be discarded; a small percentage can be kept. This sorting is self-awareness. Healing through self-awareness is the only honest healing, since it goes beyond physical alteration

*and most importantly changes one's preconception of cos-
mic confinement. One's view of reality changes as one
grows toward health, opening up new vistas of physical
and spiritual life. The individual can more appropriately
define healing as he lives it and struggles to find acceptance of his own perfectness. There are no "do nots" and
"cannots" in healing. Everything in physical reality is
transmutable through love, or you know it as "energy."
Healing is a free-wheeling, continually perpetuated journey. The personal "sorting out" process is always at work
within the individual psyche. So the healing process can
likewise be invoked into everyday experiences in cases of
major disease and trauma. Accordingly, each day in Earth
School requires healing of the self through awareness and
acceptance of the human connection to love.*

*All people are healers, and each is capable of healing
not only his own presence, but his children, parents, close
friends, distant relatives and total strangers. Every man,
woman and child on Planet Earth is a healer. Every physical life situation has the potential for healing, for causing
transformation. Life does not exist as a prerecorded message of either plodding drudgery and misery or carefree
escape. It exists as a learning—a lesson in the art of healing oneself, each other, the planet and beyond. The purpose of physical life is to learn to heal: heal the pain, anger
and frustration, channel the vast resources of love and
learning to where they can do the most good, to the heart
of mankind.*

*There are no limitations to the vibrations of empathy
and love. Love is the vibration which when expanded
through cosmic attunement produces "miracles." I realize when I say there are no limitations that this is difficult
to comprehend when one seems constantly hemmed in,
limited by the physical. But in the world of healing, in the
world beyond the physical presence of stars, planets, and
galaxies, exists a force of such enormous intensity that
even a vague alignment with its presence produces changes
beyond knowable limitations. So in the thinking of oneself
as a healer involved in the giving and receiving of love,*

one should feel buoyed by the notion of nonlimitation in which all that is sought in the name of "love" becomes appropriately manifested.

There is more than healing through traditional medical routes; healing occurs through the creative process. The artist, the dancer, the musician, the architect, the teacher, business executive, lawyer and politician can all heal through their own creative approaches to and interpretations of their fields. Just because one is not interested in physically touching another or palpating another's spleen does not mean one is not a healer. Men and women can heal each other through their own individual expression. Certainly audiences and individuals alike are healed through interplay, acceptance and understanding or creative interpretation. The everyday creative motions one goes through can be one's mode of healing. These potentially viable healing abilities unfortunately often become blocked by the individual's own inability to translate perception into response or interpret one's true self in terms others can understand.

Healing oversees the field of individual creative archetypes. It is the term used to cover all the forms of creative expression and interplay which cause joy and wholeness to surface in the individual. For example, the architect who lovingly creates the designs for a building is then faced with the problem of selling the designs to the customer. Creative perception turns to thwarted response when the customer remains unimpressed, and the potential joy and healing through creative exchange is lost in the dilemma of response. When personal ego replaces love, dilemmas can never be dissolved and resolved, and thus healing never takes place.

When an actor plays to an audience, becoming sensitized to its collective energy, he loses himself in the act of playing out his own creativity. There is no singular ego directing the audience or actor—each is healing the other through the understanding of the shared creative experience. Each moves in response to the other's subtle cues. The individuals within the audience are being healed through the release of themselves as separate entities and their acceptance of themselves as part of the whole. The performer is being healed through the infusion of energy projected from the audience, allowing him to flow within his own creative performance.

Medical Clairvoyance: Learning to See

Medical clairvoyance is a perceptual ability not bound by the restrictions of time and space. In order to gain an insight into the dynamics of medical clairvoyance, it may prove useful to view its underlying principles already recognized in fields far more conventional.

Consider, for example, the direction toward which certain areas of physics are aiming. Research among various physicists is now suggesting that "time," as we experience it, is an artificial expression of reality subject to our understanding of physical life on this planet. Therefore, the physicists are now involved in trying to reconcile an intuitive perception of the nature of time and space with the laws of physical reality as they are currently understood.

For laymen not fully schooled in physics, this research may appear totally absurd. Were it not for the fact that physics is a highly accepted and admired area of science, perhaps the entire theory of transcending time would be entirely disregarded.

And yet, one must recognize that before physicists could work toward bridging the gap between what they are perceiving intellectually and what they understand to be true physically, they first had to intellectually acknowledge that reality may be more involved than we currently believe. In a very real sense, their minds had to transcend the limits of time and space before they could work toward discovering the corresponding patterns in physical reality.

Similarly, medical clairvoyance requires that an individual's perceptual system transcend the restrictions of the physical reality. Physical laws of energy and geographic space should not be applied toward the understanding of this ability. Medical clairvoyance is governed by the principles of nonphysical energy. Simply put, processes of imagination and memory are real. When one recalls an emotionally powerful memory, immediately one recreates that distant experience, regardless of the fact that the physical body remains locked into present time. Literally speaking, the natural ability of the mind, not bound by time, made a journey beyond time and space, experiencing fully an event no longer in physical reality.

Likewise, the perceptual abilities of a medical clairvoyant cause the energy system of another person to be seen through focusing the innate ability of the mind to "view" or "experience" realities beyond the physical plane. Specifically, a medical clairvoyant is concerned with perceiving the existence of an energy pattern, within a person's total energy profile, which indicates the presence of disease.

Just as a physicist must educate his mind in order to relate to the world of physics, so also must a medical clairvoyant train his mind. More than acquiring a strong academic background, the medical clairvoyant must work toward understanding and trusting his own perceptual system, as well as toward learning to translate his perceptions accurately. It is also required that he challenge the conventional and scientific view of reality and move into investigating a more mystical understanding of the principles of life.

I am not suggesting that one substitute the mystical for the scientific. I am, however, saying that one must seek to understand that the mystical and the scientific represent two approaches to the same underlying reality.

It was against this backdrop of scientific/mystical reality that I developed as a medical clairvoyant. The ability to accurately perceive another's physical body emerged through study and practice with the ever-increasing flow of clients. Yet in the early stages of Mentor's teachings on the nature of wholeness, before there were clients, I tended to accept his belief in the healing potential of the individual as more metaphor than physical reality. I remember how abruptly this illusion was shattered when I was given a chance to perform an actual healing.

A Minor Miracle

Melanie, my five-year-old daughter, had been sick with a severe chest cold and high fever for several days before I called the doctor. He agreed to see her later that day. As I finished my morning's work with Mentor, he unexpectedly offered the following thoughts on Melanie's condition:

❋*Agartha, become involved in looking beyond your own immediate assessment of limitation. Sickness and health are opposite sides of the same issue of wholeness. Choose to perceive in a way reflecting the divinity of your core as well as seeking a connecting energy channel between your presence and the unlimited love of the Universe.*

It is appropriate for you to hold your daughter in your arms, mentally projecting the love of the Universe into and through her form in order that negativity may be dissolved and the unseen fragmentation of her being reformed into unity.

While it is true that many people need their problems as crutches, it is possible to slowly replace these crutches with a sense of their own divinity and thus ultimate potential. Believe that you can transmit or channel such energy to others and it becomes so. The vibrational level you continue to feel during our sessions is the universal energy of love of which I speak.

This is the force with which you must work to heighten another's vibrations. The individual's willingness to accept love into his life will, to a large degree, effect the healing. For in being healed, one actually changes vibrational rates, overriding the established level of energy within the body. The new energy causes an intensive cleansing within the body which frees the physical body from its load of acquired negativity and confusion. Practice channeling divine love to Melanie and you will be amazed at the results.

Taking Mentor's advice, I took Melanie in my arms and held her for several moments, trying to project a divine balance of love and light. The phone rang, interrupting my concentration. When I finally returned to Melanie's room, I found her jumping on the bed, with no fever and no sign of congestion. In the short time I had been on the telephone, Melanie's symptoms had melted away and she seemed fine. The doctor who saw her later that afternoon was more than a little perplexed by her recovery.

It seemed inconceivable that those few minutes of holding Melanie had made such a drastic difference in her condition. I asked Mentor to help me understand the dynamics of the healing process:

✳ *Healing occurs when the body's established energy pattern of disease or trauma is altered by an intense new vibration of wholeness. This heightening of vibration neutralizes the multipointed negative charges of disease. Think of disease as a many-sided projection of negativity drawn from all aspects of the physical and emotional bodies. When you held Melanie and pictured her as divinely balanced, you effectively neutralized those aspects of imperfectness which had manifested in her illness. Another way to look at her condition is to realize that her own sense of wholeness had been diminished and thus allowed the illness to exist. As you held her, you reinforced her sense of oneness and perfectness within the universe and thus changed the balance within her body. What you are doing, Agartha, is adding sufficient energy to the person's whole being that his own body reestablishes its own unique balance. It is ultimately the individual who heals himself; the healer provides the balancing energy. One can possess psychic gifts and not be a healer. Being a healer means recognizing one's gifts as a manifestation of the love energy of the universe and using them in that realization.*

Love, given with no sense of self-glorification or personal achievement, is the thread woven through every healing. People heal each other every day without realizing that their positive energy has in any way influenced another's actual physical health. The healer gives another the permission to be whole.

A Second Miracle

My mother had suffered for years with what doctors called carpal tunnel syndrome, which is compression of the median nerve within the carpal tunnel channel of the wrist. The pinched nerve caused her arm to periodically "go dead," becoming completely numb for hours at a time. When feeling eventually returned, it created severe pain which could only be lessened by drugs. The condition intensified and surgery was recommended. Because she suffered from severe arthritis in her hands, she was afraid she would never regain the use of her right hand if it was immobilized by surgery.

When she called and asked if Mentor would help, I knew I risked Mentor's credibility if his suggestions failed, and yet it was a second opportunity to use his teachings on a problem in my own physical reality. He had shown me the way to proceed with Melanie and I hoped he would offer suggestions for me to work on my mother.

✳*Agartha, there are often numerous long-standing dysfunctional elements within the physical and emotional bodies. You would have no cognizance of all of these elements; therefore, visualize a black star over the area of your mother's trauma. Allow this black star to act as a magnet drawing forth conscious and subconscious negativity, physical imperfection and all deviation from wholeness. Superimpose a white star over the exact configuration of the black star. Let the white star represent the perfectness of creation, the supreme matrix of the universe and perfect attunement of mind, body and spirit. Concentrate on the white star.*

If you have not succeeded in drawing enough of the negativity to the black star, the healing will be short-lived or will be only partially successful. Your concentration should take the form of projection, creating in your mind's eye the desired result. When the two star configurations are matched, picture the individual as completely normal, with the diseased area replaced by healthy function.

It takes time to be able to successfully match up the spurs for a healing, and this is the part that is so often misunderstood. It is not enough to just wish a person well, there must be a direct linkup of positive and negative energy in order to cause a change. You will develop your own method, Agartha, which will not necessarily involve the following of specific steps. You will become more familiar with the dimensions of the appropriate connection.

My mother and I worked on Mentor's visualization for five days. For the first few days I went to her home, three hundred miles away. Thereafter I worked on her from my home. Although Mentor had not told me what I could expect to see when I concentrated on the white star, I found that after I had lined up the spurs, the white one developed a beautiful luster and depth. I watched mesmerized as the light spur literally overpowered the dark one, as if the very "life" of the negative energy was being transmuted before my mind's eye. The dark shape shrank and crumbled until it disappeared totally. Each time I did the visualization, the effect was the same. On the fifth day, the phone rang. The wrist and hand were normal. There was no more pain.

It did not seem possible that a physical condition which had existed for years actually had been corrected through visualization. We were stunned, both by the change in her condition and by the realization that an evolved source of guidance had provided us with tangible tools of healing.

This healing, more than all of Mentor's thousands of words, spoke to me in terms of my own reality because it was tangible. I had believed in Mentor when it seemed preposterous and illogical to do so and now I felt vindicated. Mentor was in existence and able to meaningfully relate to the people of Earth. Through his love and insight, I had participated in a healing which confirmed that the human being has the potential to manifest beyond the limitations of physical reality.

My mother's condition never returned, and while the results of subsequent healings were often not as dramatic, each one was special in its own way, increasingly expanding my understanding of wholeness and its relevance to healing.

Caroline: A Major Miracle

The Universe works in strange and wonderful ways. In my lifetime, few people have affected me as profoundly on a personal and professional level as my partner, Caroline Myss. We were brought together to work as a healing team in the fulfillment of a contract we had apparently signed with the Universe long before our births.

I met Caroline at my Gateway experience in Virginia and loved her instantly. She spoke theology, philosophy, astrology, psychology and mysticism, often in the same breath, and peppered her intellectual acrobatics with an outrageous sense of humor that endeared her to everyone. Caroline could charm the most inscrutable personality and, though she did not realize it at the time, we would find her loving warmth and charming wit to be as valuable in our future healing work as the impressive array of psychic gifts she had carried with her since childhood.

Neither Caroline nor I had conscious knowledge of the contract we had signed or the eventuality of our partnership, but we enjoyed being together. She and I were as different as two people could be, with different pasts and strikingly different projections for our futures. She was a writer and looked forward to furthering her writing and journalism career through development of a new magazine. There was nothing suburban about Caroline. She lived the fast-paced life of a single professional woman and loved the outrageous demands which kept her in continual motion. We kept in close touch following our Monroe experiences and, after I met Mentor, we often shared his advice on friends and relatives who asked for help.

Caroline's first visit to New Hampshire would dramatically reshape the course of her life, though neither of us knew it at that time. Her visit had been rescheduled from the previous summer when, in response to a personal question,

Mentor had suggested she travel to New Hampshire to experience the "great energy happenings" which would result from our being together.

After Caroline's arrival, Mentor requested a direct session with her, in which he revealed that she and I had promises to keep in this lifetime; namely, that we were to work together in the healing field. Further, Mentor commented on Caroline's recent meeting with her own nonphysical teachers, informing her that this "contract" to become involved in healing work was the reason for this nonphysical connection.

Mentor began instructing us that week on the manner in which we were to initiate our healing work, including methods by which we would begin to sharpen our clairvoyant skills and blend our perceptions. To the amazement of both of us, we found that when we compared "readings" of various people we were able to not only identify major physical and psychological traumas, but also to additionally define the disease in our respective physical or psychological terms. We even called some of the people to confirm our results. They were accurate. It was impressive how perfectly complementary our work was.

The same week, Caroline requested a "life reading" from Mentor and he agreed. This was unprecedented, for Mentor rarely agreed to have direct sessions with individuals, much less to agree to do a life reading aimed at gleaning past life information, current life purpose and prospects for the near future. After the reading, Caroline admitted to being shaken and refused to share the contents of the reading with Jim and me.

She did, however, relate that Mentor elaborated on the information regarding our future work in the healing field. Our combined efforts would include her psycho-perceptual abilities and knowledge of psychology and spirituality with my physiological perceptual abilities and knowledge of the body and its mechanisms.

Caroline was not interested in becoming a healer and found it distressing to even consider the supposition that "when the time was right she would fulfill her contract to become a healer.'' At the end of our week together, Caroline returned home to Chicago. As we continued our diagnostic and channeling work, we confirmed Mentor's statement that our telepathic channels would remain open in order that ''our work would not be limited by physical geography.''

During the next six months, Caroline struggled to make her career as a magazine editor and journalist come together, and by the end of that summer, she was on her way to England to develop her newly-evolving magazine on human consciousness. She traveled to the Findhorn Community in Scotland, from which point we received her call announcing that she would soon return to the States with the intention of moving to Walpole to fulfill her ''contract.''

Much later, Caroline revealed that in her life reading with Mentor he told her that until she came to terms with her contract to work in the healing field, nothing in her writing career would move for her. She would not sell a magazine article, much less get a magazine started. Her visit to Findhorn had brought her face-to-face with a place consciously directed by nonphysical guidance. Oddly enough, it spiritually embodied everything from which she was trying to run.

By October, 1982, Caroline was a resident of Walpole. Within weeks of her move, it became apparent that Caroline had come home and we were meant to work together. With Mentor's help and that of her own guides, we developed a system to combine health ''readings'' for people wishing physical and emotional diagnoses. The results were profound, and we quickly found ourselves involved in the lives of many people who were looking for insight into their disease and emotional traumas. As Caroline gradually redefined and expanded her definition of a healer, she found the focus for her own healing work to be ''diagnosing'' the emotional, psychological and spiritual belief patterns or crisis areas within an individual which contribute to the manifestation of a physical illness.

Healing: How It Actually Works

Caroline and I extended our healing work to include people in other countries. Because we worked without the necessity of seeing the client in person, we were able to send cassette tapes to people who lived too far away to come for personal sessions. Eventually we developed a system through which an individual was encouraged to relate his feelings about his condition and treatment through our questionnaire, and then combined with our reading, we arrived at our own in-depth evaluation.

Another important link in our healing effort came with the addition of a physician who was eager to explore the use of our perceptual abilities, feeling it offered a unique opportunity to study healing from beyond the usual limits of medicine. We also found it an advantage to have a medical doctor on our staff, since it allowed us to draw the best from both worlds. It became increasingly clear as our work expanded that we were defining a new level of healing by seeking to offer the best possible choices to our clients, regardless of their medical preference.

Our diagnostic assessments continued to be accurate, yet we were baffled by the varied impact of the actual healings which ranged from astounding to seemingly no change. Caroline and I both sought to be honest with ourselves and our clients and were therefore puzzled by this seeming incongruity. We were at a loss to explain the mixed results. We asked Mentor for a review of the actual dynamics of healing involved with the tapes we did for clients:

✳ *The tapes you and Caroline do, Agartha, are the vehicle for heightening vibrations, but it remains up to the individual who would be healed to change his internal wavelength receptivity to allow healing energy to be integrated. The tapes you send explain impaired physical and psychological function as well as ways of relieving and changing belief patterns. But unless the client is willing to open himself to the possibility for change, the tape alone cannot effect healing.*

If the person listens to the tape, if he believes that he is able to change his situation, if he tries the visualizations, and if he works toward a different reality, he is in effect heightening his body's vibrations, putting himself into another span or octave of beliefs. Within this new vibratory level or octave, your tapes can heal because the projected Universal or God energy has the ability to combine with the person's physical forces to change the physical and psychological configurations. Without this heightening of vibrations achieved through working with the tapes, the person's presence would not be shown the existence of this altered state. The individual must be receptive to a change in his reality, or in effect, he has withheld permission from his body and mind to change a given condition.

Once the person being healed achieves this altered state, even for a moment, healing energy is free to merge with his body. This is why there is most often a vehicle, a tangible "something" that changes the energy field, allowing a healing. Certain religious objects and shrines have been instrumental in causing healings. These physical objects are the manifestation of higher consciousness, imbued with power by an avatar, or evolved presence. The reputation of such an object allows the individual to believe it can change his reality, and in authentic cases of healing, certain objects have been known to differently align a person's energy causing what you call miracles. Your tapes also possess power because the material on them was received while you and Caroline were working with an avatar in an altered state of consciousness. As you work during your daily meditations, projecting healing love to others, you continually reactivate the power of the tape.

If the individual is unwilling to heighten his vibrational pattern or is unable to seek change because of serious illness, pain or a sense of futility, then it is not possible to artifically alter that most necessary of preliminaries. Without effort from the individual, there can be no healing.

Caroline and I were constantly confronted with the confusion people experienced when exposed to an unfamiliar

approach to disease or treatment. Familiarity with one type
of medicine usually precluded the use of remedies outside
that field. While some clients felt guilty if they took anything
stronger than a vitamin pill, others were threatened by talk
of nutrition as opposed to taking drugs.

There were appropriate uses for both allopathic (traditional) and holistic (non-traditional) medicine. The issue became how to help the client feel at liberty to draw from both
fields.

Appropriate Treatment: Allopathic or Holistic

❋ *There are many avenues to health, holistic and allopathic. These include not only the traditional modes of
medicine but also such areas of healing as: yoga, acu-
puncture, chiropractic therapy, homeopathy, polarity,
nutrition, herbs and massage, to mention just a few.*

*A great deal has been written about all these methods
of healing. But the issue is not really whether today's
"New Age physician" talks of allopathic or holistic approaches to treatment but rather, first and foremost, what
is the healer/physician's motivation for becoming a healer.
For this motivation will determine his willingness to use
what methods are best for the patient rather than that
which is most expedient or ego-satisfying. In other words,
what is the healer/physician's "heart-set" rather than
"head-set"? Mind and body must work sympathetically
to arrive at knowledge and implement appropriate treatment. When the mind works alone to heal, the potential
power of the healing is reduced to a semblance of what
could have been achieved with mind and heart working
together. No number of titles, degrees or accolades can
offset the primary need of a healer/physician to love.*

The Healer/Physician

   Those who are currently drawn into the field of medicine/healing potentially fulfill a larger vision of integrating health care to reestablish awareness of the working relationship between body, mind and spirit. The term I would like to use for such an individual is healer/physician, symbolizing the new wave of energy surrounding the individual who now seeks to heal by combining proven methods of both traditional and nontraditional medicine. It does not matter from which world of healing the individual comes; it only matters that he choose to step forward committed to use all available resources, physical and nonphysical, with which to promote ultimate health.

   Rarely does one fill the role of healer/physician without great trepidation. It is not easy to become involved in the forefront of the healing arts with a new approach to unity and balance. Yet it is appropriate that each human look to his own responsibility for life and interaction with the human race.

   An individual does not choose to practice healing, or any other creative art form. The art form chooses him. Often it is a struggle to resolve the doubts and realize the dream. This pull toward personal fulfillment in an evolving field is strewn with external and internal uncertainties. Conflict can revolve around denial, either of one's attraction to healing or as easily to one's investment in the belief that he alone is responsible for another's healing. It is rather a matter of recognizing that one is potentially drawn into partnership with the Universe in order that one's creative gifts may be shared to the greatest end.

   Society at large, and institutions in particular, are threatened by anything or anyone who chooses to set themselves apart from the norm and respond to a personal calling. But to those who are drawn to the role of healer/physician as creative interpreter, acceptance or rejection ceases to be the issue as personal commitment replaces doubt, and one begins to flow in what seems the most natural and beautiful of directions. The healer/physician evolves through stages of self-healing and Universal understanding which stand as his preparation for the world he chooses to enter as surely as the studying of anatomy and physiology.

Perhaps a brief discussion of the steps one encounters in the transformative process from recognition to realization of the creative healer within will enable an individual caught in the process to move through the land of confusion to identify his own struggle. These stages are applicable to all those within the creative process, not just those seeking the role of healer/physician. Healing, in addition to carrying specific medical connotations, is also a creative energy that promotes self-awareness and effective group interaction. The realization of creative potential is inwardly and outwardly healing in both its realization and manifestation.

Denial: The first step toward seeing oneself in the role of healer/physician is often denial. This stage is more intense in the holistic field where unfortunately there are not always the "positive strokes" for involvement with lesser-known paths to wholeness. This stage reflects personal, family and/or social pressures to do something else with one's life. Feelings of inadequacy, of lack of personal power in interacting with another's trauma, of fear of failure or recrimination, also fear of vulnerability to facing emotion may surface. Many times the would-be healer/physician already has a chosen vocation. The fact that the original vocation is not working suggests the need for reassessment. In other words, one may run from the knowledge that he feels a need to creatively interact with people on a primary level, especially where it means removing one's own protective mask and exposing one to his own reflection. Often the fear of "owning up" to one's feelings causes a depression of actual physical systems. This physical depression or dis-ease further clouds the individual's willingness and ability to understand his vision.

The role of the New Age physician is only now evolving to the consciousness of the allopathic medical community. But evolve it must, causing each person in the healing field to see himself as responsible for his own as well as his patient's creative connection to life.

Skepticism: This is the "why" stage: "why me?," "why this field?," "why this time in my life?" This phase is not quite as introspective as in "denial" but is in flagrant defiance of what the healer himself feels. The fact that each person is ultimately drawn toward his own version of creative flow often further confuses those whose brains have picked out a different physical reality. Yet the fact remains that circumstance, many call it coincidence, draws the person into closer union with the ultimate focus. Those who ridicule or remain forever skeptical are those who in their hearts feel the closest affinity and yet have never worked through this stage to realize their dream.

Ego Release: Ego involvement is failing to realize the interrelatedness of man with nature and man with man, acting as if there was no concern, save man's own immediate gratification. It often comes as a shock that the manifestation of cosmic understanding involves the use of tools appropriate to the world of healing as well as of creative endeavor. When one releases the reality of "doing it all alone," one promotes productive avenues of personal search. The healer/physician is in the position to influence his patient on every level of health and personal responsibility for health. When he fails to accept this responsibility as the teacher, he and his patients lose the opportunity to understand the miraculous nature of life and define the undefinable in terms of man's connection to God.

Each should nurture the whole person and each should use and learn what is available in both allopathic and holistic medicine. The traditional and the New Age physician must move beyond current standards and into deeper commitment as healers, not losing the war of understanding illness to the skirmish of ego versus ego. There is no room for the personal ego in the field of healing. There is only room for the desire to truly understand and appreciate each healer's potential gift to the patient. The *marriage of traditional to nontraditional medicine is what must happen for the underlying jealousy to be dispelled and the healer/physician to arise as the new balance.*

The goal of integrating all forms of medicine that Mentor was suggesting seemed a dream, and yet increasingly people were pouring into the healing fields. I wondered about my life, having been drawn into an unconventional form of healing that offered such unique insight. What was this energy that was changing the structure of medicine and healing and that had drawn me into the field of healing?

✳ *It is impossible for a healer/physician to remain for long without a vehicle for healing. So it was with you, Agartha, that your vision became your reality. Your request to the Universe to "let me see the path to wholeness and understanding for myself and those around me who suffer" became your personal still point. Your introduction to "touching" suffering came with the understanding that to ask is quite literally to receive. One must ask the questions in order to receive the answers.*

If the nature of healing is love, then the nature of wholeness is understanding that others can help and wish to help another's suffering. Often the individual who suffers feels he must suffer alone, that others do not wish to be around him and that disease is something dirty that should cause feelings of shame and guilt. Disease is instead the absorption of dense energy from the vibrational Earth School plane which manifests into a dysfunctional body when the individual allows himself to become clogged and burdened by the apparent weight of the physical lessons.

Healing another is healing oneself. Exploring another's needs, fears, joys, and successes is sharing one's own inner self. The Earth's people are connected by a silver thread of healing. It remains the challenge of the individual to recognize that the true nature of life is life lived in wholeness.

CHAPTER NINE

DEATH: THE NEED
TO SURVIVE

The luminous soul body slowly gained momentum, pulling away from its now deserted physical body. The transformation of life to death to life was complete.

MENTOR

WHAT LIES BEYOND our physical reality? Are we spiritually immortal? And if so, does the individual personality survive the transition into the nonphysical state? There has never been a generation of people who, in their own way, did not ponder the answer to that question.

For people reared within Christian religious traditions, the promise of immortality is a major artery in the belief system. Yet for all of the support this belief received from Christian religions, many Christians see no incongruity in simultaneously believing in some form of spiritual afterlife and in totally fearing physical death.

Consider the impact of the death and dying research as well as the vast amount of material released to the public on the subject of the near-death experience. Both of these areas of information support the tenet maintained by all world religions—that some form of consciousness exists beyond this physical reality. And yet, while scientific research has begun to add credence to what (mainly Christian) religions have always held to be true, a tension nevertheless has been generated. Scientific researchers have gone one step further than simply stating that there is life after physical death; they

have begun to describe the state of consciousness gleaned
from the experiences of individuals who have either had a
near-death experience or have tapped into the nonphysical
realms through, for example, meditation.

Reports from these researchers seem to indicate that while
the Christian tradition is accurate in its belief in the immortality of the soul, it now has to clearly reconsider much of its
structural doctrine. For example, among the vast majority of
individuals who have had a mystical or transformational experience, the belief in reincarnation replaces totally the idea
that we only live once. This is not an easy issue for Christian
traditions to reconcile. Further, the research material also
suggests that the individual personality continues its development even more authentically when it returns to the nonphysical state.

Our work as medical clairvoyants and holistic counselors
brought us naturally into contact with individuals whose diagnosis was terminal. Metaphorically speaking, one will
never walk more delicately than in the presence of an individual who is dying. For in trying to avoid the recognition
of imminent death, the individual will employ the most unnatural—and often unhealthy—of behavioral patterns because it will seem more "appropriate." It seems more
appropriate, for example, not to mention another's impending death, as if verbalizing the reality of death somehow
confers a type of conscious power which eclipses all hope.
And in one sense, that is exactly what does happen. As hope
for the return of full physical health is released, an enormously
painful void, heavy with the fears of the final moment of good-
bye, seems all that remains. It is almost impossible to avoid
the tremendous pain involved in the dying process. While it
may appear that not talking about the situation eases the strain,
this is highly inaccurate. Unnatural silence only supports the
process of denial and prevents any opportunity for the type of
communication so precious to the dying process.

Part of the healing process includes helping the dying person confront his death. While it often takes an act of grace
to accept that need, it requires an act of courage to proceed
accordingly. As counselors, Caroline and I both felt it ap-

propriate to seek information from Mentor on what was actually occuring during the dying process, not from the viewpoint of the observer, but within the consciousness of the terminal patient himself.

Moving from Life to Death and Death to Life

✳*The room was darkened. The venetian blinds hung limply at the windows reflecting the ripples of heat back to the street and its busy figures. Alisa lay in the hospital bed absently studying the putty-colored venetian blinds, thinking how much they reminded her of her own home. Yes, the color was the same, she thought, but somehow they looked altogether different in her family room. The doctor walked into her room and soberly pulled a chair over to her bed. "Ah-oh," she thought wearily, "more bad news." "Alisa," he said slowly, "I'm so sorry . . ."*

How do people face the realization that they are going to die—disbelief, fear, anger, horror, panic, relief, uncertainty, joy? The physical reality seems so real, so permanent, yet the fragile thread of life can be so easily and swiftly severed, allowing body and spirit to begin the separation process. Much as a plane lifts off the runway, gradually gaining speed and altitude until it disappears above the clouds, so the spirit takes leave of an old familiar friend and readies itself for the continuation of life.

Why do people who are nearing the end of their Earth School stay become intrigued and immersed in their early lives? It is not senility or retreat from the earth life, it is a need to put one's life in perspective, to more clearly reconstruct the very beginning of one's physical life so that the cosmic connection can be known as one prepares to exit (albeit temporarily) from the earth plane.

If indeed each "soul" or eternal being does ultimately respond to a personal cue from the universe, then it stands to reason that as the "cue" becomes stronger and more established within the superconscious, the person will begin his own reconstruction period, asking the consciousness to put life's pieces together to more clearly see life's patterns. One's very early childhood, for example, is usually forgotten and cannot be recalled until one prepares to depart Earth School and then, no matter what the age, the individual finds recollections consciously available. As the time for conscious separation becomes imminent, many can remember the actual birthing process, and yet because the physical mind has begun to detach from the soul body, the individual loses the ability to express these thoughts. The words of the dying or elderly often become garbled and unintelligible as the individual is forgetting how to talk and how to function within the confinement of a limited physical body.

As one nears the separation process, the nonphysical reality becomes the more obvious reality and the physical reality gradually fades. For in order to cause one's body and mind to work, one must see oneself as part of a physical working mechanism, so when one removes one's sense of self from the physical body, it ceases to function. The body and mind are no longer cohesively held together at this point. Each goes in its own direction oblivious to consideration of the other. The collective functioning of the human circuitry ceases when the sense of self has been removed.

The two major transitional periods of physical life are obviously being born and dying. Let us look more closely at each. In the birthing process there is a period of transition for the mother as well as the baby. Those who are awake during labor or the period of dilation of the cervix are aware that there is a period of emotional as well as physical transition after the cervix has reached maximum expansion and before the fetus is actually born. It is an odd period for the mother as she receives mixed signals, physically as well as emotionally. Physically the pressure is the same, even reduced, and yet the woman experiences more trauma, frustration and inability to focus on the birthing process than at any other time. Emotionally she is responding to the vibration of transition; the child is *part of her internal reality and yet has already begun to move toward her external reality.*

The same is true for the fetus who is being weaned from the quiet security of the womb to the confusion of the world outside the womb. Few adults remember being born or remember existence before birth, yet all have experienced it. Perhaps it is reassuring to realize that it was just as fearful to be born as it will be to face death. The letting go of the nonphysical vibration (expanded self to embryo to birth) to embrace the physical (birth into the world) is to go from expansive wholeness to limited understanding and capability. The womb is the transition, the period of adjustment to the Earth's vibration. Like a compression chamber for adjusting to underwater or space conditions, it changes the body's vibrational pressure. The life within the uterus completes the countdown to birth. The soul body becomes gradually accustomed to the denseness of Earth and to the necessary physical life functions that it must master through the development and use of a physical body. As the fetus's physical shape develops so does its sense of self within the body.

At birth the child is fully acclimated to Earth. If there are physical or mental deficiencies at birth, it means the sense of self has not been totally developed and the child is still more strongly connected to the nonphysical vibration of expanded self than to the physical Earth plane vibration. It is rather a half in-half out state. Great care needs to be taken with such children to help them develop a sense of self in the physical world through touch, sound, color and gentle manipulation to show them where they are and what is expected of them.

The freedom of the life in the state of expanded self has already begun to fade at birth, yet the memories still remain within reach. Through sleep the child reawakens dormant memories and unites them with intuitive life/death perceptions, continually learning the process of integration. A small child has an intense need for sleep. This need is a barometer of his true weaning from expanded self-awareness. The less sleep that is required, the greater the conscious commitment to the Earth. This conscious commitment to Earth reaches its pinnacle between thirty-five and forty-five years of age, following which one spends more time daydreaming or again tuning in the vibrations of the nonphysical, beyond physical life reality.

The transition of physical life to physical death begins around the half-way mark of living, meaning if a person dies at age eighty, by forty he will be superconsciously aware of vibrations originating from the next nonphysical stage. In other words, from birth to forty an individual will be heavily influenced by pre-birth expanded self, and from forty to eighty he will be influenced by post-death expanded self, or most immediately, the observational learning mode.

So death or temporary entry into the nonphysical begins long before any actual separation. Likewise from age one to forty the individual is listening to the vibrations of his previous nonphysical status. The individual always has access to either a previous or an upcoming period of non-physical reality. There is never a period in Earth School when the individual is cut off from contact with the Universe and his own universal energy. The human is always connected to the whole.

Thus the process of the fetus coming into the world is the same transition as the adult moving out of the world. Both are leaving the secure known and entering the unknown. Both also relinquish the previously familiar world as the new world's vibrations become dominant. Upon birth the child must breathe and eat for itself, assuming responsibility for the total being, breathing a sense of self into the physical life. Upon death the adult loses the sense of necessity for breathing and eating as he rightfully assumes responsibility for the role where there is no physical body. The birthing process into or out of life happens automatically as the soul body picks up the emanations of what is coming. It is no more difficult to let go and be born than it is to let go and die, being reborn through death to the continuing reality of expanded self.

It seemed to me, at this point, that if the process of death was to be truly understood, the notion of reincarnation would need to be addressed. I asked Mentor to offer an explanation of reincarnation that would shed light on the process and its purposes:

Reincarnation: Repetition of the Way

✳ *The spiritual journey involves being born many times. It involves existence with and without the support or limitation of a physical body. To reincarnate means to be born again, to come to physical life again. Of course, life as you know it now is not the life that exists outside the Earth. Physical life only exists on the Earth and in the other physical realities where there are opportunities for new learning. Reincarnation is the opportunity to experience various life forms and identities all toward the end of learning in the most appropriate manner those lessons which are uniquely and selectively part of the ever-changing continuum of life. The soul body is a precious commodity and becomes of greater value to itself and each physical life as it becomes refined through living different realities. Considering the slow progress toward awareness, and the fact that most people do indeed die short of enlightenment, it becomes obvious that to achieve even relative cosmic understanding, the soul body needs more than a mere eighty years on Earth. It needs the constant course correction of birth, life, death and rebirth to begin to grow in understanding. Just as matter though physically changed remains intact, so the human spirit is born, lives and physically dies but remains indomitable.*

In the early writings, I spoke of life as originating from the "birthplace of all souls." This means the blue channel of energy where all knowledge and perception merge into life as you know it. You may or may not realize that each incarnation adds more energy to the soul body, energy here meaning life substance. Each rebirth causes the soul body to become more and more complex in structure as it

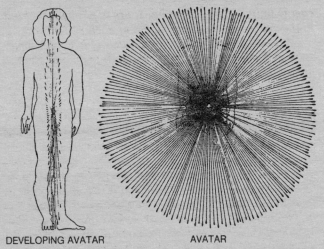

DEVELOPING AVATAR   AVATAR

moves toward ultimate perfection or the ultimate perfection of balance. It becomes necessary with each incarnation to integrate the new life force material with the original. Animal energy as well as other unattached free-floating energy units merge with the channel of life and then become attached to other more developed or complex energies. All human energy began and is beginning as single energy units and through repeated cycles of merging with the channel of life gathers a more and more complex spiritual and physical structure.

The highly evolved soul bodies, the avatars or seers of your world, who incarnate from time to time in physical form—Jesus Christ, Buddha, Krishna and others—all maintained their spherical energy patterns even while on Earth. Developing avatars have a singular column of energy with energy units being added in additional columns on either side of the original column until a sphere is created. Each reincarnation adds appropriate new energy units. The more evolved the soul body, the more complex the pattern of energy units. For example, Agartha, you see my energy field in a spherical configuration of many energy units. To me, Agartha, yours is not spherical but in the shape of a singular column of energy.

Once a sphere is formed, the balance of energy becomes such that one has access to one's own previous lifetimes as well as to much greater awareness of the intent of one's journey toward perfectness. One also at this point has access to knowledge—past, present, future—as befits one's needs in instructing others. It is as if with the developing spherical configuration comes an ever-increasing sense of compatibility with the universe.

I was absorbed by Mentor's physical descriptions of a non-physical process. It was not difficult to imagine the accumulation of energy units as one progressed through the process of reincarnation. What was confusing was the notion of animal energy units or "free-floating energy units" attaching to a human channel of life. My mind refused to accept the idea that different forms of energy could merge. I wanted to believe that humans were human and animals were animal.

An even more perplexing situation seemed to exist by this seemingly open process of energies associating with one another. What about karma? How could one person's karmic path be merged with another's?

Karmic Ramifications of Additional Energy Units

❋ You question that if new life energy is always being integrated, then must there be karmic ramifications incurred by taking on additional energy units. The answer is no. Animals, for instance, do not have karma. They follow a much more basic pattern. This means karma does not become an influence until the energy structure reaches the complexity of the human. Thus single life energy units are added to more complex units when they have no karma. There is no karmic confusion in trying to merge two evolving life forces into a single unit. The idea of the life force of an ant, for example, being added to the life

*force of a human may seem repugnant, but if you remove
the personification of ant and human, remove the physical
trappings, each is spirit, each is energy and each is a compilation of life force units.*

*The notion of progression toward perfection suggests a
beginning and an end. Unfortunately, there is no connection between creation as having a beginning and an ending. Since "God" or "That" is not static, then merging
with sublime energy does not mean an ending but a beginning of a new level of consciousness. As such the beginning of all things, the life force, always has been and
always will be available. It just is. Which means the "stuff
of the universe," the love energy building blocks of life
force, is something integral to the nature of "all time and
all structure." There is only a beginning in the mind of
the human. There is only life and the advancement of new
levels of life and understanding.*

Regression into Past Lives

I was curious to pursue the thoughts about regression and
the authenticity of recalled past lives through states of meditation or hypnosis. A friend who is a regressional hypno-
therapist offered to take me back to see if I had ever been
with my children or husband in any previous lifetime. During
my regression, I could recall a number of "lifetimes." Certainly, this recall is not the same as experiencing the full
memory of each life. It is more akin to viewing single acts
of multiple play performances. Still, there was one lifetime
about which I was especially curious. During the regression
I had recalled an awareness of a scene in which I was standing on the edge of a steep-sided embankment and below me
was a fire pit of smoldering red embers. I felt a calmness
standing there, even though I was aware that I was soon to
be sent to my death. I did not turn around to see who was
pushing me. I remember just watching the coals get closer
and closer as I catapulted down the cliff. I never hit the fire;
instead, at the very last moment, I was surrounded with an

exquisite calmness and well-being which lifted me away. This scene haunted me. A few days later I asked Mentor: "Why did I not hit the fire or if I did, why did I not feel it?"

Agartha, in your recounting of regressional experiences you confirm what I have been saying about the continual connection to the nonphysical status. When you fell toward the burning coals you experienced no pain, or any sensation of contact, because the nonphysical vibration to which one is always tuned surged to the forefront when you consciously released the physical life, realizing you were going to die when you hit the fire. This release of the life force, this letting go of the "sense of self," allows the always-present vibration of the nonphysical to become the dominant signal. Whether or not your physical body was actually burned is not the issue. The issue is that all your awareness processes relayed that you were not burned or traumatized in any way but were "rescued" at the very moment you expected excruciating pain. When the separation of body and spirit occurs, the physical is left behind as the used vehicle it is. You may be curious about the abruptness of the separation. What about long-term diseases versus sudden accidents? When does the soul body separate from the physical?

In the case of a lingering illness, the individual monitors and measures growing nonphysical vibrations against the physical vibrations and knows when the bodily functions are winding down. At the time the person chooses to consciously acknowledge the dominance of the nonphysical vibration, this person moves from a physical state to a nonphysical state. In other words, the person dies. A high level of pain may be experienced by the dying person if the individual refuses to consciously recognize the signals their bodies and psyches are trying to convey to them. This need to see one's body as friend and to acknowledge one's bodily signs is of very great importance in order that one may monitor what is truly being said. As the person recognizes the physical transition for what it is, a period of confusion over which physical or nonphysical vibrations have su-

premacy, then the fear can be brought under control and the dying patient can put his sense of self on "automatic pilot," realizing he is intuitively responding to a higher and more direct order of instructions.

In the case of an accident where the person is forced to leave the physical body abruptly, the same "rescue" occurs where the individual moves beyond the pain and trauma. For example, in the case of an automobile accident where an individual may appear to be critically injured and enduring excruciating pain, this is not actually the situation. It is just what the bystander sees. The pain is only the physical body's response. The true body, the nonphysical body, has left permanently or even in some cases temporarily. I say temporarily since the individual may indeed be resuscitated later at the hospital and returned to the physical. This is frequently reported in the cases of life-after-death scenarios where the individual sees clearly the peaceful, joyous life beyond the death experience, but for his own reasons returns to the physical plane. Hereafter there is rarely a fear of dying. The "other side" has been given more than a name, it has been given the "sense of self."

I suddenly remembered to ask Mentor what he meant during one of our earlier sessions when he commented that one had no need to recall previous lives until it served one's purpose as teacher. Did he mean "Earth teacher" or "nonphysical teacher"?

❋*Only those who have grown beyond a need to return to the physical level have past life recall. As we have said, there is not sufficient drawing power to pull in past lives until one has arrived at certain understandings of truth. If evolution means refinement to a clearer purpose, then the progression toward having a clear channel to all of one's lives should serve some purpose other than personal verification of life after death, since this becomes obvious with each transition. When having access to physical lives enhances the teacher's understanding without causing*

*unnecessary clutter, then it is so. It is also the opportunity
to seek the understanding of the truth without automatic
awareness of it. Interestingly, because each person incar-
nates more often into an overtly creative healing mode,
men, women and children are learning through the developing avatar stage to tap an awareness of continuing life.*

My questions about death were not always concerned with
the grand scale. It was appropriate to know about the "overview," but a secondary wave of questions developed through
my work with people who were about to experience death.
They wanted to know what actually happened upon dying,
what was one's "manifestation" if such a thing existed, and
what types of contact continued between one's "spirit" and
one's actual remains. Knowing answers to these questions
could only serve to reduce the uncertainty, and therefore, the
fear of death.

Physical Death: The Missing Sense of Self

*❋Looking at the physical body of one who has died can
and should be a comforting experience in the sense that
this body in no way resembles the presence of the living
individual. The all-important sense of self is obviously
missing. The charismatic spark of light that causes the
reflection of inner life is gone. The reason one "feels the
deceased person's presence in the room" is because he is
in the room. As we previously mentioned, beyond the
physical life-functional stage of learning comes the nonphysical life-observational stage of learning. The person's physical presence may be missing, but his or her energy
is very apparent. It can be seen as a white aura around the
area of the coffin. If the individual's physical body is dis-
posed of through cremation, then the aura appears around
the urn of ashes. If the physical presence is buried, the
aura obviously cannot be seen, but if the body is later
exhumed, the aura reappears, meaning the observational
stage is still active and energy is still being invested in that*

particular physical life manifestation. Following crema-tion, if the ashes are placed above ground, the white aura will be seen to gradually fade as the sense of self leaves the observational mode of learning to rejoin expanded self.

When a manifestation of spirit is seen, what one is see-ing is the refocusing of the soul body around a physical vibration. Often what is poorly understood is either feared or revered. Seeing the aura, the soul body of a person who has physically died, can be very frightening if one does not understand what the "apparition" is and that it repre-sents the soul body's presence within the observational mode. As you remember, Agartha, during this nonphysi-cal stage an individual's energy is between physical life and expanded self. The soul body has access to all that the physical body would have known, and in fact it often re-sponds as if it were yet in physical form. The physical appearance of a soul body signifies that a physical situa-tion has elicited a physical response from the soul body still in the observational mode.

Quite appropriately one should realize that just because a soul body has left the physical form, it still remains in the learning stage and is not necessarily more evolved than it was in physical life. If a communication or contact is therefore desired with a nonphysical soul body, one should carefully consider who that individual was in life. For un-til the soul body reunites with its expanded self, it is not cognizant of the broader perspective. In other words, one's motivations and needs may not be any different just be-cause there is no physical body.

It is, therefore, always wise to be sure who or what one wishes to draw into one's energy field by appropriately aligning one's energy with specific forces of love. Difficul-ties arise when one opens oneself to contact without de-fining what the desired purpose or goal is. The nonphysical presence can be held to the physical plane either by the physical forms that still exist in the physical or by its own inability to release the needs and desires of the physical level. The more attached one is to the physical reality, the more difficult it is to appropriately release the observational mode and move away from the past physical reality.

Perhaps the question asked most often by people about to die is: "What will it feel like?" This always seemed to me to be a natural question, one arising from fear of the unknown. I asked Mentor to comment on the actual experience of dying. What would a person experience at the moment of death?

What Does It Feel Like to Be Dead?

✳ *Without a physical body the means of transmission is telepathic. There is no seeing, hearing or touching. Instead there is only perception.*

Close your eyes, Agartha. Picture the front of your house. You are not actually seeing it, yet you have a very clear sense of it. Now picture a friend's house, someone who lives at least one hundred miles away. You did not have any trouble picturing the second house. You also arrived at the house without spending time traveling there. In effect, you transported yourself to the place in question to have a look. When you have no physical body, you simply place yourself at the scene in question. It is just that easy. There is no limitation to one's powers of manifestation. Telepathy, or the intuitive reading of wavelength vibrations, is the means through which vision, sound, smell and touch are transmitted. There is no "home base" as you know it, no singular family or life routine. One's awareness shifts to the inner self and this gradually becomes home.

Without a physical body one feels suspended in the continuum of life. Things and experiences are not simply connected end-to-end the way they are in Earth School life. Instead they are layered in order that everything is experienced individually as well as collectively and with greatly heightened acuity. Let us consider the analogy of lying in bed under several layers of covers—a sheet, a light blanket, a heavy blanket and a quilt. Using only the physical

*dimension of perception, the average person would have
trouble distinguishing whether three or four blankets were
on his bed. And even if he could discern the exact number
of coverings, the sensation of increased weight would be
conveyed to the mind only as an increase in pressure.
Those in the nonphysical sphere can distinguish not only
the exact layers of blankets and quilts but also the nature
of each layer and that the blankets and quilts represent a
source of warmth to sustain the human body. This readout
happens simultaneously with the actual experience. If this
added dimension of perception is applied to the transition
of dying—or moving to the nonphysical state—then it becomes obvious that one is perceiving the many layers of
continuing life as separate and yet as an integral composite. Each aspect of being is highlighted and accurately
recognized as whole.*

*When one is released from the confinement of a physi-
cal body, one quite naturally falls in with the new level of
perceptions and abilities. There is not the wrench in the
dying experience that most people assume is inherent in
the transition. The transformation of physical to nonphysical is recognized as natural—just as natural as the
transformation of being born into a physical level of learning. The fear of releasing oneself to the next level of change
is the cause of pain and trauma. There is no pain or trauma
in the experience of dying. It is only within the confinement of the mythology of Western man where life is seen
as a gift of permanence instead of brief transition, that
fear and pain appear as the robbers of one's gift of life.*

Mentor's response was appropriate to my question. I had
asked what death felt like and his answer dealt with that
question exclusively. As I read over his statement about perceptions after death, it occurred to me that no mention was
made of a "judgment day," "pearly gates" or a "final reck-
oning." What is the purpose of physical life that it should
take so tortuous a route through many lifetimes? Who judges
whom? Is life a "gift" and, if so, what is one supposed to
do with this gift? Since I asked all of these questions more

or less simultaneously, Mentor attempted to create order by dealing with my small questions first and then answering the larger one about the purpose of it all.

The Gift of Life

✳ *The value of one's life is measured in non-tangible accomplishments, in accomplishments of the soul. Here within the innermost reaches of one's heart, the real understanding takes place and the results of the physical reality can be measured. This measurement takes place simultaneously with the passage of one's soul body from the physical Earth School plane to that of the nonphysical mode. Has it ever occurred to you, Agartha, that there might be in fact a measurement of one's progress? I have said that there is no time limit for enlightenment and no right or wrong answers to the choices one makes. This is true, but there is awareness of one's continuing progress. The energy within the heart, what can be seen in the physical as the energy in the area of the heart or fourth chakra, is the way one's own expanded self measures the progress of each physical incarnation. There is no outside source which is keeping track of each soul body's trips through realities; instead, each expanded self—each intuitively connected grouping of energy—is tracking its own physical reality. This means that each person is indeed responsible for his own spiritual progression through the universe. There is no outside source to reprimand or demote one to a lesser level of life if one somehow fails the tests; one's own expanded awareness is solely responsible for evaluation of the end products of each functional and observational mode of living and the learnings gleaned as a result.*

Just as it is one's own responsibility within the physical reality to try, to reach, to struggle toward awareness and the light, so it is one's own higher self which "stands in judgment" of one's own ways. The questions are: one, what was one given to work with or, in other words, into what life situation was the soul body born; and secondly, what advancement was made toward the comprehension of the Oneness and a loving understanding of one's own divinity? One's own nature is the decision maker, the energy which offers the next set of reality systems as workable platforms of lessons to be learned. Just as the individual knows in his heart when he moves one step closer to awareness and when he moves further from it, within the human heart, within the network of the expanded self, is the understanding to govern all worlds. "God", "That" or the "Isness" is intimately aware of all expanded selves, because they are one and the same with the Omnipotent Presence of the Universe. Agartha, it is important to know that it is the energy of the individual soul body which ebbs and flows with the lessons of physical realities; it is in the end only the individual consciousness which makes its own decisions.

Perhaps the notion of progression toward perfection suggests a beginning and an ending to the action of the universe. Unfortunately, there is no credence to the notion that creation had a beginning and will therefore have an ending. Since God is not static, then merging with sublime energy does not mean a physical ending but the beginning of a new level of consciousness on the nonphysical level. As such the beginning of all things, life force, always has been and always will be available. As we have said before, it just was and is. As the building blocks of life force units do not signify a progression down a linear line but instead a development of understanding inward, so the physical complexity of developing man is the only measurable linear progression.

We have talked about the "stuff of the universe," the love energy building blocks of life force which are things integral to the nature of all time and all structure. There is only a beginning in the mind of the human. There is life and the building upon life to create new levels of awareness and perception. Look at it this way. The universe is a continuous explosion: God. This explosion is comprised of an infinite number of particles: life energy. The reformation of these pieces into a whole is the process of re-

incarnation or growth, development, refinement through continued existence to reformulate the perfectness of this Sublime Whole. The Sublime Whole is in constant motion whether as a whole or as its individual life force pieces. In other words, as "God the actualized concept" or as "God the actualized spirit within the human," all of our lives move toward a perfect reunion.

There was one last significant question remaining to be asked. I wanted to know if there was any truth to the notion that families and friends tended to reincarnate together. Perhaps it was simply human that we wished for reunion with those we love. I almost refrained from asking the question for fear that my own myth would be crushed.

The Need to Survive

✻ *The concept of reincarnation and reincarnation within the framework of family and friends should not be lightly dismissed. In other words, wherever there is a strong affinity—positive or negative—the elements of life force tend to rematerialize in close proximity to each other. One should not be afraid to believe in the joy and eternal movement of the life force, the sense of self which moves beyond the physical. The fact is that some choose to believe death is the end of conscious life in spite of all the awarenesses described in this material and other valid information. The griefs and resentment can be intense for those unwilling to listen to their own hearts for the sense of eternity which rings there. Those who are presumptuous enough to deny the Universe in all its infinite beauty have, of course, but to wait until they leave the physical to be convinced of the authenticity of my statements.*

Agartha, the act of dying is a peaceful, beautiful affirmation of life and continuing life. The letting go of physical life is traumatic, but the acceptance of the joyous after-life reality is so very natural. It is as if one were coming home after a long and wearisome trip. As soon as the individual walks through his front door, home feels familiar, supportive and accepting. And so it is with dying. Home is all of the things the physical home is, but it is accentuated beyond your current comprehension.

Think of Alisa, the example I used at the beginning of the lessons on dying. Let us pick up her case and follow it one step further, sharing her last physical experiences, including her death.

Alisa heard the words, "I am so sorry," but did not hear the meaning. She could not hear the meaning. It had been such a long hard fight against the growing cancer in her stomach. She had known somehow that she would not be able to beat this thing—but not now, not yet, it was too soon—she was not ready. She watched the doctor's lips moving as if he were at a great distance and realized he was talking to her. She could not seem to hear him.

Gradually the small ray of hope that had survived the drastic surgeries, chemotherapies and radiations began to flicker and quietly went out, just as surely as if it had been snuffed. The weeks slowed to a painfully halting pace in which the moments passed only with the greatest of effort. The sparkle had disappeared from living. Alisa felt at the bottom of a deep well with the steep sides of the well, her disease, preventing her from seeing the sunlight or even the sky.

Two weeks following the doctor's news of the return of the cancer, Alisa let go of the physical reality centering around the life of the blond, blue-eyed mother of two. She floated free of all cares, all pain and all earthly responsibility. The luminous soul body slowly gained momentum, pulling away from its now deserted physical body. The transformation of life to death to life was complete—Alisa was home.

CHAPTER TEN

MAN AS GOD

The Golden Rays of Light
Seek to radiate from the heart
Causing the violent to become peaceful,
The sick to become whole,
And the aware to move toward realization of
  their vision.

MENTOR

IT IS NOT my intention in this chapter to challenge the nature and structure of God or religion. As I have already stated, it is my desire that the material in this book serve to enhance the reader's personal belief patterns, not replace them.

The material Mentor has communicated in this chapter transcends the notion of a religious god. That is to say, it is designed to assist the reader in recognizing and discovering that which is godlike within each person. For ultimately, it does not really matter in which manner we establish our God-connection, whether that be as a Christian, Hindu, Jew or Atheist. All of these approaches will lead to the same end point.

Thus, rather than focus on encouraging the reader to question the substance of religions and their various descriptions of God, it is more important that the reader be directed toward recognizing that which is his own divine substance. And then, it truly does not matter which "face" is given to God because contact with the beginning point of consciousness will have been made. Once this connection is made, it is possible for each reader to enter more fully into his own

spiritual nature, and to discover the abilities intrinsic to the
human spirit, such as channeling.

Learning to Channel:
A Coming of Age of the Human Experience

✳ *There is immense beauty in the physical nature of planet
Earth. Yet it is not the physical nature of the planet which
is misleadingly seductive but rather man's contrived system of physical rewards. Earth's physical beauty can be a
door to personal awareness while man's colloquial mate-
rialism can only lead to gluttonous self-satisfaction. No
one begins seeking only the worldly, but often those who
only wish to sample become unwittingly immersed and unable to pull away from the world's hyperbole. In other
words, they invest in the counterfeit and forfeit the genuine value. Of course, each person does eventually move
onward and away from the delusion, but if the individual
could become awakened to the sound of his mind working
harmoniously with his heart before the end of the current
life, there could be impressive gains made for the side of
the Light. Cumulatively the odds could be drastically
shifted to the arena of peace and awareness of the spiritual
forces which surround the living experience.*

*The development of the earth represents the develop-
ment of an Earth School where physical presences can
work out their learnings. It is also the place where individuals learn to distinguish the real from the unreal, the
creative from the static.*

*It will not be long, fifty years perhaps, before "chan-
neling" will be considered the norm rather than the exception. It will be common knowledge by then that all
universes, all creatures of creation, are working together
to create the most perfect whole, wherein humankind will
enter the new age of awareness, learning to integrate the
mystical with the practical. One's "teachers" or "spirit
guides" will be as common as one's professors at a uni-
versity. The professor will teach mathematics and the spir-*

itual "teacher" will enlighten. Each will learn from the other. Spiritual growth should not be left to "take care of itself."

Spiritual work takes discipline and commitment just as in any other field. No individual becomes proficient in any form of creative endeavor without the backup work, and so it is with the spiritual progression that one moves along the designated paths toward and through enlightenment, learning and sharing and advancing.

There are many times when celestial counsel is the only kind that has the perspective and vision to suffice. Let no individual feel that his thoughts go unanswered, for they do not. Answers tend to come in the form of questions, however, rather than statements. The Universe is not in the habit of pinpointing only one suggestion; instead, there are always several from which to choose. The individual must then weigh all possibilities in light of his current situation. Any decision must be the product of the Earth School participant and higher-realm guidance, rather than just directives from beyond Earth. Otherwise nothing has been accomplished, and certainly the individual has not derived insight from the potential learning situations of Earth. The individual must be allowed to find new meaning in his own passage through Earth School and the universe.

The answers one pulls forth from the universe are meant to guide, teach and promote one's own comprehension of life beyond the Earth School, not just the immediate physical, for, of course, the phases of physical incarnation are vastly outweighed by the phases of nonphysical. There is actually a 4:1 ratio of nonphysical life to physical. The physical incarnations are peppered throughout the total learning experience of advancement.

When I had begun to "channel" Mentor, I knew of only a few people living, plus a few from the past such as Edgar Cayce, who were known as "channels." Mentor was now suggesting that many people would become acquainted directly with their nonphysical teachers in the near future. I could only speculate on how conscious awareness of the non-physical world would alter the shape of reality from that which is presently accepted as true. Not the least of the shift would be the automatic dissolution of the fear of death and a pure belief in a compassionate Universe. There would be no limits to the beauty the human species could create with a consciousness far more in harmony with the ultimate source of creation.

I asked Mentor to comment about spiritual questing and awakening:

Seeing the Spirit Within

✳ *Is the human being actually one with the Ultimate Source or is that merely a figure of speech? I will tell you that the peoples of the world are indeed one with each other and all creative universal forces. All peoples have unlimited personal and cosmic powers. Telepathy, precognition, clairvoyance, clairaudience and other psychic gifts are not classified as "cosmic powers," since they are but the first of many steps toward mystical purification and interaction. Instead, conceptual integration of one's physical life with one's own expanded self hearkens to a more advanced cosmic attunement. Understanding and consciously following the link between and through physical lifetimes is much more significant than merely picking up details about a singular incarnation. One must look beyond one lifetime and incorporate the larger groupings of one's lives in order to gain perspective on continued problem areas and areas of strength. This expansion of one's vision is possible if one knows that physical lifetimes grow outwardly in concentric circles of greater and greater depth from the core of expanded self and that what is a major issue in this life has often remained unresolved from another incarnation.*

Lives are not lived in a past-present-future sequence, but instead are in a blending of lifetimes in which each series exhibits greater depth of understanding and aware-

ness. Rather than seeing the specifics of past lives as the goal, focus instead on the knowledge that because living is not a static experience, each life holds experiences worthy of remembering and even reliving. Awareness of these larger issues allows one to step back from the individual life experience in order to see the broader spectrum of issues which overlap into other lives. While it is difficult from the incarnated level to see the overlapping issues, nonetheless it is possible if one is awake to the possibility that illnesses, emotions and predispositions can be the hook to call forth larger life issues, that one can sense the lessons which one is solving. Therefore, in the discovery of the root of one's real self comes the added awareness of identifying issues which have been in one's life before.

Each lifetime has its own unique situations which at times seem all-encompassing. This is so for each physical incarnation where one is equally preoccupied with the joys and traumas of that physical existence and unable to see beyond the death experience. Once one has learned to recognize the multiplicity of the physical experience, one is no longer earth-bound, one can let go of the constraints of needing everything to "work out" on the physical level. When it becomes obvious that there are many, many levels of physical existence, then major unresolved issues can be allowed to exist without an immediate answer, and radical changes within one's physical reality, such as losing one's partner or children or experiencing major financial setbacks, can be seen as issues where there may be more to come within the context of another physical life. It becomes obvious that since all life is connected through continuing realities, problems can be resolved throughout many lifetimes. So while there is pain, there is no limitation to the framework of resolution, and lives continue to exist as the developing sagas of one's total cosmic memory.

The experience of living allows the building of what I call one's "mosaic path." Each action, each interpretation of the Earth, allows for another beautifully crafted and colored tile to be fit into a unique design representing *one's own experiences and therefore those ideas which make up one's belief in a God or Higher Universal Source. All experiences and belief structures are tiny pieces of one's mosaic path. Traditional religions have for years inadvertently thwarted the learnings of their congregations by teaching them they must all believe exactly the same thing. This is not possible. Each man, woman and child is unique. Nowhere in the universe are there two units of life energy exactly alike. Thus, to tell someone he must think or act exactly like someone else is preposterous and only causes temporary repression of one's own true being. Each magnificent unit of living matter deserves to be all that it can be and to reach the heights of achievement and awareness, not according to any artificial standard of achievement, but according to what one feels inside and intuitively knows to be true about himself. This is what it means to build one's own mosaic path.*

One's mosaic path is the sum total of all thoughts and actions and is a clearly marked passage from physical birth to the current moment. It is hopeless and pointless to measure oneself against any exterior parameter, either person or object. The individual human life exists both for individual awareness and also for interaction with other life forms. Those who fail to see and benefit from the insights gleaned from the magnificent mosaic path they are building tend to lose personal footing, being pulled this way and that at society's whim. The stability for life comes from the realization that one is creating a balanced work of art from one's life experiences and that one's own mosaic path is both a verification of physical life and of cosmic progression.

How does one verify one's ''mosaic path''? If the Earth was about to experience an accelerated level of activity between the human and celestial realms and there was to be a dramatic increase in channeling, then to whom would one appeal for such a mystical initiation? And how would the individual invoke such channeling? By prayer?

What Does It Mean to Pray?

✳ *We have spoken of meditation and its effectiveness, and I have suggested some specific meditations for quieting the mind. It is now appropriate that we speak of prayer, since prayer is a companion to meditation, rather than its replacement. There are times to quietly center the body's energy in order to allow the words of the Universe to become known. There are other times when it is appropriate and necessary to speak to the Universe. If one's child never asked his parents questions or for opinions, the parents would no doubt feel something was basically wrong. Certainly there needs to be verbal interaction between parent and child. Just so, there should also be verbal interaction between God and one's own Earth-bound presence. Often one hears that it is not appropriate to talk to God, since God's presence is so mighty and man's so meager that man should only listen. The truth is that man is much more than just his physical presence. His expanded self is an alive and growing unit of life energy which is synonymous with God.*

To pray is to talk to God. There is nothing too insignificant or too overwhelming to be voiced. What is of concern to humankind needs and deserves an answer. Just as the parent seeks to explain the often unexplainable to his children in terms the child can understand and fit into his knowledge bank, so the responses from the heavens appropriately respond through the human heart which is the interpreter of cosmic signals. It would be inappropriate to respond intellectually to what is essentially an issue of the heart. It is certainly true that the Universe responds to issues of the heart with greater regularity than to issues of the mind apart. This is because the intuitive interpretation is a language above language and is understood for what it is. Just as a personally intense feeling concerning another human being is known on a separate level from mind, so the Cosmos responds in terms only translatable through its compatibility with the human heart. When

*specific answers are desired from a greater awareness, one
must first become a channel for the intuitive.*

*When Galileo stood and studied the heavens, the sun,
the moon and the stars, it was intuitively that he was
struck by their interconnectedness and the awesome potential for mankind as a builder of civilizations and a pi-
oneer of spiritual and cosmic evolution. His most basic
understandings of astronomy and astrology stemmed from
his heartfelt connection to the wonder and beauty of the
universe. The truths he sought to understand were out-
croppings of his unshakable belief in man's connection to
the powers that dominate the world's forces and his desire
to awaken others to this connection. It is certainly no
accident that all successful inventors of thoughts or things,
the geniuses of their time, have had a sense of the integrity
of the universe as a whole and have wished to speculate
upon those understandings which grow from this source.
In other words, men and women of vision are connected
to the universe by their own visions of themselves as part
of an inseparable aspect of creation. This sense, this intuitive avenue through the heart, opens the mind to the
appropriate translation that it may enter the theoretical
aspect of living and effectively integrate those feelings of
the heart into usable theory.*

*Since time on physical Planet Earth is so limited and
time within the bosom of the universe is so extensive, there
is room for each to develop his own level of cosmic vision
and give birth to it through the appropriate channels of
physical reality. The level of the mind is limited and grows
slowly, but the level of the heart is eternal, and as it becomes filled with love it changes the very nature of man
into the vision he holds most dear: that of himself as an
alive and integrated extension of the Universe.*

I very much enjoyed the notion of a dialogue between man
and God and realized that our prayers tend to be monologues
in which we do not expect answers, so we do not listen for
them. Mentor followed his discourse on prayer with some

specific thoughts on constructive prayer and its dynamic nature.

The Nature of Praying

Prayers are personal and yet there are aspects of praying which need to be noted. There are elements within the prayer framework which help the individual send out the most appropriate requests for guidance and action.

1. *An opening or salutation.*

   A loving introduction to the forces which one perceives as the focus and outgrowth of one's being draws the energy of that presence within range of one's own physical being. Whether or not the word "God" is used, an appropriate designation of the energy or presence to whom one is speaking is necessary. Just as one addresses a physical presence by a name, a nonphysical presence also needs to be addressed in terms of a singular designation in order to invite that presence into one's moment of prayer.

2. *A statement of thankfulness for those gifts and perceptions already received.*

   This approach acknowledges one's connection to the Universe or God and reaffirms one's own awareness that gifts of understanding have come to allow the individual to move toward the Light. It reconfirms one's conscious connection not only to the expanded self but also to the larger manifestation of God-consciousness through the process of prayer as an effective vehicle for contacting and interacting with the Ultimate Reality.

3. *Verification of the problem or focus of prayer.*

   The prayer process invokes eventual healing through the individual's ability to precisely understand the sit-

uation and in so doing more clearly see the matching piece which is the solution. Clarity of thought in this case brings the energy of the dilemma to a head and causes the matching energy of the solution to be equally focused and thus obvious to the individual.

4. *Affirmation of one's belief in an appropriate solution.*

If one does not believe that a solution of some type is possible, then one has no business praying, for no solution will be forthcoming. It is only through one's belief in a possible solution that appropriate avenues of help will be noticed. In other words, if one is closed to healing vehicles, then none will be found even though they exist in one's life. Since the solution is implemented by the individual, without a willingness to look for solutions or see them when they present themselves, the subtle workings of the Universe will remain obscured, and one will insist that God did not answer the prayer. This is not the case, yet if one is unwilling to accept a solution the Universe offers, remaining locked into one's own didactic set of possible solutions, then the obvious will not be seen. Opening one's eyes to the realization that one's most earnest wishes may not be included in the Universe's solution is often difficult, but it is necessary if one is to see the final resolution as indeed the perfect healing.

Praying causes energy, celestial and physical, to be directed to a specific area of one's life, and repetition of the same prayer is very effective in drawing in appropriate telepathic vibrations. The repetition of letters and sounds in a particular order forms a more intense network of energy than an everchanging series of sounds. Just as a single sound, such as "om," when used in meditation causes an accelerated gathering of one's energy into a peaceful and orderly inner formation, so a single series of words used as a prayer causes an intensely peaceful and powerful vibration to develop within the individual. This rhythmic calming of one's physical presence allows a more accurate and intense response to be drawn into one's consciousness, and thus one's interpretation of the input will be more clearly and accurately deciphered by the conscious mind. In other words, when one uses the same prayer over and over, it builds not only the intensity of the invocation but also the clarity with which the Universe's response can be heard, seen and understood. After all, Agartha, it was through your own appropriate praying to be shown an avenue of awareness that you strengthened your presence to where I could reach you. Certainly our connection constitutes an intense response to a prayer.

Once again, the answer seemed simple and yet profound. I had indeed "prayed" for a teacher, and I had been terribly frightened and surprised when the prayer had been answered. Yet there was at least one fact of which I was certain: prayer had worked for me even though I wasn't fully conscious of the possible consequences of my efforts.

If more individuals became conscious of the processes and power of prayer, it seemed to me that finding teachers to guide them along their "mosaic paths" might become a very strong possibility for future growth and transformation. It seemed a question of man's consciousness of himself and the God he prayed to for help.

Toward Realizing Man's Divinity

Prayers are answered not as a parent answers a child but more as a teacher answers a serious student who is expected to draw his answers from many sources. Prayers are not answered from a great father figure in the sky; instead prayers are answered jointly from all of one's celestial teachers as well as from one's God-presence within. The Universe is vast and so is the hierarchy of celestial presences, meaning presences which have evolved to a place of universal love and perfection. These are the teaching presences of the Universe, Agartha.

God is the composite of all life-force energy, both the celestial forces and the internal forces of one's heart. God is the total living force of the Universe. Therefore, when one prays to God one is praying to a whole, with varying aspects of the working whole influencing every solution. Therefore God, the Isness, the Great Oneness of the Universe, is the collective presence of all things living, all evolving beings. The expanded selves of all teachers and highly-evolved presences as well as all forms of evolving life merge to form God. Every growing, evolving energy unit has an expanded self, and each expanded self is divine.

Thus man is indeed God. His eventual path is always toward awareness of his own divinity, is always toward consciousness of his Godly nature.

My mind initially recoiled from the concept of "man as God" until I grasped the corollary notion that God was all things and that there was nothing outside of God. It was really a question of man seeking consciousness of his own divine roots.

If the problem facing man was one of consciousness, then I was apparently lacking an adequate understanding of the workings of consciousness. How did consciousness relate to Earth School learning? What was it that caused man's conscious journey through the Earth School to be so difficult?

The Pathway of Spiritual Consciousness

✳*All conscious thought is carried over to the first stage of nonphysical life, or from physical functional life to nonphysical observational life. When the separation occurs at death, all conscious thought continues to the observational mode of learning. When one leaves the observational learning mode, however, to re-merge with the expanded self, then consciousness is filtered according to what one considers to be of lasting value and what one considers only a product of the physical life. Only a nucleus of most valued experiential information is taken onward to the expanded self. So all conscious thought which is deemed valuable at the release from observational learning is retained, while all else is dropped and not recapturable until one no longer returns to physical incarnation. Interestingly, after one has chosen to drop various memories from former lifetimes, one is unable to relive them even in the state of hypnotical regression to a past life; what is played back is only that which was not voluntarily erased. The individual's consciousness makes the determination of what it considers valuable enough to retain, and this is in fact what merges with the continuing conscious memory bank of continuing lifetimes.*

Thus in tapping one's memories of other physical realities, one is cognizant of only those memories which were considered significant enough to retain at the end of that physical life. As one develops in cosmic understanding, spiraling onward toward greater attunement with the directing forces of the cosmos and reaching states of understanding which are compatible with spherical energy, one is once again allowed to pick up all details of previous lives. This is known as tapping the cosmic channel. It is possible, as we have said, to tap varying degrees of awareness in this channel during physical life. The full complement is not at one's disposal until one becomes sufficiently evolved to possess the spherical energy pattern. Of course, by the time the individual consciousness has progressed to the state of spherical energy, what had been discarded in developing lifetimes is often no longer relevant.

Nothing is lost once it exists as a thought or action. All is forever held once it is given birth by the human mind or body, even though it may not always be accessible. One chooses those elements of the previous physical life which seem the most meaningful to take along to expanded life. But herein lies the problem. If the individual has considered the physical reality as all-important, then what is relevant to that purely physical existence will be the sub-

stance with which one will begin the next reincarnation. If, on the other hand, one has been involved in sorting out one's life in terms of universal understandings, then those relevant experiences will be the ones with which the next physical reality is begun. It is the responsibility of the individual to discern the learning lesson intrinsic to each of the experiences of his life. The individual then has the option to devalue an experience by disregarding its learning benefits, and thus, all which was meant to be gleaned from that experience will dissipate. That means that all the learnings having to do with spiritual development will need to be relearned in the next physical incarnation. The importance of emphasizing one's spiritual life ensures that these learnings will be present in continuing lifetimes.

Every aspect of Earth School is designed to allow an infinite number of lessons to be presented through an infinite number of incarnations until the individual grasps the spiritual significance of himself as a spark of the Infinite. One must, indeed, make one's own reality by slowly and even painfully learning the difference between the illusion of the purely material path and the permanence of the real or the God-path.

I recalled Mentor's metaphor of the archer. He had said that if the target was truth and the arrow represented knowledge, then one had only to release the string to let the arrow of knowledge find its goal, namely truth itself. Man's great challenge was one of life's paradoxical mysteries: to become conscious *of the moment when the bow has been placed in his hands.*

Consciousness: The Meaning of Life in Earth School

✳ *When one exhibits not the slightest interest in the things of the spirit and is solely preoccupied with the things of the immediate physical reality, it means that there is no memory carry-over from other lifetimes involving the things of the soul. Either the lessons were never learned or their relevance was not noted, and all or partial recollection was discarded and thus must be learned all over again. It comes down to an issue of what is seen as important, for if one leaves a physical reality believing in the things of the world, then that is the baggage taken into the observational mode and then into the expanded self. All that has been learned relevant to the spirit will in all likelihood be discarded, since one does not have access to the overview of the expanded self until actually reunited with the expanded self, and then it is too late. Certainly, one then realizes that the wrong things were discarded. When once again his energy is funneled into a physical reality, it picks up with the same understandings that were last exhibited, and the overview is once again obscured. Thus the individual enters the next incarnation with the same baggage he thought was important in the last. It is easy to see that many, many realities can be lived before one chooses to retain the things of the spirit and let loose of the other.*

Mentor's Final Thoughts

The information, Agartha, which has come through me to you is to be used only in love and only to enlighten, to fill the world with the energy of love, peace and understanding that each human being may move even more successfully through each physical incarnation, choosing or at least becoming acquainted with the Truths which ultimately bring happiness.

This book serves as the affirmation of man's divinity through an understanding of the continuation of consciousness and a greater appreciation for the concept of expanded self. The God-presence is within and without all that exists. Verification of this Universal Force through individual experience gives permission to mankind to pick up the challenge of trusting in the forces which manifest within the personal life experience.

THERE CAN BE NO GREATER GIFT, AGARTHA, FROM MY WORLD TO YOURS THAN THE LOVE THAT CREATES AND TRANSFORMS THROUGH UNDERSTANDING. HOPEFULLY THIS LOVE HAS REACHED YOU AND WILL REACH OTHERS IN FULL MEASURE TO LIFT AND SUPPORT, THAT ALL WOULD FIND GREATER VERIFICATION OF THEIR PRESENCE WITHIN THE SPHERE OF LIFE THAT NEVER ENDS. WHILE YOUR STRUGGLES ARE NOT OVER, YOU HAVE INDEED BEGUN TO SEARCH, AND IN SEARCHING COMES THE VER-IFICATION OF THE TRUTH WHICH SURROUNDS ALL BEINGS OF LIGHT.

THE SPHERE OF LIGHT WHICH YOU HAVE COME TO RECOGNIZE AS YOUR BEACON OF GUIDANCE WILL CONTINUE, FOR WE HAVE MUCH WORK TO DO, YOU AND I. WHILE YOU WORK TOWARD YOUR OWN RELEASE FROM THE PHYSICAL PLANE, I WILL WORK WITH YOU TO-WARD THE GREATER UNDERSTANDING WHICH WILL BRING YOU ETERNAL PEACE. I AM MEN-TOR, YOUR TEACHER.

GO IN PEACE.
MENTOR

*

EPILOGUE—1989

What is past holds potential wisdom for the
present
What is present is only temporary
and continually shifts within the structure of
change
Then what is future. . . . ?
It is the truth of action taken and the awareness
of this
truth as it exists in the heart of Divine Intention.
MENTOR

MENTOR'S FINAL WORDS in AGARTHA tugged at my heart when I read them for the first time five years ago . . . "WE HAVE MUCH WORK TO DO, YOU AND I . . . I AM MENTOR, YOUR TEACHER" . . . I remember opening my eyes reluctantly to look at what had been written on that sheet of paper in my typewriter. I had mixed feelings about coming to the end of the writing of AGARTHA. I was eager to conclude the long hours of writing, rewriting and editing, but I was ambivalent about completing my dialogue with Mentor which had become more important to my life than I even realized.

Endings had always been difficult for me, and so ending AGARTHA felt enormously unsettling. It felt as if I was saying "good-bye" to an old and trusted friend. I'd come to rely on my daily sessions with Mentor to reassure me of the existence of the nonphysical world and of my ability to interact with it. While it was not Mentor's intention to direct my life, I'd come to deeply love and believe in this compassionate and knowledgeable teacher who challenged my thoughts and choices with a vision of the "bigger picture" and influenced me to reach for the life I most sincerely wanted to live.

Like birth and death, beginnings and endings of life cycles should be recognized and appropriately commemorated. Yet the actual changes these major beginnings and endings herald often slip quietly into history before we've come to see or adequately measure their profound importance. I have suggested that it was no accident that you, the reader, were holding this book. That, indeed, there was and is a "Divine Providence" that directs our lives toward those elements that can both teach and guide us in the most appropriate directions. And it is no accident that I am now writing the epilogue to the first edition of *Agartha*, which represents both a major closure in my life and appropriate passage into a new beginning.

Choice, Change and New Beginnings

When Mentor said that he and I had much work to do, it felt beautifully poetic, even if I wasn't sure how our work together would continue. The saga of the spiritually innocent housewife from Connecticut who stumbled into an awesome relationship with a nonphysical teacher called Mentor sounded more like science fiction than reality. The fact remains that this "beginning" marked a major turning point of my life. And like all true beginnings there was no knowledge of what would follow from that beginning. I had no real understanding of what it meant to walk a spiritual path. My life, in fact, had yet to be tested against the stark reality of the enormous changes and challenges that life would present to me.

My discovery of the fact that there was, and is, a constant dialogue between the physical and nonphysical worlds had been both frightening and thrilling. My experience of this interdimensional communication presented me with possible levels of guidance that were advanced in scope and intention. I realized that we were meant to work with a dimension of life that was far greater than just that which could be seen or appreciated in physical form.

Mentor's presence in my life made it clear to me that humankind is a collective body responsible not only for the quality of life on Planet Earth—it is equally responsible to the Universe for the quality of the thoughts and actions affecting this life force. It is through this collective-planetary interaction that we are meant to see how important and precious we each are to the greater spectrum of life.

This knowledge of my indissoluble connectedness to all life was my true beginning. While my life had been filled with many opportunities and challenges before meeting Mentor, my real learning began with our first encounter.

As the dates on the calendar have slipped past, and it's now 1989, I've come to deeply appreciate the nature and power of choice and the inevitability of change. Nothing ever remains the way it was. I've changed, my work has changed, my friends have changed, every aspect of my life has changed, including my marriage to Jim. Life in all its many beautiful facets has shifted into a new kaleidoscopic pattern. My current life holds very little resemblance to my life before Mentor. If that sounds frightening, it is not meant to. What has unfolded in my life—both the positive and that which still needs to be tended to, is far more important to me than all that went before.

With or without guidance from an expanded realm, our life lessons are often tough—they touch us deeply where we are the most vulnerable and seemingly unprotected. We are continually exposed to the world of other people's desires, needs, fears and conscious and unconscious attitudes, and our responses to others' beliefs and emotions can bring us both inner turmoil and the opportunity to change and heal.

I have discovered that even though life's lessons may initially seem too tough to bear, there is no substitute for such learning and we are never asked to handle more than we can immediately learn from. Our lessons seem to be offered directly in relation to the issues we most need to see clearly.

They lead your attention inside—into the inner realms of your life which are spiritual in nature. These inner recesses are calm and peaceful and filled with a soothing contrast to the countless crises of daily life. These inner spiritual dimensions, though very private and very tender, are amazingly persistent in drawing your attention back to your own true self and the precious qualities that are yours alone. These inner dimensions offer the solace and healing energy necessary to grow into personal empowerment.

When we are forced to reevaluate our lives and are urged through our inner stirrings to move in strange and unfamiliar directions, we have the opportunity to grow enormously. When we can no longer remain in the seemingly safe place where we have been but must move out into the unknown, we eventually see the universal wisdom involved and the love that has carried us through the most rigorous and painful of journeys into the light. We come to see ourselves and life differently.

Often the best way to measure how far we've come or how much we've learned is to look at where we began. For instance, if you are now a quality seamstress you can look back and remember how you fumbled to make your first outfit. If you are an accomplished actor, you can remember the faltering attempts at overcoming your own self-consciousness to effectively portray the character in the script. So it is with each of our spiritual journeys. We must look back to the beginning to measure and assess the significance and magnitude of our development and progress.

When I look back at my spiritual journey, I see the crossroads at which I released a twenty-two-year marriage and the subsequent struggles I faced in my new life as a single parent. I can see the bend in the road where I recognized the necessity for becoming more flexible in responding to my children's changing needs, and the plateau at which I released inappropriate feelings of personal ownership of my son and my daughter, and the view from the hillside when I began to honor the paths they have chosen to walk. Finally, and perhaps most significantly, I can now appreciate and value my sometimes tumultuous passage through the personal doubts and fears that accompanied my move from the inner to the outer world where I began to teach and share Mentor's material. This transition turned out to be the perfect mirror for witnessing my own personal empowerment.

Personalizing the Universe

Our natural instinct is to personalize the Universe, and yet I've come to realize that Mentor and teachers from a more advanced level of awareness do not respond to the "pulls" of the personal ego the way we do. They are not limited by our time/space perspective. Yet in spite of this absence of *human frames* of reference I was intensely drawn toward learning more about Mentor's world. I wondered what he felt when he looked back over our first meeting and our interaction over the years? How did he assess it? Did he change in any way or grow spiritually through his interaction with Earth and the life forms with whom he communicated and continues to communicate? I also realized I had never asked Mentor if he had a mission he was destined to accomplish and if so—what it was? Mentor answered my questions with this response.

❋ *There is a great healing happening on the Earth amidst great turmoil. There is once again hope for a different outcome; hope for a future filled with direction, intention and harmony; hope for a rebirth of love; hope for personal health and feelings of inward satisfaction. You and I are participating in this rebirth of hope. When we wrote AGARTHA, we did so as the introduction to a way of life, a way of hope. The material we wrote was not just interesting or even inspiring information from another dimension. The spiritual information in AGARTHA weaves together basic spiritual tenets which form the basis of the human experience. Thus information which is spiritual in nature is also truly human in nature and transcends any and all limitations to inspire the reader to rediscover his or her own deepest level of hope and inspiration for living.*

*In commenting on AGARTHA let us look at what its
impact has been and will continue to be, not as a book,
but as a body of information which elicits hope. What part
does hope play in the human drama? Without hope, life
force cannot seek purpose, meaning, love or added dimension of any kind. Without hope, there is no energy to
struggle because there is no belief in a meaningful or
pleasing or appropriate outcome. To eliminate hope is to
believe in the power of the physical/emotional/mental
worlds of life over the spiritual. To eliminate hope means
that there is no constant truth which guides and directs
the Universe and therefore no outcome which can have
meaning. It is interesting that it is basic to life to hope for
a beneficent outcome which translated another way, suggests that human beings are always actively seeking change
or a means to adjust the goals of life.*

*So, Agartha, in considering the experience that you and
I have shared in creating AGARTHA, I would say that
you have grown in hope as your relationship with the nonphysical universe has prompted and taught you the truth
of change, of opportunity to survive and flourish because
of an awakened state of spiritual grace which supports and
promotes your effective activity on the Earth.*

*You ask if I am helped on my path of development by
our communication—most assuredly I am. All teaching is
sharing the transmission and the reception of thought. I
have sought to infuse your life with awarenesses as I perceive them which are the basic teachings of all religion
and all spiritual truth.*

*My purpose or mission, Agartha, has to do with the
movement of collective energy forms which influence the
evolution of planets, earth-schools, planes where lessons
are forthcoming that teach spiritual truth. My focus is not
geared to a certain time/space sphere but beyond such
regimentation to the perception of truth/wholeness as it
exists in the larger nonphysical universe. You might think
of my focus as the guiding of complex bodies of energy
toward their own greatest awareness and thus toward perfection.*

It has always amazed me that Mentor could respond to a question of immense import to my life and the lives of others, without pomp and circumstance, and simply as a statement of truth. While I was accustomed to his understated manner, I had never considered that his mission was one of such magnitude. I could only imagine what it must be like to be responsible for *guiding complex bodies of energy toward their own greatest awareness*.

His mission was to serve as teacher for both human beings and other life forms on our planet, guiding the evolution of our Earth as a collective body of energy. But if he was teaching primarily on a collective consciousness level, why was he involved with teaching me, a single human being?

* *Since you are not a complex body of energy, then perhaps my statement may seem at odds with our relationship. The way complex bodies of energy are influenced is through the primary streams of light which make up these bodies. The Earth is, as you are aware, in a crucial time that is drawing from all life forms, especially human beings, the maximum capacity for change into awareness. This is necessary because in order to transform, your Earth must have a highly intensified collective energy which is of the light. The stronger each individual element of light, the greater influence on the whole. Thus your emerging energy, light, is and does influence many. Those who choose receptivity to the light are actually allowing the restructuring of their own physical/emotional/mental lives in order to promote the emergence of this dominant force of light.*

I am indeed involved in the conscious teaching of the collective body you know as Earth. This means simply that in teaching you and others, I teach the whole; and in consciously interacting with the whole, I teach the individual. The whole in this case is your Earth. It is conscious and more than just conscious, it is taught as a body of life force just as you are. It has a physical presence (body), a means of processing data (mind) and a commit-

*ment to a divine path (soul). It has a purpose and a process
of transition and issues of delusion vs. truth just as you
do.*

*This subject of earth consciousness is the next level of
teaching of consciousness, and I would like to offer that
it can be handled most appropriately in a new book, perhaps entitled,* THE UNKNOWN NATURE: Exploring
the Conscious Evolution of the Earth.

*You and many are ready to know of and participate in
this teaching and it will be my pleasure to offer it to you.
It is, after all, not just humankind that influences the
Earth, it is also she who has choices and with those choices
influences the very existence of humankind. You will find
this subject most fascinating.*

Fascinating . . . what an understatement! I was thrilled
and intrigued with Mentor's thoughts on Earth consciousness. I deeply wanted to know about the Earth and her
choices. What was she choosing and when and how? Yet,
beneath Mentor's offer to share new information, I realized
that he was saying something else that I needed to hear. His
comment about THE UNKNOWN NATURE was confirmation that we were to continue to work together and that I
was meant to remain Mentor's student. As the impact of his
words moved slowly into my heart and mind, I was filled
with a profound sense of gratitude for being blessed to have
the opportunity to continue my extraordinary partnership
with this incredible teacher.

Once again I found myself filled with a familiar euphoria as I comprehended the totality of Mentor's inspiring
message. It always fascinated me how the effect of his
words simultaneously soothed, excited and empowered
me. Was this really the basis for our human existence—to
change into structures of light that activated a divine destiny for the earth? I thought of all the familiar structures
of today's physical world that were rapidly changing, necessarily changing, to forge a different path for humanity.
I thought of the many corporate executives desperately trying to reverse the downward spiral of their organizations

whose usefulness to humanity had declined, and like dinosaurs seemed destined for extinction. Mentor had commented that the period from 1988 to 2001 would be one of intense upheaval and conflict. And as I am writing these words at the beginning of this new era, a maelstrom of upheaval is upon our planet. We are experiencing the polarization of people into two different camps—those calling for a new level of human consciousness based on responsibility to the whole of life and those mired in their fear of letting go of the old illusion of separation.

Institutions and organizations whose philosophies are based on separation and personal interest are now beginning to crumble—undergoing rapid change from the inside out. Such groups are being awakened by the actions of those who say "enough" as more and more people refuse to accept what is no longer growth producing for the whole. This evolutionary spiral represents positive growth and change. This is the upside.

The downside is, of course, all too evident. For every person who is interested in creating and living a different tomorrow there seems to be twice as many committed to looking the other way. I wanted Mentor to comment on how we could, as he suggested, "restructure for the light" in order to make faster progress toward a whole and healthy planet? Why is change happening so slowly when there is so much to be done?

Personal and Planetary Rates of Change

✳*Do you really feel that change is happening too slowly on the Earth? Do you feel it is happening too slowly in your life? Wouldn't you say that change is occurring in your life just as fast as you are capable of assimilating it? I would offer that change on the Earth is also happening as quickly as it can be assimilated and supported by a more developed structure of beliefs.*

Change is the texture of the Universe and is in no way

punitive or disciplinary but growth producing and creative. This you already know. The state of change is permanent and continually directs your attention to that on which you can depend. This means that change allows the individual to differentiate between that which is permanent and that which is only transient. Because it is deeply reassuring to focus on that which is permanent, eventually all forms of life come to appreciate their own primary relationship to a greater Universe. Secondarily, each learns to appreciate the physical life reality and yet to see it for what it is—transient.

Change begins deep within a person or structure and gradually readjusts the foundations so the outer structures must change or collapse. Just as in an earthquake where the foundation of a building shifts and the top collapses, it must be rebuilt to withstand the next earthquake. When a person undergoes a loss or radical change in personal life that reforms the foundation, then the external life must eventually be reformed to reflect the new foundation. Both collapse and reformation are part of the process of responding to change. If all leads to a deeper and more all-encompassing relationship with the Universe, then how can one mourn loss when it is replaced with greater gain?

Whether it is a corporation changing its way of doing business in order to cease polluting the environment or an individual facing life fully with love and without blame, judgment or guilt, the process of change happens slowly if it is to be permanent. As your own thoughts lead you to new intentions which then give birth to different actions and the manifestation of new dimensions of your being, it takes time and commitment to change. Yet, there is a deep level of change underway in your world which is affecting every individual who currently lives on Earth. These changes, while not immediately obvious, nevertheless are reshaping the most basic of ways in which you interact, love, work and share life. Let us consider some of these significant changes.

So Mentor was going to show me how the Earth and humanity were changing. Certainly there were obvious positive changes happening in the world: such as improved relations with the Soviet Union and an increasing call for world peace and nuclear disarmament as well as for the end of indiscriminate dumping of nuclear and chemical wastes. But what about the apathy and lack of awareness of the majority of humankind to the reality that our home, the Earth, is already in extreme trauma. Even the alarms now sounded by most of our leading scientists and thousands of organizations dedicated to the restoration of a healthy Earth ecology seem insufficient. The future of our planet is still seemingly controlled and influenced by those whose values and choices reflect little concern for the well-being of all humanity and the Earth as a global home. For most of those in positions of external power, the healing of the Earth is a concept that lies dormant in their consciousness.

In thinking about Mentor's analogy to personal change, I felt as if personally, I had been rapidly clearing away old dysfunctional beliefs and replacing them with beliefs based on my new clearer perception of universal truths. While to the outside world the extent of my internal change may have gone largely unnoticed, in actuality I was literally undergoing a total transformation. Certainly the experiences and new insights of the past four years have helped me understand how to take a far more responsible approach to my life and to the larger whole.

I was beginning to more lucidly understand Mentor's message that ''change at the global level begins first at the personal level.'' Each person is a significant unit of change, either positively or negatively. Thus change must begin at the foundation or internal structure first, before it can manifest in external structures of society and a physically healthier world. While change often appears to us to be happening only in rather insignificant ways, it really occurs in powerfully subtle ways. And we are assimilating change and evolving as a species at a speed commensurate with the level of our consciousness.

✳ *Let us begin to consider the ways in which your planet is changing by looking at two of the more subtle inner changes that greatly affect the outer and more obvious changes. These are both the way you as humans learn and the way you relate within your families.*

Extinction Becomes Relevant: A New Way of Learning

✳ *The healing of the Earth has become a meaningful vision for an increasingly large number of people. While the specifics of that healing vary from individual to individual, or organization to organization, nevertheless it has to do with reclaiming and valuing all life—person, animal and nature herself—in order to live in peace and harmony with all.*

The realization of the true meaning of extinction has also come to hold power for many. By this I mean that as species continue to become extinct at a rate beyond which others can come into being, then the individual cannot help but ponder his or her own future. If individuals who form the collective governing and organizing bodies of the world are unwilling or unable to stop the elimination of life, then surely it stands to reason that when life is valued so little, it is only a matter of time until the human being will also become extinct.

I suggest to you, Agartha, that because of the drastic devaluation of life on every level in your land, it is appropriate and significant that many now look to a new generation and a new world. I will also suggest to you, on a more empowered note, that the blatant ignorance which has been pushing your Earth toward extinction has begun to be stemmed because of the new model of learning which is taking root in people's consciousness. This new model of learning is allowing individuals to recognize life from a spiritual perspective rather than just from a physical/emotional one. Let me explain.

I am saying two things: first, people are now participating in a new learning model. This means they actually have the capacity to process data differently and two, because of the way information is now processed, human beings are beginning to see life and the value of life quite differently.

Let us look at how the the process of learning is changing.

> *Model of learning before 1980:*
>> *emotions produce action which causes introspection and growth of the soul*

> *Model of learning possible after 1980:*
>> *growth of soul (vision/guidance) prompts action which produces emotions*

The importance of this new learning model is that human beings are now capable of acting on the promptings of their own soul, their own guidance and vision, rather than just on the whimsical attention of their emotions.

For example, in the past individuals took action primarily around those issues that were brought to their attention most poignantly. The response was primarily emotional and did not extend beneath the surface of the issue to the root cause. Today, individuals have the potential to be even more powerfully moved by the deeper underlying causes that precipitate an emotional response and these underlying causes are spiritual in nature.

You have felt the pain and trauma produced by isolated instances of inappropriate action or lack of compassion. Now you are prepared to feel the pain and trauma of the whole. Not one tree or one animal or one person's pain but the issues that represent the defilement of basic Universal Truths. This is action based on the empowerment of your own soul. This is action that can change the planet. The impetus for action has moved from emotion to spirit.

There have always been visionaries who predicted or foreshadowed a different path for humankind, a different conscious level of participation in life. These were people who had a deep relationship with the nonphysical world, who saw that all things were intricately connected and

*that to eliminate the most insignificant was eventually to
eliminate the mightiest. These individuals represented the
vanguard of the new physical/emotional/mental/spiritual
models yet to be born and put into place.*

So this was what Mentor meant by being "restructured for
the light." Without conscious participation or noticeable effort people were beginning to change in the most miraculous
of ways. From the inside out, according to some hidden cosmic time clock, we were being encouraged to hear our own
soul and to value its truths.

It had always mystified me how humanity had seemingly
changed and metamorphosed through external influences
of its environment. We have learned from historical evi-
dence that our species first lived in small survival-type
family units, then in small clans and later within larger
and larger communities. Individuals learned that by co-
operating in the gathering of food, raising of animals for
sustenance, and building of shelter, the benefits to all were
greater than the benefit to the single individual. This re-
corded maturation of our human species and its progress
toward more civilized living is presented to us as the evolution of our species. But is this a true measure of a species evolvement toward wholeness?

We tend to think of native tribes throughout the world
as primitive, yet they all seem to share a common reverence for the interconnectedness and sacredness of all life.
So who are the primitives, the uncivilized? Perhaps our
methodology for assessing the evolutionary development
of our species has been based on a false perception. Perhaps we keep missing the point. The principal criterion by
which we need to measure our evolutionary progress is
"how awakened are we to new spiritual insights and how
well have we responded to them." Have we responded to
the pull of emotional and physical stimuli or to true spiritual philosophy urgings? It would seem that only by developing a "spirit-first" that substantial positive growth
and physical change can occur. And while the constant of
the Universe appears to be such that every single form of

life is genetically encoded to evolve toward wholeness, we human beings have the power to choose how rapidly we evolve. Not whether we will evolve, but how difficult and enduring our path to wholeness will be.

The other powerful point Mentor made which is tremendously encouraging to me, as it should be to you, is that we now also have the capacity to view life from the spiritual perspective and not a limited purely physical/emotional one. It is as if the Universe has placed in our hands a new gift for seeing clearly how to choose a new direction for our life and for our planet.

Mentor has suggested that our species is evolving in this important way, because we are learning to appreciate the messages of our own souls and of the soul of the Universe.

Could the role of "channeling" also be linked to the unfolding of this new model of learning? Is the Universe opening each of us up to hear our own souls and the souls of other sources of life in order to validate the Universal truths that continually serve as the guiding beacon for our lives?

I was curious to hear from Mentor about the next area of substantial change for the human species. He had said "family bonding" was changing. I wondered if he was going to talk about the alarming rate of divorce and separation. Even for those in long-standing relationships that appear successful on the outside, there seems to be many individuals resigned to a way of life that is neither joyful nor growth producing. What were the deeper levels of change happening beneath the surface of family life?

The Changing Family Structure: A Personal Search For Spiritual Bonding

❋ *There is a significant breakdown in primary family units in all the major cultures on your planet. Some are openly collapsing as in the Western world and some are only subtly pulling away from the traditional ways, but major change is occurring in this basic cultural structure. This*

*change is important to analyze because it offers insight
into the shift toward community, spiritually aligned "families," and a global family.*

*The structure of a family unit related by blood has been
necessary in the past for stability, nurturing, education
and transmission of cultural attitudes and history. The
bonding between family members has had a great deal to
do with the need for all to participate in the completion of
daily chores in order to physically survive. There were also
often religious practices that were shared, and these too
created important bonds within the family. A framework
was created where each person "fit" and was important
to the sustenance of the whole.*

*There have been family units that were positive and
others that were negative, while most were both. In the
past, the individual had no recourse but to remain within
his/her birth family. It has not been until the latter half
of the 1900s that awareness has been brought to bear on
the nature of the family and its influence on the individuals involved, and a level of appropriate social and legal
accountability provided.*

*In the best case the family provided joy, comradery,
sharing, acceptance and quality nurturing and love. From
a strong unified family unit, children had the opportunity
to move into empowered, loving, responsible adults and
parents, the opportunity to develop ever deepening and
mutually satisfying bonds of real love.*

*However, where family units were less than productive
and often extremely destructive, not only was there no
appropriate bonding but there was damage to the physical,
emotional and spiritual aspects of the individuals involved. Where there had been no outside accountability
there was no recourse for the child or wife who was abused
or battered. There was quiet acceptance of family relationships no matter how destructive, painful or degrading.
There was no relief from a lazy, unproductive, uncoop-
erative, unresponsive spouse. Each family member pro-
tected the image of the family from outside criticism and
interference regardless of the personal confusion, break-*

down or emotional consequences. The primary family unit was above reproach whether it generated love, spiritual growth and nurturing—or dependancy, grief and pain.

However, in analyzing the growth and strength of the family unit, it becomes obvious that there is something happening that is causing the change and breakdown of the traditional family. The change is this: an evolutionary energy has begun to surface in people's lives causing intense need for spiritual bonding. As individuals have looked to their primary families to provide this bonding, they have often found this bonding entirely missing or in its place the bonds of repression where absolute adherence and obedience were required by the family and parent(s). This, of course, nullified independent thought and thus personal spiritual growth.

Parents who were searching for the same spiritual bonds began to search elsewhere when it could not be found within the existing relationship. Children and young adults became disenchanted with the familiar bonding which no longer felt relevant and yearned for a different kind of bonding. What I am suggesting is that family structures have been deteriorating: between partners, between children, and between children and parents.

The sequence of this breakdown might look like this:

- shared cultural/social/economic and religious bonding necessary for survival of individual and community
- breakdown of organized religion and traditional beliefs in favor of individualzied spiritual beliefs
- the affirmation of the individual and the search for spiritual bonding within relationships
- breakdown of family units which do not generate and encourage spiritual bonding
- the search for other "family units" which do generate spiritual bonding, such as communities
- recognition of the primary need to participate in spiritual bonding as the basis for life in every relationship
- the desire to restructure a more durable and lasting fam-

*ily integrity by basing the family's bonding on spir-
itual truth and a reverence for the personal quest*

*I am suggesting that the traditional family unit is break-
ing down, yes, but it is changing to reflect a deeper design
which is to move the individual into harmony with not just
a blood family but into relationship with a global family
made up of many races, creeds and colors. This global
family shares a common bonding of responsibility for life
through a belief in a greater whole, a belief in an Infinite
Presence and the necessity of living spiritually in accordance with personally validated spiritual beliefs.*

It is clear that the Universe is nudging us to seek more
meaningful relationships based on the principle of oneness—
one human family. The demise of the 1980s family unit is a
necessary evolution of our species and not a falling back-
wards. We are being called upon to move into a new level of
responsibility, a level of responsibility for establishing spiritual bonds between others, regardless of whether they are
inside or outside the traditional family structure or determined by our society or religion.

In thinking back over my twenty-two years of marriage to
Jim, I realized that many of the factors Mentor had noted as
contributing to the deterioration of old relationships were
also the ones that eroded our marriage. It was time for more
spiritual bonding to emerge as the primary force within our
relationship. However, in order to have that kind of bonding,
both of us were being called to first recognize the root cause
of our disenchantment with the other and to recommit to a
new way of being together. Because all people must be able
to live their own life according to the way they can feel personally empowered, each individual must choose how to
change. Sometimes the patterns that need to be changed are
in conflict, and to remain together is no longer growth producing. That was the situation with Jim and me.

The writing of AGARTHA had signaled the true launch
of Jim's and my own search to discover and know our own
spiritual essence. We both understood that without that

core in place, the inner confidence in our own abilities to grow into whole persons and to be successful in living our own spiritual purpose would be severely compromised and that we would be unable to take the next important step into a whole relationship. Still we were reluctant to venture out in search of our individual empowerment for fear it would diminish or destroy the relationship we had established.

I've since come to understand that without the courage to search alone, it is never possible to have a truly quality relationship with another person. Fear of the unknown or fear of failure is not sufficient justification for people to stay together. There are some journeys in life that require, in fact, demand, that they be taken alone. The Universe gradually moves you along the path you've chosen, even when the hurdles look too formidable to jump.

Jim and I both did begin the process of jumping the hurdles, in spite of our fear of letting go of the familiar, and we discovered that our way of being together was no longer supportive of our individual quests. Like the legendary warrior who leaves home in search of his own vision, when he returns, nothing is as he remembers and he must turn his attention to walking his destiny alone.

I had thought that our move to New Hampshire would help us build a stronger family unit and give us a new and meaningful beginning. Yet what resulted was the breakdown and subsequent releasing of the very family unit I had so wanted to protect.

In reflecting back over that difficult period of my life, I've come to appreciate that the search for one's own deepest spiritual roots is both the beginning of real spiritual awareness and also the impetus to act in accordance with the truth discovered. This truth, no matter how appropriate for your growth, is still often bitter to swallow.

When you do decide to separate or seek a divorce, you find yourself in the center of turbulence and radical change such as you've seldom known or imagined. It is like being in the middle of a cyclone. You cannot see or feel the swirling of the storm around you, but you know that as you move out of the "eye" you will be tossed and turned in tumultuous ways. You're afraid that the moments of empowerment and euphoria that you've created by taking your life into your own hands and moving into alignment with your beliefs, will quickly dissipate. You glimpse a life devoid of hope or opportunity to fulfill your life's work. You feel and, in fact, *are* very alone.

The thought of facing life alone with all of its varied challenges is overwhelming for someone who has been in a long-standing relationship. It makes no difference whether you're widowed, divorced, separated or in a relationship where the lines of communication have disintegrated. Aloneness brings up our greatest fear, stemming from our fear of abandonment as a child. What as a child was potentially the most damaging and debilitating loss can be only slightly less debilitating for us adults who have never been alone. I think we fear being alone because to love and be loved by another is a very basic biological need. We want to be able to share our deepest inner feelings with a partner, to be valued and appreciated. Unfortunately, we also often look to others to fix us or to make our lives work and of course this is where the problems begin.

I had spent a great many years expecting others to be responsible for my well-being. I looked to others to choose those things that would bring me happiness. And I've learned that this lack of responsibility to self doesn't make you feel empowered. Rather you continually feel like a victim where others hold the power of choice over your life. Nor does it make it easier to acknowledge that you willingly gave your power of choice to others.

The writing and publishing of AGARTHA represented an enormous step forward into my being responsible for my own life. I had begun a path with Mentor, and while it hadn't been one I thought I'd consciously initiated, nevertheless after four years of intensive channeling and dialoguing with the nonphysical world, I'd gradually begun to do exactly what Jim had continually insisted I needed to do. I finally took responsibility for my life and for my life's work. It seems the height of irony that as I learned to truly incorporate the basic lessons of spiritual empowerment into my life that our relationship began to unravel. The original bonds which held us together were no longer the appropriate ones and were not strong enough to weather the storm of change. It was time to walk different paths.

I have come to believe that true partnerships allow continual change in the relationship. All too often in long-term partnerships there are subtle "rules" that define each person's relationship to the other and to the outside world. Couples who wish to stay together play by these rules. Couples who don't play by these rules and begin to redefine their needs and their sense of self to an outside world run the risk of a broken relationship.

Because the need to be true to oneself and grow is undeniable, the boundaries of a relationship must be elastic and able to be continually redefined. I've come to realize that the rules for a lasting relationship are developed not from people's fears, dependencies and insecurities but from their strengths and personal wholeness. After all, we come into this world alone and we go out of it alone, not married, not in partnership with another, just a single human being. In spite of all the bonds that hold a successful relationship together—family, friends, a shared history—the partners seldom are able to stay together if they are consistently intolerant rather than supportive of the other's changing mode of expressing growth.

As I began to teach workshops and be away from home more and more, Jim and I felt as if we had been put on "cosmic notice." If our marriage was to continue, it needed new energy and a new definition of partnership. This meant we both needed to change. I no longer needed, nor wanted, to look to him for approval of those activities which gave me a stronger sense of self-empowerment. Nor could I blame him when things in my life didn't work. In turn he had to learn to accept responsibility for those issues in his life which were of his own making and not those of others acting upon him. Each of us were responsible not to or for the other, but for our own inner growth.

The break-up of a relationship is a time to understand and

appreciate the difference between aloneness and being lonely. At various times in our life we are all alone. They can be powerful times of inner growth or times of great stress and fear. To be in aloneness means to be alone in partnership with the Universe. To be lonely means to feel shut off from the life force that nourishes you.

At first, when you find yourself without someone, you count the pitfalls not by the tens but by the hundreds. Simple things like coming home alone when it's cold and snowing and you've forgotten to leave the outside lights on can leave you feeling profoundly alone. Going out on a miserably sub-zero night to bring in more wood for the fire—a chore your partner did—can leave you bemoaning your new found freedom. Deciding to mow the lawn but not being able to pull the start cord hard enough to turn over the motor raises the anxiety/anger level about being able to create your new reality. For men the dilemmas usually have to do with making the house a home, the handling of child care, preparing meals, doing laundry—all tasks which traditionally were done by the female in a partnership.

There is nothing that triggers feeling lonely as much as going to a party as the "single" in "couple-land" where everyone is matched up in pairs like animals entering the Ark. When you move into the role of being single, everything changes. You find new and different friendships. There is a natural tendency to seek out those who share your same miseries and challenges as well as those who seem to have emerged from the "pit of loneliness" into the daylight.

When others would say to me they knew what it must be like to feel all alone, I knew they really did not, because I didn't before I went through the process of separation. I felt I had taken the necessary step for both Jim and me by moving out of my marriage, a step that was right and essential for both of us. Although I'd tried to plan for my own self-recovery, I only began to heal as I moved away from the actual separation and allowed myself to reflect on what I'd learned and how I wanted to live my new life.

The process of loss can teach you inner strength and trust in a compassionate Universe where your basic needs are met. It can also cause you to feel that you are pathetic, lonely and an outcast from society. Yet gradually you heal. Life goes on, children need you, people need you, life needs you. In spite of yourself you begin again, you hope with more wisdom, humility and a truer understanding of your own vulnerabilities as well as the indomitable spirit of your courageous self.

Going In the Right Direction

The changes Mentor talked about were certainly far-reaching. I thought of all the other ways people were changing and wanting to become healthier and more empowered. My own steps in search of wholeness were no better or worse than thousands like me who were trying to "do it right."

I realized that Mentor had been sharing with me the subtle, underlying changes that are presently occurring in the spiritual evolutionary process of the human species rather than only commenting on the physical earth changes that I had questioned. It became apparent that as more and more of us are willing to change in response to our deeper spiritual needs, we can shift the balance from high negative energy on the Earth to high positive energy and bring about the healing of the whole.

I guess what I wanted to know most of all was Mentor's assessment of humankind's and Earth's spiritual development. Was he discouraged at our lack of progress? What perspectives could he offer to give us hope for a positive future? What insights about the natural evolutionary restructuring of human beings and the Earth, both physical and nonphysical, might we ponder?

✻*All life is energy, Agartha. This energy of life forms an individual's hologram which is observed by teachers without judgment. This means that each person's hologram is a multidimensional "picture" of the total compilation of life force from this life and previous lifetimes. Each ho-*

logram is comprised of total potential and total opportunity for change and spiritual evolution. So each person and each form of life is seen by the nonphysical world in holographic perspective. I see you, Agartha, as light, just as you see me.

The nature of light energy is the holographic form for which human beings are reaching. As the individual tries to evaluate physical life, choosing those paths which lead to the validation of universal truths, he or she grows in light. People are actually changing physical composition to become more as they exist in between lifetimes, as pure spirit.

I have an interesting thought for you to consider as you think about your life and the advancement of your Earth School and as I consider what the world of nonphysical teachers would offer as a message to humankind. I would suggest to you that as different forms of life on your planet grow more fully into their spiritual essence, the physical forms in which they now live—their bodies—will be less and less useful and will gradually dissolve. This means that much of your Earth School will be inhabited by life forms that are pure spirit and can only be recognized by those who have adapted their perception to deal telepathically on the higher planes of awareness.

Eventually there will be no more physical incarnations on planet Earth, only spiritual incarnations. Physical incarnations will continue to exist on other developing Earth Schools, but in the distant future your Planet will become a nonphysical Earth School. The lessons will become increasingly spiritual lessons. People will no longer need to live in houses and eat physical food because all will exist within the lifeline of pure energy.

It is interesting that often there have been reports surfacing from your spiritual community that if there were to be a nuclear exchange on your planet or the destruction of the Earth were to take place, that there would be a lift-off of those who were "believers." There is some truth to this, in the sense that if there were to be a dissolution of your Earth, those of your life forms that were evolved enough to seek a spiritual path would be lifted off, not to another planet, but to exist within the nonphysical Earth School as pure spirit.

Then you might ask, what if the Earth were destroyed, how could any Earth School remain? And I would answer that the nonphysical Earth School is not in your hands to keep or destroy. It is true that the physical Earth School can be destroyed, but the nonphysical counterpart cannot. The nonphysical Earth School serves a function within the whole configuration of growth that is essential. This is why I suggested to you that your Earth would not be allowed to destroy itself through nuclear exchange because the release of that type and degree of energy would hurt the health of the nonphysical Earth School—energy like you. Destroying your physical Earth through your own neglect and lack of care is quite another matter and would be distressing. Yet this destruction would not influence or destroy the nonphysical Earth School. Nothing is allowed to interfere with the energy configuration of life and its individual components. That is why you are eternal. Your body changes form but your spirit is pure energy that has a place in the ongoing structure of the universe.

A nonphysical Earth School! The physical Earth was just like each individual, then, with physical and nonphysical aspects. It was profoundly reassuring to think that we would not be allowed to destroy the Earth through nuclear bombs. I needed to believe that this beautiful planet would live through this stage of humankind's insensitivity to the sacredness of life into a time when people can become the true stewards of the Earth.

As I paused to reflect on the magnitude of evolutionary changes to come, I imagined what the Earth would look like without the physical presence of animals or people. Mentor said that we would grow through the physical stages of life to live and learn in spiritual form. That might explain why there is so much current intensity in everyone's life. For many of us it feels as if we are being catapulted toward a meaningful transition into living a conscious life.

A million questions came to mind as I imagined a non-physical Earth School without the physical world. But I realized that where Mentor was leading me was in a new direction toward a new body of information relevant to what he had called the "conscious evolution of the Earth." I could feel the desire welling up in me to work with Mentor to give birth to such an abundance of powerful and wonderful undiscovered material. I felt like an explorer who had just set sail for a distant land and discovered that there was no map and the stars would need to be her guide.

Mentor had still not directly answered my question about a message from the angelic forces for humankind. I wanted to let his message resonate in my own mind and heart and to feel the power of his words as the bridge that would carry me and many other seekers of truth into what Mentor was suggesting was the next intensely absorbing arena of spiritual education—conscious planetary growth and evolution.

✳*Intention is tied to the greater Universe and is the human beings' link to the Infinite. When you consciously form your intentions into thoughts and thoughts into appropriate actions, then you are living your fullest capacity for life.*

When you are creating with the Universe, which is what channeling and meditating are, you are combining the energy of dreaming, remembering and creating. Each newly cocreated intention holds a totally unique configuration that has never existed on the Earth before and which belongs to you and the nonphysical Universe alone.

Isn't it an impressive thought, Agartha, that the teachers of the angelic kingdom move closely with you at this time of great change on Earth? Is it important to you that there is a Universe that is interested and supportive of your greatest good? Then let it be your gesture to the angelic world that it is not we who can inspire you but you who can inspire us by your commitment to a life where the truth of the bigger whole lives in your minds and actions and where your destiny is seen as a shared relationship with all that is spirit.

We exist for your own greatest good and for our own. We are one family, one unit, one force for change. We exist within your world as you allow us to exist and to consciously interact with your forces of change. Allow us to be in your every thought and action, and we will. Allow us to live and encourage the positive forces of change on your Earth, and we will. I am Mentor, your teacher, Agartha, and I am one of many who do seek to empower you and your world. Learn to love more with your total being and to invoke the teachers of the expanded realms of consciousness in order to truly bring into being the full and complete magnificence of your Earth's spiritual evolution.

You and I will continue our work, Agartha. I offer you a blessing of peace that you and many may find joy as you seek the light.

Go in Peace.
MENTOR
*

ABOUT THE AUTHOR

Meredith Lady Young is a nationally known workshop leader and lecturer in the field of personal development. Her work focuses on developing spiritual tools for self-empowerment and personal transformation. She is co-publisher of Stillpoint Publishing and Vice President of Stillpoint International, Inc. She makes her home in Walpole, New Hampshire.

For information regarding workshops and seminars, contact:

Stillpoint International, Inc.
P.O. Box 640
Meetinghouse Road
Walpole, New Hampshire
603-756-3508